Art Spiegelman
Conversations

Conversations with Comic Artists
M. Thomas Inge, General Editor

Art Spiegelman
CONVERSATIONS

Edited by
Joseph Witek

University Press of Mississippi
Jackson

www.upress.state.ms.us

The University Press of Mississippi is a member of the
Association of American University Presses.

Copyright © 2007 by University Press of Mississippi
Illustrations copyright © by Art Spiegelman, permission of
The Wylie Agency.
All rights reserved
Manufactured in the United States of America

First edition 2007
(∞)
Library of Congress Cataloging-in-Publication Data

Art Spiegelman : conversations / edited by Joseph Witek.
    p. cm. — (Conversations with comic artists)
Includes index.
ISBN-13: 978-1-934110-11-9 (cloth : alk. paper)
ISBN-10: 1-934110-11-6 (cloth : alk. paper)
ISBN-13: 978-1-934110-12-6 (pbk. : alk. paper)
ISBN-10: 1-934110-12-4 (pbk. : alk. paper) 1.   Spiegelman, Art—Interviews.
2.   Cartoonists—United States—Interviews.   I. Witek, Joseph.
NC1429.S5687A35 2007
741.5′973—dc22
                                                        2007006712

British Library Cataloging-in-Publication Data available

Contents

Introduction   ix

Chronology   xvii

Art Spiegelman   3
Alfred Bergdoll

***RAW* Magazine: An Interview with Art Spiegelman and Françoise Mouly   20**
Dean Mullaney

Slaughter on Greene Street: Art Spiegelman and Françoise Mouly Talk about *RAW*   35
Gary Groth, Kim Thompson, and Joey Cavalieri

Art's Father, Vladek's Son   68
Lawrence Weschler

From Mickey to *Maus*: Recalling the Genocide through Cartoon   84
Graham Smith

Interview with Art Spiegelman   95
Roger Sabin

Art Mimics Life in the Death Camps 122
Michael Fathers

The Cultural Relief of Art Spiegelman: A Conversation
with Michael Silverblatt 126
Michael Silverblatt

The Man Behind *Maus*: Art Spiegelman in His Own Words 136
Chris Goffard

Art Spiegelman 143
Noami Epel

"Words and Pictures Together": An Interview with
Art Spiegelman 152
Susan Jacobowitz

Art Spiegelman 163
Andrea Juno

The 5,000 Pound Maus: On the Anniversary of Kristallnacht,
Art Spiegelman Revisits His Legacy 191
Ella Taylor

Interview with Art Spiegelman 196
Brian Tucker

Art Spiegelman: Walking Gingerly, Remaining Close to
Our Caves 220
Natasha Schmidt

Art Spiegelman and Françoise Mouly: The Literature of
Comics 223
Calvin Reid

Pig Perplex 230
Lawrence Weschler

"The Paranoids Were Right" 234
Alana Newhouse

A Conversation with Art Spiegelman 238
Gene Kannenberg, Jr.

Art Spiegelman, Cartoonist for the *New Yorker*, Resigns
in Protest at Censorship   263
Corriere della Sera

Interview with Art Spiegelman   267
Joseph Witek

Comics as Serious Literature: Cartoonist Spiegelman Has Seen
Change since Pioneering *Maus*   301
Laura T. Ryan

Index   305

Introduction

When Art Spiegelman first began publishing his drawings as a teenager in the early 1960s, comics as a form of popular art in the United States were well on their way to cultural obsolescence. With newspaper monopolies fast eroding the economic function of syndicated comic strips, and with comic-book circulation figures plummeting as young audiences switched to television and other electronic media, cartooning in the United States had become for the most part a low-prestige backwater of the commercial illustration industry. Forty years later, however, the concept of comics as a serious art form for adults is widely accepted, and a substantial subset of comics and their creators has been increasingly integrated into the world of the contemporary arts. Comics for adults have been published in general-circulation newspapers and in small-press literary journals; comic art is routinely included in library collections and museum exhibitions; comics are discussed in literary reviews and academic treatises, and cartoonists are honored with prestigious artistic awards and financial grants. Most observers agree that no single person has done more to achieve this cultural repositioning of the comics medium than Art Spiegelman. Indeed, the special Pulitzer Prize awarded to Spiegelman in 1992 for *Maus: A Survivor's Tale*, his account in comic-book form of his parents' experiences as Polish Jews in the Holocaust, is almost universally cited as the defining moment in the emergence of comics as a serious art form.

Yet had Art Spiegelman never published *Maus*, his accomplishments as an artist, editor, publisher, critical thinker, teacher, and public figure would still make him one of the most influential figures in the history of the comics medium. As a pioneer of the underground comix scene in the 1960s and '70s, he created a sustained body of formal experimentation in comics, work that helped to clarify the place of comics in the aesthetic history of modernism and postmodernism. He has founded and co-edited no fewer than three seminal comics anthologies, each of which has played a crucial role in the modern development of the comics form by providing what Spiegelman has called "a visible rallying point" for groups of creators and for readers of comics alike.[1] In the 1970s the anthology *Arcade: The Comics Revue* (co-edited with Bill Griffith) sustained and extended the artistic breakthroughs of the underground comix movement. In the 1980s the oversized magazine *RAW*, co-edited with his wife and frequent collaborator, Françoise Mouly, was a lavishly and innovatively produced vehicle that nurtured new cartooning talent in the post-underground comix era, exposed U.S. readers to the vital work of established cartoonists from around the world, and explored the formal boundaries and conceptual overlaps between comics and other visual and narrative arts: *RAW* ultimately formed the locus of an international explosion of new approaches to comics. Since the publication of its first volume in 2000, Spiegelman and Mouly's *Little Lit*, an anthology of comics for children, has reconnected young readers to the pleasures of comics narrative at a time when comics are no longer a popular mass medium. In addition to this important work, Spiegelman's critical essays on comics, some in comics form, and his championing of classic and neglected comics and cartoonists have strongly influenced current understanding of comics history, helping to ensure that the story includes figures as disparate as Rodolphe Töpffer and the anonymous pornographers of the Tijuana Bibles. As the following interviews serve to demonstrate, comics today are made differently, marketed differently, read differently, and discussed differently than ever before, and Art Spiegelman has been central to every one of those changes.

The shift in cultural ideology concerning comics and the many ways Spiegelman has figured in that reshaping can be illuminated by considering a watershed moment in Spiegelman's career, one that is evoked several times in the interviews that follow. For much of his professional life, Spiegelman subsidized the creation of his groundbreaking but hardly lucrative comics by serving as an artist and creative consultant to the

Topps Bubble Gum Company, for whom he created such popular card series as Wacky Packages and Garbage Pail Kids. Spiegelman has called Topps "my Medici," since the regular income from Topps "gave me an incredible amount of autonomy in my life by paying me so well for so little of my brain, and so little of my time, relative to the time I needed to make comics."[2] Spiegelman eventually broke with Topps in 1989 over a number of issues, in particular the ownership of original art and public credit for artwork. The precipitating incident for this rupture was a public auction by Topps of original artwork, where Spiegelman found himself angered that the art was being sold rather than returned to the artists and was, as he reports, doubly humiliated at being outbid for his own drawings then asked to sign them by successful bidders.

In this particular moment in 1989, with *Maus I* meeting widespread critical acclaim and *Maus II* not yet completed, Spiegelman was confronted full-force with the contradictions inherent in straddling two different models of cultural production. On one hand, the Topps company worked under the assumptions of the industrial mode of anonymous mass production, with its direct, albeit unequally distributed, financial rewards. On the other, the underground comix and their successors pushed cartooning toward the mode that the French sociologist Pierre Bourdieu calls "the field of limited production," where producers themselves define the nature and scope of their productions and where rewards are first symbolic, coming in the form of reputation among one's peers, critical approval, and cultural respect, before being converted into economic power as grants, awards, and professional opportunities.[3]

That is to say, Spiegelman's frustration at the Topps auction marks a point when he was leaving behind the world of anonymous mass-produced cartoons, but the world of comics-as-art for which he had so long labored was yet to be fully born. Thus the professional freedom to work on his comics in his own way was paid for by the loss of autonomy in his work for Topps, creating the bitter irony that Spiegelman's own signature, like a signature on a gallery painting or limited-edition lithograph, had the power to raise the economic value of his original drawings, while he himself, like a factory worker on an assembly line, was unable to assert control over the work of his own hands or to benefit from the proceeds of its sale. Just a few years later, however, Spiegelman's career demonstrates that the transition of comics to the world of limited production was nearly complete—a 1990 Guggenheim Fellowship, the famous Pulitzer Prize and a one-person exhibition at the Museum of

Modern Art in 1992, and a professional position as contributing editor and artist at the *New Yorker* magazine are precisely the kinds of symbolic rewards made possible by the re-conceptualization of comics as a form of art.

Spiegelman described his perspective on the process in 2004 when discussing the genesis of *RAW* magazine,

> At this point, it's as if everything was far more visionary and conscious than it was. It's all as a result of the same impulses that got *Arcade* magazine going finally, and that got *Breakdowns* into the world, and that got me to pursue the kinds of comics that I was interested in. Bizarrely enough, I can see so much of what's going on now as having its gestation and birth in *RAW* magazine, as if it knew it was going to succeed in its mission. Kind of uncanny, because what's still seen as cutting edge is what was appearing in *RAW* number one and two, twenty-five years later. It's kind of scary that things move so slowly. But, from where it sits now, it seems like: mission accomplished. We did that in a void. We did it because there wasn't anything else happening, and there was a crying need for something to happen. So we by default were put into the position of doing exactly what we did. But the notion of comics as being something like what they're becoming now is just part of what I, even then, was calling a Faustian deal: very specifically trying to find part of an existing cultural fabric that would allow them to be stitched in.[4]

A large part of that "stitching in" has meant getting the word out about comics, and in his role as the standard-bearer for adult comics Spiegelman has become one of the most widely interviewed cartoonists of all time. The selections in this volume represent only a fraction of the scores of question-and-answer interviews and feature articles based on interviews with Spiegelman (many times along with Françoise Mouly) that have appeared around the world in newspapers, on television and radio, in general-interest magazines and specialist comics periodicals, and in academic, literary, and art journals. As a result, this collection can aspire only to be representative rather than comprehensive. For instance, the often-exhaustive interviews with Spiegelman published in the foremost English-language periodical of comics criticism, the *Comics Journal*, would exceed the page count for this entire volume by themselves. The single *Comics Journal* interview from 1982 included here, itself originally published as separate section taken from an issue-long interview, must stand as an earnest of that mass of material until a complete reprinting of it appears, a project promised by its publisher for the near future. Yet another future volume could be collected of Spiegelman's words in feature articles and transcriptions from audiovisual media and from a number of panel discussions and public presentations.

Because the unprecedented popularity of *Maus* brought comics to the attention of a wide and varied readership, Spiegelman routinely, and like no cartoonist before him, has found himself in the position not only of discussing his own creative work but of explaining, and sometimes defending, the fundamentals of his chosen métier. Over the years Spiegelman has also been queried on the historiography and psychology of the Holocaust, on the interrelations of biography and autobiography, on censorship, on the politics of the *New Yorker* magazine and the politics of the Middle East.

And always he has been queried on comics—on the art and craft of their creation, on their history and future, on their strengths, weaknesses and artistic potential, on their marketing, and their legitimacy as a form of expression. Many early reviewers of *Maus* were astonished that a comic book, let alone one using cats and mice as characters, could convey such a convincing and emotionally compelling account of the Nazi death camps and the psychic scars inflicted on the survivors and their children; some commentators were dumbfounded to the point of denying that *Maus* was a comic book at all, since, "after all, comics are for kids."[5] That Spiegelman's standard public lecture is entitled "Comix 101" signals his perhaps rueful acceptance that the enormous cultural success of *Maus* has cast him as a comics educator as well as creator.

In fact, Spiegelman's years of experience teaching at New York's School of Visual Arts often are in evidence in these interviews, many of which find the cartoonist on the road in support of a recent publication. Over his career the immediate topic at hand in any given interview moves from the various numbers of *RAW* magazine (and the ongoing serialization of *Maus* contained within them), to the published *Maus* over the course of its two separate volumes and then the collected edition, to his illustrated edition of Joseph Moncure March's narrative poem *The Wild Party*, to the ongoing *Little Lit* project, and most recently to *In the Shadow of No Towers*, the collection of his comic-strip responses to his experiences in the 9/11 attacks and their emotional and political aftermath. But while a book-touring novelist can assume that even the most unprepared interviewer at least knows what a novel is, Spiegelman often has needed to enfold his comments into an *ad hoc* introductory course on comics form and comics history.

This collection of primarily full-length interviews highlights Spiegelman's strengths as an interview subject. Many cartoonists have been notoriously reluctant to theorize their art form, but throughout his career Art Spiegelman has been articulate and analytical about his wide-ranging interests. He engages his interlocutors, and is alive to the nuances of ideas as they arise in a discussion. While Spiegelman is so closely identified with his award-winning graphic novel that he at times must struggle to prevent every interview from devolving into yet another *Maus* piece, his restless intellect and wide-ranging artistic ambitions have made his career as wildly eclectic as the many incarnations of his drawing style, and, as these interviews show, he is an efficient polymath in conversation as well. Spiegelman tells the story of how his father, forcibly attuned to the possible need of sudden flight, insisted that his son learn how to pack a suitcase, and his responses in these interviews showcase the cartoonist's ability to efficiently arrange many disparate items into a limited space. He likewise has the good teacher's knack of delving beneath the literal question to address its unspoken premises, and in many of the interviews included here he works to fully develop his ideas over the entire course of a conversation.

Interviewers have often inquired about the exact relationship between the creator and the autobiographical persona in the story, and at times Spiegelman has had it both ways at once, as when he told a radio interviewer: "In order to draw *Maus*, it's necessary for me to reenact every single gesture, as well as every single location present in these flashbacks. The mouse cartoonist has to do that with his mouse parents."[6] Certainly the human being who emerges from these interviews shares much with that "mouse cartoonist." He is a chain-smoking, sometimes neurotically intense intellectual, with a sardonic wit and a passion for words, images, and ideas. It seems significant that the central work of Spiegelman's career casts him in the role of an interviewer as he collects his father's memories of the past, and perhaps his experience on the other side of the tape recorder helps to account for his generosity with his time and mental energy, and for his practice of responding thoughtfully and patiently (most of the time) to questions he's fielded a hundred times before. Like any veteran interview subject, he reuses favorite anecdotes, illustrative examples, and convenient phrasing, but his answers rarely seem rote. Nearly every single interview considered for this volume, no matter how brief or how familiar the questions, contained at least a notable new phrase or two, or a refinement of his thinking on an old topic.

The interview I conducted with Spiegelman in the summer of 2004 took place, as do a number of the interviews in this volume, in his South Manhattan studio, as an air conditioner battled the ubiquitous cigarette smoke to a draw. A newly arrived advance copy of *In the Shadow of No Towers* on a nearby table served as harbinger of an impending book tour. Having read, heard, or transcribed scores of previous interviews with Spiegelman, I had intended to use the opportunity to ask follow-up questions about some of the recurrent issues that had been raised in other interviews over the years. Like many others before me, however, after only a few prepared questions I found myself in an exchange of ideas about our mutual interest in the history of comics, about the minute details of comics form, about the books on his shelves and the artwork on his studio wall. Our session ran out of time (in fact went an hour over schedule) well before we ran out of topics, and I was left with the strong impression that conversations with Spiegelman come to a pause rather than ever really stop.

The blizzard of interview requests in the immediate wake of *Maus* made Spiegelman feel, as a fellow cartoonist tells it, like he was "giving up his career as an artist for one as an interview subject."[7] If so, since then Spiegelman has succeeded in folding each of those roles into the other; his many public utterances have helped to create the cultural climate in which he can create the kind of comics he wants to make. Read individually, each interview shows the cartoonist, as he told one interviewer, "just trying to deal with what was important to me in the medium that was best suited for me to tackle it through."[8] Reading the pieces together, however, one can make out the underlying story of how the cartoonist Art Spiegelman made himself possible.

The interviews in this volume are arranged by the date they were conducted, when that can be determined, rather than by when they were published; in most cases the gap between the conversations and their publication was brief. In keeping with the editorial policy of this series, the interviews are presented in full as originally published, with the following exceptions: obvious typographical errors and mistakes in transcription have been silently corrected, and the use of italics and quotation marks for titles of works has been regularized. The transcriptions of previously unpublished interviews have been edited for clarity and coherence with the permission of the original interviewers. Errors of fact and memory in the interviews have not been annotated or corrected; information in the interviews should be checked for accuracy against standard reference works.

This volume was made possible by the generosity and assistance of Art Spiegelman, for which I am deeply grateful. I would like also to express my thanks to all the authors whose interviews appear in this volume, and to Stetson University for its consistent support for my scholarship; special thanks also go to the staff of Stetson University's DuPont-Ball Library. The index was prepared by R. W. Scott; I thank him for his extraordinary generosity and collegiality. I have been helped in many different ways by series editor Tom Inge, and by Gary Groth, Todd Hignite, Mike Rhode, Artie Romero, and Brian Tucker. My appreciation also goes to Gene Kannenberg and Roger Sabin for their generosity in allowing their unpublished interviews to appear and for their assistance in transcription. I would like to thank my friend and editor, Seetha Srinivasan, for her many years of patience and support; I have also been greatly assisted by the staff of the University Press of Mississippi, in particular Anne Stascavage and Walter Biggins. I would like to dedicate this book to Donald Ault, who showed me that thinking hard and reading comics could be the same thing, and to my parents, Pat and Joe Witek, who did not throw out my comics.

JW

Notes

1. Bergdoll, *Cascade Comix Monthly* #14, p. 7.
2. *Comics Journal* #180, (1995), p. 88.
3. Pierre Bourdieu, *The Field of Cultural Production* (1993), p. 39.
4. Bill Kartalopoulos, "RAW: A History." *Indy Magazine*, Winter 2005. Online at http://64.23.98.142/indy/winter_2005/raw_02/index.html
5. Elizabeth Hess, "Meet the Spiegelmans," Village Voice (14 Jan. 1992), 87.
6. Art Spiegelman, Interview, "Fresh Air," National Public Radio, December 1986.
7. Eddie Campbell, *How to Be an Artist*. Eddie Campbell Comics (2001): p. 97.
8. Ryan, *Post-Standard*.

Chronology

1948	Art Spiegelman is born on February 15 in Stockholm, Sweden, to Vladek and Anya (Zylberberg) Spiegelman.
1951	The Spiegelman family moves to the United States and settles in Norristown, Pennsylvania.
1957	The Spiegelman family moves to the Rego Park section of Queens, New York.
1960	Spiegelman begins drawing his first cartoons.
1963	Spiegelman's drawings begin to be published in a variety of outlets, including his fanzine *Blasé*.
1963–65	Spiegelman attends the High School of Art & Design in New York City, majoring in cartooning. He meets Woody Gelman, art director of the Topps Chewing Gum Co., who urges him to apply for a job when he graduates from high school.
1964	Spiegelman begins to sell his drawings to the *Long Island Post*, among other publications.
1965–68	Spiegelman attends Harpur College (now Binghamton University) in Binghamton, New York, where he is

staff cartoonist for the college newspaper and editor of a college humor magazine.

1966 Summer: Spiegelman begins working for Topps as a creative consultant, developing and illustrating novelty cards, stickers, and candy products. He begins creating his first underground comix, at first distributing them on street corners, then publishing in the *East Village Other* and other underground newspapers and magazines.

1967 Spiegelman writes and draws the first series of *Wacky Packages* for Topps. He travels to San Francisco where he spends several months before returning to college.

1968 Spiegelman is hospitalized for a psychotic episode, ending his university studies. Anya Spiegelman commits suicide.

1969 Spiegelman begins working as a cartoonist and illustrator for men's magazines, including *Cavalier, Dude,* and *Gent*.

1971 After a number of previous visits, Spiegelman moves to San Francisco. His underground comix work eventually appears in numerous underground titles, including *Gothic Blimp Works, Bijou Funnies*, and *Young Lust*.

1972 An underground comic anthology, *Funny Aminals*, includes Spiegelman's "Maus," a three-page story using cats and mice as characters to depict his parents' experiences as death-camp survivors.

1973 Spiegelman co-edits *Short Order Comix*, the first issue of which contains "Prisoner on the Hell Planet," an autobiographical account of his mother's suicide. He co-edits *Whole Grains: A Book of Quotations* with Bob Schneider.

1974 April 1–3, Spiegelman lectures at Harpur College on "The Language of Comix."

1975–77   Spiegelman co-edits *Arcade* magazine with Bill Griffith; the magazine lasts seven issues.

1975   Spiegelman moves back to New York City. The three-page "Maus" is reprinted in *Comix Book*, an underground comix anthology published by Marvel Comics.

1977   Spiegelman marries Françoise Mouly on July 12. *Breakdowns*, an anthology of Spiegelman's experimental work from the underground comix and *Arcade*, is published.

1978   Under the imprint of "Raw Books and Graphics," Mouly begins publishing various projects, including a local neighborhood map/street guide, postcards, stationery, and cartoon pamphlets.

1979–87   Spiegelman teaches at the School of Visual Arts in New York.

1980   *RAW* #1, an anthology of comics and graphics, is published in July; it includes "Two-Fisted Painters," a color insert by Spiegelman. Eight issues of *RAW* magazine are published by Spiegelman and Mouly in oversized magazine format from 1980 to 1986. Three more paperback-book sized issues of the magazine are published in association with Penguin Books from 1989 to 1991. *RAW* #2 is published in December containing the first episode of *Maus: A Survivor's Tale*. *Maus* continues to be serialized as an insert in succeeding issues of *RAW*.

1982   Vladek Spiegelman dies on August 18.

1986   *Maus I: My Father Bleeds History* is published by Pantheon Books and is nominated for a National Book Critics Circle Award in biography.

1987   Spiegelman travels to Poland to research *Maus II*. Daughter Nadja is born to Spiegelman and Mouly. A reprint anthology of material from *RAW* magazine, *Read Yourself Raw*, is published by Pantheon.

1988   Spiegelman appears in a documentary film on comic books, *Comic Book Confidential*. He publishes "Commix: An Idiosyncratic Historical and Aesthetic Overview" in the graphic design magazine *Print*. *Maus I* wins the foreign category Prize for Best Comic Book at the Angoulême International Comics Festival in France. *Maus II* is awarded the same prize in 1993.

1989   *RAW* vol. 2, #1 is published by Penguin in the new format. Spiegelman ends his relationship with Topps.

1990   Spiegelman is awarded a Guggenheim Fellowship. *RAW* vol. 2, #2 is published. Spiegelman's critique of the "High/Low" exhibition at the Museum of Modern Art, "High Art Lowdown," is published in *ArtForum* magazine.

1991   *Maus II: And Here My Troubles Began* is published by Pantheon and earns a second National Book Critics Circle Award nomination for Spiegelman. Son Dashiell is born to Spiegelman and Mouly. Mouly joins the *New Yorker* as art editor. *RAW* vol. 2, #3, the magazine's final issue, is published by Penguin.

1992   Spiegelman receives a Pulitzer Prize special award for *Maus*. He joins the *New Yorker* as contributing editor and cover artist. An exhibition of artwork, sketches, and research materials for *Maus* is presented at the Museum of Modern Art in New York. Spiegelman's journalistic comic strip about a trip to Germany, "A Jew in Rostock," is published in the December 7 *New Yorker*.

1993   Françoise Mouly succeeds Lee Lorenz as art editor of the *New Yorker*. Spiegelman's first *New Yorker* cover, "Valentine's Day," (February 15) depicting a kiss between a Hassidic man and an African-American woman sparks public controversy. Spiegelman's September 13 *New Yorker* cover, "The Guns of September," depicts heavily armed schoolchildren returning to school. A comic-strip collaboration with

Maurice Sendak, "In the Dumps," is published in the September 27 *New Yorker*.

1994   Spiegelman participates in a *Village Voice* roundtable discussion on Steven Spielberg's film *Schindler's List*. Spiegelman is series designer for Dave Mazzucchelli's graphic novel adaptation of Paul Auster's novel *City of Glass*. A CD-ROM, *The Complete Maus*, containing the text of the published *Maus* along with sketches, drafts, historical documentation, and commentary by Spiegelman is produced by the Voyager Company. An edition of Joseph Moncure March's 1923 narrative poem *The Wild Party: The Lost Classic* designed and illustrated by Spiegelman is published by Pantheon. An abridged version of the work appears in the June 27 *New Yorker.*

1995   Spiegelman is awarded an honorary doctorate of letters from his alma mater, now Binghamton University. He co-edits, with R. Sikoryak, *The Narrative Corpse*, a chain-story by sixty-nine artists. Religious groups protest Spiegelman's *New Yorker* cover of April 17, "Theology of the Tax Cut," depicting an Easter bunny crucified against a tax form.

1996   A one-volume edition of *Maus: A Survivor's Tale* is published by Pantheon. "Mein Kampf," a comic describing Spiegelman's reaction to the success of *Maus*, is published in the May 12 issue of the *New York Times Magazine*.

1997   Spiegelman publishes *Open Me . . . I'm a Dog!*, a children's book. He writes an introductory essay for *Tijuana Bibles*, a collection of vintage sex comics. His essay "Getting in Touch With My Inner Racist" appears in the September 1 issue of *Mother Jones*.

1999   *Comix, Essays and Graphics and Scraps (From Maus to Now to MAUS to Now)*, an anthology of Spiegelman's work, is published as a catalogue to accompany La Centrale dell'Arte's traveling exhibition

Comix, Essays and Sketches. Police groups picket the *New Yorker* offices to protest Spiegelman's *New Yorker* cover of March 8, "41 Shots 10¢," the cartoonist's response to a police shooting of an unarmed citizen. Spiegelman's essay on Jack Cole, "Forms Stretched to Their Limits: What Kind of Person Could Have Dreamed Up Plastic Man?" appears in the April 19 *New Yorker* accompanied by Spiegelman's cover, "The Plastic Arts." Spiegelman is inducted into the Will Eisner Award Hall of Fame.

2000   February 14, Spiegelman publishes a comic-strip essay on Charles Schulz, "Abstract Thought is a Warm Puppy," in the *New Yorker*. Spiegelman and Mouly publish *Little Lit #1: Folklore & Fairy Tale Funnies*, an anthology of comics for children; contributors include a number of *RAW* alumni as well as several noted creators of children's literature.

2001   September 11, the Spiegelman family witnesses the destruction of the World Trade Towers after finding Nadja Spiegelman at her school near the base of the Towers. Spiegelman's black-on-black image of the World Trade Towers appears on the September 24 cover of the *New Yorker*. In 2005 the American Society of Magazine Editors ranks the cover at #6 on its list of "Top 40 Magazine Covers of the Last 40 Years." *Little Lit #2: Strange Stories for Strange Kids* is published. Spiegelman's *Jack Cole and Plastic Man: Forms Stretched to Their Limits*, with Chip Kidd, is published by Chronicle Books.

2002   Spiegelman is invited to create a series of comic strips on topics of his choice by *Die Zeit*, a weekly German broadsheet newspaper. Ten installments of "In the Shadow of No Towers" appear in *Die Zeit* and the *Forward* from 2002 to 2003 and are reprinted in several European newspapers and magazines and in small-press outlets in the United States. Major American media outlets decline to publish the strips.

New Yorker readers object to Spiegelman's July 8 cover, "Fears of July," which depicts an atomic mushroom cloud amid holiday fireworks.

2003 *Little Lit #3: It Was a Dark and Silly Night* appears. Spiegelman resigns from the *New Yorker*, citing differences in sensibility between himself and the magazine in the contemporary political climate.

2004 The collected volume of *In the Shadow of No Towers* strips are published along with a supplement of thematically related late nineteenth- and early twentieth-century newspaper comic strips.

2005 France names Spiegelman a Chevalier de l'Ordre des Arts et des Lettres. *Time* magazine names him to its "Top 100 Most Influential People" list. The first chapter of a projected longer work by Spiegelman, "Portrait of the Artist as a Young %@?*!," appears in the *Virginia Quarterly Review*.

2006 Spiegelman is interviewed in the March 6 issue of the *Nation* along with comics journalist Joe Sacco on the controversy concerning the Danish publication of cartoons of the prophet Mohammed. Spiegelman's fuller essay on the topic, "Drawing Blood," is published in the June issue of *Harper's* magazine. *Big Fat Little Lit*, a paperback collection of selections from the three volumes of *Little Lit*, is published. The second and third installments of "Portrait of the Artist as a Young %@?*!" are published in the *Virginia Quarterly Review*.

Art Spiegelman
Conversations

Art Spiegelman

ALFRED BERGDOLL / 1979

From *Cascade Comix Monthly* #11–12, February 1979, pp. 28–34, and #14, April 1979, pp. 4–9, 17. Reprinted by permission of CityStar Group, Inc.

Mr. and Mrs. (Art and Françoise) Spiegelman live and work in the ultra-fashionable Soho area of Manhattan on the third floor of a roomy loft. It is comfortable, tasteful, but all business—artistic business, needless to say.

Raw Books, Françoise and Art's imprint, is quartered here. The offset press, about eight feet long, gleams and glistens, apparently ready to go at any time, like a locomotive in a station. A large, very professional guillotine paper-cutter stands against the wall. These people are not dependent on imbecilic publishers and printers. Such a demonstration of independence and power is exhilarating.

Cascade: You were talking about the problems of distributing comix.
Spiegelman: Well, actually it was only part of something else that I was talking about which was that living in New York, it's very easy to be skeptical about underground comix continued existence, in a way that my compatriots in San Francisco don't. It's different than when I was living in San Francisco, and different from the reports I get from some friends in San Francisco, in that they have a much lower profile here in general. There are only maybe two or three places you can buy underground comix, so you have to be a real aficionado to follow it up or order by mail. On one level it feels like a very, very small-scale thing, just in its tangibility, and then there's also the problem of content. For the most part, the work is not as inspired as it was. There are a few people who are doing really fine work, the same people, for the most part, that have been doing really fine work for about eight or nine years, and there's no surprise anymore. There's not that many new people coming into it and that's a sure sign of decay, and the people who have been are into refining, myself included, refining their own corner, cultivating our own gardens.

But I don't feel that sense of breakthrough, that tingle when I pick up a book that I did at one time. I think that one of the biggest problems is this thing that I just mentioned about no new blood. For instance, Mark Beyer, who, as far as I'm concerned is one of the most important third-generation cartoonists, has a very difficult time of it. He wouldn't have if he had just been born five years sooner, but now he has a small book, he had to print it himself because none of the traditional underground publishers could handle it because of their economic situations. Even more sad, once he's gone through the struggle of putting his own book together, he's having a hard time finding a way to get it distributed. He's written to all the regular distributors and most of them haven't answered—I think Denis Kitchen answered him and said that it wasn't possible for him to distribute anything but mainstream underground comix. The idea of a mainstream underground is a boggling one to me. I understand economically and realistically where that idea comes from, but if someone like Mark can't find a reasonable outlet for his work, then there's no chance for new artists to really develop.

When most of the underground cartoonists started working, for the most part we were all pretty crude. It was only by having a chance to see our work in print and believe in ourselves as cartoonists that we were able to explore whatever we were doing far enough to develop a set of skills and a set of interests that were personal; develop our own personalities as artists. It's very difficult to do that if you have to work in a vacuum. I don't have that much contact with a lot of the new artists that are coming along, but just Mark as an example: very good work and no place to put it.

Another thing that really did shake me up was—I'm teaching now at the School of Visual Arts. I'd say that most of my students are taking comics studio courses; the other teachers at the school are Will Eisner and Harvey Kurtzman. I'm teaching a course in the language of the comics, an aesthetics and history course, and most of the people in the class have never heard of underground comix. They're about nineteen or twenty years old, they're intending to be professional cartoonists, but they not only hadn't heard of underground comix, but when I started exposing them to them this past week, I really got shaken up. I started showing them this R. Crumb story, "Whiteman Meets Bigfoot," and all of the underlying presumptions of the themes were alien to them; the idea that people might want to drop out of society—they didn't get it. They also found it very difficult to deal with the idea of comics that were personal. I find that one of the struggles I've had in the course was weaning these people from their Marvel Comics tit, and onto real tits or whatever. Like their idea of integrity is wanting to use a finer brush to feather the muscles.

To me, the fact that they could possibly not be aware of underground comix, the fact that the idea of a personal comic should be so shocking to them is all too bad. I suppose New York is a special case. . . .

Cascade: They look at themselves as shoemakers, rather than as artists?
Spiegelman: It's hard for them to look at themselves as artists because no alternative exists for them. Best I could tell them was that they're going to have to fight it out, they're going to have to set up their own little comic books and distribute them by taking them to stores, taking out little ads in comics fanzines, finding a route for themselves to express themselves. I kind of sympathize; I remember how it was in 1965 when I was drawing comics and the best I could do was some fanzine stuff, college newspapers; I think I started making up comic strip leaflets and passing them out on the street just as a way of exposing my work.

Cascade: How did you get started in art in the first place? Were you always doing cartoons as a kid?
Spiegelman: Yeah, I wanted to be a cartoonist specifically from about the age of eleven, and pretty diligently went about copying everything I

admired, and was actually doing cartoons for my junior high school newspaper, and then there was a local weekly newspaper in Queens that I didn't realize I should be getting paid for, I was just real happy that they were letting me illustrate their sports column with caricatures, and do an occasional cover illustration and lettering—they kept me pretty busy as a fifteen-year-old kid, and I learned a lot doing that.

And then I went to the High School of Art and Design in New York City, which is sort of a trade school, the way an automotive high school might be, and took academic courses plus a half-day each day of commercial art stuff. That's pretty much my art training.

Cascade: Which pens and brushes do you use most?

Spiegelman: Well, first of all, it's impossible for me to know because part of the way I've always worked is I think of each strip as having its own requirements visually, and therefore each strip has also required different tools, so that a strip like "Don't Get Around Much Anymore" I did with a rapidograph because I wanted the kind of sterility of line that that could provide. On the other hand a strip like "Prisoner on the Hell Planet" was done with scratchboard tools and brush. A good example is "Ace Hole," where each character was done with a different tool as indicated in that splash panel—there's a crowquill pen for the Picasso woman, and a rapidograph for the child's toy, Mr. Potato Head, and a brush for Ace Hole, so it would be drawn more like a pulpy detective illustration style.

Cascade: I guess that's one reason that a recent issue of *Alternative Media* called you the ultimate cartoonist.

Spiegelman: Oh, that's sort of embarrassing, but yeah. They were at least sensitive enough to record on the first page that I didn't want to be called the ultimate cartoonist.

Cascade: But I think it brings out your resourcefulness, which I think is pretty unique.

Spiegelman: It actually is trying to turn a possible weakness into an asset; I never developed any really strong one way of drawing, at least to my eyes. I've had people tell me that my artwork is very recognizable, and there are people whose artwork I find very recognizable who don't think of themselves as having a style. In any case, the fact that I don't find my work as having a clear trademark has made me decide that the best way for me to proceed is not to try to be a star, but rather to be an actor. What I meant by that is that a star is somebody who, no matter what role they're in, they're always Marlon Brando, or whoever, and an actor is somebody who finds his way into each role and convinces you that he's that character. And therefore to me it's most important that each comic strip be a fully realized world, rather than that they're all obvious slices of the same masterwork.

I think that until I saw *Breakdowns*, which was a collection of all my work, I didn't quite even know what all my underlying themes were, or what connectives there were between strips, and *Breakdowns* made it clear to me and to other people as well, I understand.

Cascade: How is the extension of the "Maus" story progressing?
Spiegelman: Slowly but surely I suppose. I find that it's the most challenging thing I've ever undertaken. So what I'm doing with *Maus* is . . . I don't think extension is the right word. I don't know what the right word is, but I'm doing *Maus* for the first time. I sort of had this little sneak preview that excited me to work on this project, which was the *Funny Aminals* three-page "Maus," but what I'm doing now is so much more extensive that it's something else completely. It has different requirements, a different rhythm, completely different work. What it will be is—I'm guessing now—maybe a 200-page or more comic book novel, for want of a better word, that will be the story of my father's life in Nazi Europe, actually starting from about the 1920s and taking him into about 1946 or '47. It will also be the story of my relationship with my father as expressed through that; in other words it will take place more or less in the present, with the bulk of the book being the flashbacks into his life.

I'm finding it very, very difficult going. For one thing, concentrating on the subject matter is difficult, and doing the research is difficult because it's just so painful. And yet I feel it's very important for me to grapple with those demons, and also insofar as there are stories still left that people should know, this is certainly among them. One of the reasons I got to work on *Maus* was that I found that some of the other directions I was heading in were becoming very specialized. I found myself speaking to fewer and fewer people. A certain kind of comics, comics that are interested in the form itself, that deal with the form as its subject matter, one could only take so far without really losing the bulk of the people who would otherwise comprise my audience. The reason, maybe, is that comics have always been so tied in to entertainment, story, humor, never going far beyond traditional narrative, that it's very hard for people to stretch for it. In other mediums it's possible to do work that it really isn't possible yet to do in comics. In painting, underground films, and most of the arts a degree of sophistication is presumed on the audience's part that one can't safely presume on the part of a comix reader.

Therefore I wanted to at least move back to home base, which is narrative. Comics are certainly a narrative medium and it's very hard to stretch them beyond it, and under the circumstances I didn't feel I could stretch much further. So I wanted to go back into narrative and tell a story, and then the problem was what story is worth telling. I think, for the most part, people are saturated with story. There's whatever number of comics come out a month, novels, TV shows, movies; all of these are usually one of Polti's eight plots presented one more time with various permutations. If I was going to go back to telling a story, I didn't want to just do one more inconsequential narrative. Doing a comic strip is just too difficult for me to try to do the same thing one more time; if I'm going to expend that kind of effort, it's got to be for something more challenging than that. This was a story that could ignite those things in me, and I find that it's very interesting in that it's possible to still be as concerned with form and structure as I always have been, but marrying it to this work so that it forms the subtext rather than the primary text of it.

Cascade: Well, I think you're too modest about "Maus," to tell you the truth. I think that the original story was the first, and I think only, successful treatment of the Jewish experience during second World War.
Spiegelman: You mean in comics.

Cascade: In any form that I've seen. I don't know of any artistic treatment of it that is successful—
Spiegelman: Oh no, there's a lot of literature; I've been finding out about it now.

But the problem, and one of the reasons I'm doing Maus is that people won't read this stuff, for the most part. I think that it offers such a threatening aspect of human experience that the natural tendency, and very forgivable tendency is to want to avoid it.

Cascade: Well isn't it the function of art to make this acceptable or tolerable?

Spiegelman: I don't think that it's possible to make it palatable or even understandable, but I think it's something that one has to grapple with, and one has to be given hooks with which to grapple with it, and maybe the best a work of art can do is give you some of these hooks with which one can try to come to grips with the ungrippable. One thing that this may do is by doing this story in comics form, maybe I'll reach people who can't be reached through some of these other media, and hopefully more honest than that bullshit TV series.

I'm working from tape-recorded conversations with my father, and supplementing them with current conversations with him. I'm having some major difficulties, and what I'm wrestling with in *Maus* is, first of all, taking a life and putting it in rows is very difficult, and therefore I find that it's useful to have a very flexible idea of what comics can be. Life isn't as sequential as comic strip panels would like it to be. I'm finding that all the things I've been doing in other comics, like where text and picture are apparently unrelated, and where things are cutting back and cutting forward are all really necessary as structural elements to propel a complex narrative.

At this point I think I've got about two or three chapters in breakdown form, and lots of notes for the rest of it, and I'm just inching forward. I don't know how long this project will take me. It's going to be a long time coming, in any case.

Cascade: Do you have any plans to publish, say, segments of *Maus* in magazine form?

Spiegelman: It's premature for that now because I'll first have the whole book done in breakdown form before I can get to drawing, and that's at least another year or two away. And then maybe as I finish it I'll just get too eager, because it's very hard to go that long without the gratification of seeing something in print. Maybe I could make some arrangements. I wouldn't mind making arrangements in Europe if I can. There's a possibility of that, but again, it's premature. It's hard to delay gratification that long, but I think it's the only way a project like this can be done, just to wait until it's finished and comes out as a book.

Cascade: I guess you haven't got many plans beyond the *Maus* thing. I mean in a current publishing context.

Spiegelman: I have plans concurrent with *Maus*, even for drawing, but nothing serious. I'm interested in trying some lithographs on our press, because evidently that can be done. And I'm interested in doing some

Unpublished sketch of *Maus I* cover (1979).

little cartoon projects. But there's not enough energy to do more than one serious comics thing at a time. I'm also involved in some more commercial art type comics stuff just to keep myself going.

Cascade: Yeah, I see a very accomplished etching here on the wall. And considering you've done only, you know . . . it looks like a master etcher's work.

Spiegelman: Well, I'm interested in trying some more graphics because one problem with *Maus* is that it is so consuming. It is so consuming that I need to take some time off and I think that lithographs now will be a way to relax from *Maus*, and also just to allow myself a head of steam in another direction, to do some of these strips for *Playboy*, some illustrations for the *New York Times Book Review* and they let off some energy in other directions. Otherwise I think I'd crack if all I was working on was *Maus*.

Cascade: Yeah. That's such a long-term project. Do you think comics can be fine art?
Spiegelman: Well . . .

Cascade: Actually, I don't see any distinction.
Spiegelman: Yeah, I get a little lost here too. Sure, of course comics can be art, but so can pencil sharpening.

Cascade: That would be a craft, I'd say.
Spiegelman: No, I think it would be possible to sharpen a pencil in such a way as to make a work of art out of it. It might then move over into the realm of whittling . . . I don't know . . . any vehicle can be steered toward the making of art, and comics are as open to that as any other possible medium. It's just as possible to make junk in painting as it is in comics, and it's just as possible to make art out of comics. I think the problem is one of the seriousness of intent. I don't think comics encourage the making of art in a way that painting does, let's say. It's a more fugitive medium; it's born in the sawdust, you know, rather than fertile soil.

Cascade: Yeah, and it's also that the drawings are created for reproduction.
Spiegelman: Yeah, but that doesn't mean a separate set of limitations and requirements. You know, like that's not necessarily a liability. Novels are set in type and one reads them in book form and it's possible to make art for reproduction. I think maybe that's part of the power of comics, that you don't have to go to a museum and stand in front of it for fifteen minutes until your arches start aching.

Cascade: Well, I know that if you get your art from museums exclusively you're not going to get much art, because I think you have to live with art to get the benefit of it. That's why I collect it, as a matter of fact.
Spiegelman: And it's much more possible to live with a . . . much more affordable anyway . . . to live with reproduced art. We were just reading

in the Sunday *Times* about how Rockefeller was selling these . . . did you read about this? . . . selling these expensive . . .

Cascade: Yeah, the art guild associations are against it. So am I.
Spiegelman: They're just selling regular old reproductions as the original. And I think it's much more to the point to make art for reproduction, rather than to produce art and pretend that it's the original. And that's one of the assets comics has going for it. There's a funny thing about comics which is that you've got to simplify your drawing because you're working with, more often than not, sharp black and white. You can't even too successfully, usually, work in grey tones. So you have to simplify drawings for that reason. You also have the fact that most panels are very small so even if you're drawing twice as large, you're still working in an area that would be considered a very small etching, let's say, with a maximum five or six inches high. And you also have the fact that you have to simplify the gesture to make it communicate quickly because it's a kind of picture writing. And you also have the fact that you can't fit that much text into any one panel, so you have to simplify your text and therefore, to do something really potent you have to suggest much, much more than you can actually state. And in that sense, maybe comics have more in common with poetry than with prose. And that's merely a limitation that the medium presents, but every medium has its limitations and it's incumbent on the artist to deal with those and make the most of it. Limitations can be turned to an advantage. And on the other hand, one of the problems with comics is, well, for one thing, they're called comic strips so they're expected to give you a boffo laugh, or I guess at most they're expected to give you some escapist super hero entertainment or something, but they're not really expected to do more than be a vehicle for mass medium entertainment. So it doesn't really attract artists to come along and grapple with the material because that's not what it's billed as. And it also doesn't attract an audience who's serious for the most part. Serious audiences are probably at least as important as serious artists.

Cascade: Yeah, I think that maybe numerically there are not many more serious comics fans than there are comics artists.
Spiegelman: Yeah, I think that the problem of audience is a major one. It's very important for people to be willing to stretch themselves to meet the work rather than to have the work poured down their sleeping, open gullets.

Cascade: Why do you think that R. Crumb dislikes the view of comics as high class art? He seems to want to stay away from high class art.
Spiegelman: Well, the first and natural answer to that is, "Gee, you should really ask R. Crumb why." But beyond that I think I can say that I find his suspicions understandable, even for myself, in that high class art just leads to a lot of sham as often as it leads to real art. And there is as much junk in galleries as there is in comic books.

Cascade: If not more . . .
Spiegelman: One of the reasons I guess I'm attracted to comics is that they are such a fugitive medium. It is such a despised form. That's kind of exciting, you know?

Cascade: Actually, I don't make any distinction between one kind of art and another. Certainly the African tribal artist . . . to him distinction between art and craft is nonexistent. *Arcade* in retrospect seems more and more wondrous as we get feeble efforts like *Zap* #9. What are your thoughts about the future?
Spiegelman: There were things I liked in *Zap* #9 and there were things I didn't like that appeared in *Arcade*. But one thing that *Arcade* did that isn't happening now is it provided a least one group of artists a very visible rallying point, and it was a place where at least one group of artists could try to top each other. And maybe that's important. The fact that there's a sense of community that I don't feel anymore when I look at the comics. I don't feel that the artists are in touch with each other the same way they used to be.

Cascade: Yeah, everybody at *Arcade* seemed to be doing his very best, that was evident, I think.
Spiegelman: And as far as the future goes, I don't know. I think that the artists that were in *Arcade* are still doing fine work and finding their own outlets for it. What's much more problematic to me like I said, is what new artists are going to do. Well, for me, it's so specialized I end up seeing what the future is for me rather than what the future is for comics. For me right now the future is to do a long, extended book of my own work. The comics format doesn't really excite me that much per se. I'm not that excited about seeing my work printed on newsprint in thirty-two small, blurrily printed pages that are sold in head shops. It's not very stimulating for me. The press that we alluded to a little bit before might provide an option for certain kinds of things to be produced. It's not an easy period.

Cascade: When and how did you get your offset printing press? I see you also have a heavy duty guillotine paper cutter.

Spiegelman: Well, it's not my press so much as it's our press. Françoise is really the steam engine behind this one. She's the one who took a course in how to use a multilith and is really struggling with it; learning what she can pull out of it. And, well let's see, the way it came about was out of Françoise's desire to do that and I'm very excited by what opportunities that affords to me and some of my friends as part of this. I'd really like to emphasize that Raw Books is Françoise's project—through proximity and shared interests I'm involved as partner and advisor. The way we got it was by doing the Soho map project. We were able to get enough money together by selling ad space to the "chic" stores of this "chic" neighborhood, and publishing a map of the area. And the money, the proceeds, went into the press for the 1978 map. And the proceeds of the 1979 map are going into paper, ink, binding costs and whatever costs to set up the publishing projects that come out of it. What those will be, we're just beginning to find out now.

Cascade: I see. Could you give us some figures say for the people who might be interested in going into something similar?

Spiegelman: How much the press would cost? Well, we had to shop around quite a bit. I think that the press itself cost $2,000.00, and I think the paper cutter was another $400.00. These are used pieces of equipment and we really had to shop around to get those prices and we still don't have other fairly rudimentary things like . . . maybe we won't even get them for a while . . . like a plate maker and an offset camera, but we have connections to people whose equipment we make use of. And . . . that's I guess the costs of that stuff, but that doesn't tell you how much a plate would cost and how much a neg would cost and how much the paper costs and it's relatively expensive, I guess.

Cascade: What have you done with the press so far?

Spiegelman: So far very little. What we've done is an announcement that the press existed, that said fine printing since 1978 on a very badly printed announcement . . .

Cascade: I saw your letterhead and your letterhead is beautifully done.

Spiegelman: We did some nice stationery and we did a little . . . Françoise invented this format of mail books which are sort of an eight-page postcard. The first one is a reproduction of sorts of a comic strip by

Caran D'Ache, a nineteenth-century French cartoonist with one panel per page and Mark Beyer just completed our second mail book which will be *Manhattan* . . . seven scenes of Manhattan. And hopefully Spain will do one, and Lynch, and Bill Griffith, and I just completed one, "Every Dog Has Its Day." This was originally a bunch of doodles made by me in a copy of a book called *The Literary Dog* as a gift for a hospitalized friend. Françoise selected some of my drawings and decided to make a mail book out of it—in color yet. Then I just did a piece of work that may appear as the cover for this *Cascade* that was turned into a note-card. These are all small projects just to learn how the press operates. But beyond these card projects we also intend to do various peculiar items like a Zippy the Pinhead project in the works, and we want to do a book translating the work of a very important nineteenth-century cartoonist named Rodolphe Töpffer who could be considered to be the first comic strip artist in the 1830s. This work's never been printed in America at all and Françoise is translating it. I'll write a monograph and we'll put that out as a book. Then Françoise is interested in translating French authors like Alfred Jarry's essays that have never been in America and maybe we'll illustrate those and issue them as chap books. There's a number of wonderful cartoons and illustrations from the early twentieth century that I think should be retrieved and put back into print like things from the French magazine, *L'Assiette au Beurre* and from *Simplicissimus*, a German illustrated magazine from the turn of the century. And I'm interested in trying some peculiar little books, maybe one panel a page books, of my work. One, *Work And Turn*—a kind of "modernistic" eight-pager, eighteen pages long. It should be in print before this *Cascade*. We're open to doing things with some of our cartoonist buddies as they come up with projects. One thing we just found out is that the press is actually capable of pulling a legitimate lithograph. It's just sort of used a little bit differently. Therefore, I know that Mark Beyer and myself will be doing some of that work on the press too.

Cascade: It sounds like an ambitious program. I didn't realize you were going to set up as a regular publisher.
Spiegelman: Well, a small scale publisher. Incidentally, if *Cascade* readers would like to be kept posted on Raw Books stuff as it appears they could send some stamped self-addressed envelopes to: Françoise Mouly, Raw Books, 27 Greene Street, NYC 10013 and receive announcements.

Cascade: What is this program costing, say, for your initial year of publication?

Spiegelman: It'll be easier to tell you that next year because we're just starting. We have some dough earmarked for projects this year and we'll see how far it goes.

Cascade: Then you're in business as a real publisher, I'd say.

Spiegelman: Well, we're still setting it up. We don't really have a distribution arm set up, and we'll have to deal with that as each project comes along. Find a way to distribute it. And it's just being born right now so we don't know where it will go or how far it can go. It's just that the press feels like a good rallying point for some possible artistic energy.

Cascade: It sounds exciting to me. What do you think of the younger artists? You said there weren't very many. Like Mark Beyer.

Spiegelman: Well, he's come up in this interview fairly often.

Cascade: Okay, let's get to Aline Kominsky.

Spiegelman: I like Aline's work very much, I just hope she keeps doing it. Last conversation (it was a while ago) she indicated a reluctance to keep drawing, and I sure hope that's not the case. I don't know. I just haven't seen that many younger cartoonists, you know? I know when we were doing the *Arcade* thing we did open up a side show specifically, that section in the back, to try to find new work and there just wasn't that much exciting work around. I've seen some new people cropping up in Kitchen's books and in some comics coming out of Los Angeles. But nothing that's jolted me. I think I've seen more interesting work coming out of France and Spain right now than I do from here.

Cascade: What's the problem with most female comics artists? Most are so disappointing. Now you may not share that disappointment . . .

Spiegelman: No, there's a few artists that I'm interested in that are women. Kominsky, Diane Noomin, Mary K. Brown, and Cathy Millet in France come to mind immediately. There are other women whose work just doesn't set my spine tingling as directly. The areas that they're mining are as disappointing as the areas most men cartoonists that I see are mining. I don't know if it's such a useful distinction. I know that to some extent the women have brought it on themselves like coming out with "women's comics" but it's as if you'd go into a museum and there would be one room for artists under 5'6'' and another room for work by artists over 5'6'' tall. It's a silly way to divide work up.

Cascade: What are the economics of cartooning as you and other greats practice it, that is practicing it as an art rather than as a business?

Spiegelman: Golly, I think it's quite a struggle for most people. I'm more fortunate than most in that I work for this bubble gum company and they keep me afloat with a relative minimum time investment, and it leaves me free to supplement my income here and there but not be dependent on commercial magazine exposure or trying to make a living out of underground comics. But as far as I know, most of my buddies are having a hard time of it. Justin Green is a sign painter; Spain is scuffling around looking for men's magazine illustration work; Bill Griffith has to turn out an incredible number of pages of underground comics just to make a subsistence living, where if the same energy were applied elsewhere, he'd be sitting quite pretty. Kim has a hard time of it. It's clearly not a get-rich-quick scheme.

Cascade: I'm disappointed that Justin Green isn't able to do more work because I think he's certainly as good as anybody. What can a talented beginner expect economically?

Spiegelman: Nothing but hardship, I think. In a way, what can you expect? You're not providing a commodity that most people want and therefore you can't expect financial remuneration. What I try to convince my art students to do in the class I teach is to go out and do commercial art work, or get a job driving a taxi and don't expect money from what you do. I'm fortunate in that I don't have to make money from *Maus* or from my other underground comics stuff. I just wish it just wasn't so hard to keep them afloat or keep them in the world, but that's just the way it is. If one wants to make money, one draws sex jokes, you know? I think that real art isn't really encouraged in any form. I think that the gallery scene is just as incapable of producing art as the commercial magazine scene. So it's just incumbent on whatever an artist . . . whatever that word means . . . it's incumbent on a real artist to be a fugitive, you know?

Cascade: Which artists of the past and present do you think most of?

Spiegelman: Oh, there's a long, long list. As far as artists in the past go, then we can go on all night listing photographers, painters, film makers. But in the world of comics, I would say Winsor McCay is very important. The people I teach in my class . . . it's funny, in teaching this thing I'm teaching supposedly the history of comics, but I'm primarily dealing with the aberrations in the history of comics because most comics, like most of everything else, is shit, so I try to give an overview and explain what the general climate of the comics were and then I focus on the ones that mean the most to me so that the people I focus on are therefore the people I like including Winsor McCay, Lionel Feininger, Harry Hershfield—an artist I just discovered in this series of books that Bill Blackbeard is responsible for. Great stuff! "Abie the Agent" and even more important for me is "Dauntless Durham" which is really exciting early comic strip work. But, Lionel Feininger, George Herriman, Chester Gould is somebody whose work my admiration knows no bounds for that stuff. Then, moving over into comic book land there's Will Eisner, Harvey Kurtzman, Bernard Krigstein, and to a lesser extent Basil Wolverton—and Jack Cole is very good.

Cascade: You have a comic strip, Ed Head, in *Playboy*'s Christmas issue. I think it is substantial and of course it contains no sex. How did you get in there?

Spiegelman: Well, it's funny. Like, Skip Williamson is the art director and Jay Lynch was working for them, two people I've known for a long time and Jay was trying to convince me for a long time to do something for *Playboy*, and I made a stab at it doing a half page strip that they rejected. I figured that was the end of it. And then I met Michelle Urry, who's their cartoon editor and she went through my notebook, some xeroxes of pages from my sketchbook and said, "Could I borrow this, this and this to show Hefner?" and I said, "Sure, if you think it might go over. I don't want to do any new work because I tried and I got my fingers burned." Oddly enough, this Ed Head which was . . . I had just finished reading the *Smithsonian Book of Comics* and got really turned on by the idea of the kind of pacing that a day-to-day comic asks for and as a result I did this Ed Head thing as just a series of dailies and evidently they were looking for some short takes like that and I didn't know that my daily would be appearing as maybe a monthly or a bimonthly, but it seemed to go over well with Hefner and they've okayed about nine of them at this point. And they took a couple of other one-shots and I've also scripted some stuff that some other artist is drawing up—the thing that they first rejected . . . when I got it back it was obvious to me that why they rejected it was that my drawings looked too weird. So I ended up joining forces with an artist who has a more conventional way of drawing, and he took the same dialogue, basically, and drew it up another way and they went for it and would like more of those. That was a parody of Mark Trail, Nature Facts, sexual facts of life. And they've taken a couple of one-shots and they seem to be receptive to a certain . . . I guess the lighter side of Spiegelman. I have no complaints about my relationship there, because so far they've been pretty much hands off. Either they take it or they don't take it, but they haven't made any changes in the stuff they have taken. It has its limitations. What they want is light, entertaining humor and that's what comics have always done and therefore it's hard to find a handle. I just sort of find Ed Head relaxing to do more than anything else. It's a pleasurable diversion. I don't take it too seriously.

Cascade: Frankly, I thought that your contribution was outstanding in that issue. May I ask what they pay?

Spiegelman: I think that their standard rate is pretty damned good for comics although not as high as what they pay their gag cartoonists, peculiarly enough. The pay for a one row comic like Ed Head is $300.00 in color. A half page is $400.00 and a full page is $600.00.

Cascade: That's not really very much. In fact it seems, you know . . . for *Playboy*.

Spiegelman: I guess on the other hand for anybody else, I can't think of any other market in the country that comes close.

Cascade: Like what does *High Times* pay?

Spiegelman: I think . . . all I've had there is reprints . . . I think it's about $250.00 a page, or maybe $200.00 a page . . . I'm not positive. But the rates for comics in general are always very low considering . . . compared to the amount of work that's put into an illustration. You're asking some-body to write, to draw, to do mechanical color, to letter. All the different skills involved, it's crazily underpaid work, even for the dross, even for stuff like the Marvel Comics, the pay is very poor for the work expected. But compared to underground comics, boy oh boy is it good!

RAW Magazine: An Interview with Art Spiegelman and Françoise Mouly

DEAN MULLANEY / 1980

From *Comics Feature* #4, July–August 1980, pp. 49–56. Reprinted by permission of Dean Mullaney.

Art Spiegelman has long been in the vanguard of the comics medium. He was among the first wave of underground cartoonists in the 1960s. His and Bill Griffith's *Arcade* again broke new ground during its too brief run in the mid-1970s. His collection, *Breakdowns*, released last year, once more found Spiegelman exploring and expanding the horizons of the medium. He has produced postcards, bubble gum cards, book covers for European publishers, and currently teaches at the School of Visual Arts in New York, in a department that also includes Harvey Kurtzman and Will Eisner.

It is now 1980 and Spiegelman and his co-editor, Françoise Mouly, have produced the first issue of another new magazine: *RAW*. It is related to the underground movement only in that it explores new territory. Its contributors range from Barcelona cartoonist Mariscal (with three short entries), to Allentown, Pa. artist Mark Beyer ("Dead Things"), to Spiegelman himself (a full color twelve-page insert and a one-pager entitled "Drawn Over Two Weeks While on the Phone").

RAW is a large, over-sized magazine, measuring 10½'' × 14½'' and is being printed on a high quality 70 lb. paper stock. Subtitled "The Graphix Magazine of Postponed Suicides," RAW is thirty-six pages plus the twelve-page, 5'' × 7'' insert.

The following interview was conducted in late May as Spiegelman and Mouly were in the middle of three weeks' work hand separating the color insert.

Feature: What are your goals with RAW and how do they differ from the goals of Arcade?

Spiegelman: I think Arcade, at the time that it came out, was a very advanced comics magazine. It was appropriate to its time and the geographical place, which was San Francisco, and the people who were surrounding me, who were the San Francisco underground cartoonists. Bill Griffith and I wanted to put together the best material from that group of people. But now it's six or so years later and I found a certain degree of impatience on my part with underground comics. I still scan the racks, but being 3,000 miles away, it has less immediacy for me than it did when I was out there. In San Francisco you can go into a small corner store and some of them actually have little racks with underground comics in them. Here, they don't have that kind of high profile. That in and of itself makes it seem less tangible to me and, I suppose, to other people who are geographically far away from that scene.

Also, I think there's been a tendency in underground comics for several unfortunate things to happen: one is it's not a place for new blood. The people who broke turf in 1967, '68, '69, myself included, are still appearing in underground comics. But when we were doing it, it wasn't that our work was over the top in terms of quality, it's just that we were at the right place at the right time. Now it's much harder for new talent to break into underground comics. That to me is a sign of ossification. It's not a vital scene anymore. Some of the cartoonists are still doing wonderful work, but some of them have fallen into riffs where essentially they do variations on exactly what they were doing ten years ago, with fine tuning that has been developed over the years. But that's it. The themes have tended to calcify, also. There's still the preoccupation

with sex, violence, and drugs. The Furry Freak Bros. are certainly as popular as ever, and that's still what people associate with underground
comics. So it made a certain leap, but it stopped.

Mouly: The publishers are aware of it because they only publish certain
kinds of work and certain artists.

Spiegelman: Yes. They're more prone to publish the old artists or certainly the old titles. Turner would rather do *Slow Death* #7 or 8 than
Whatever #1.

Feature: Do you think the publishers are responsible for things becoming
stale?

Spiegelman: They're responsible, but I wouldn't hold them culpable
because it's really the audience's fault. The publisher is only responding
to the marketplace and that's what people have come to expect from
underground comics. One of the things even with *Arcade* that was really
hard to break out of was that people expected sex, drugs, and violence.
Hardly any of those things were covered.

Feature: Was the reason for doing *Arcade* in a larger format an attempt
to differentiate its appearance from underground comics?

Spiegelman: There were several reasons. One of them was because at
the time underground comics were going through a recessionary cycle,
and we just wanted to have a life raft that everybody could climb on to.
Another reason was that *Comix Book* was coming out and we wanted
to respond to it. *Comix Book* was this compromised underground comics
magazine coming out from Marvel, and I was even to some degree associated with it. But it wasn't satisfactory. It didn't do the job and we
wanted to do it up right.

Feature: What was your initial involvement with *Comix Book*?

Spiegelman: Originally I was going to do a cover and several interior
pages, but when I found out what the copyright situation was, I allowed
them to reprint my work, but I couldn't do new work. One of the major
inroads that underground comics made was the possibility for artists to
have the right to own their material and do whatever they saw fit with
it. I think the battle fought then allowed magazines like *Heavy Metal*
and *Epic* to consider similar arrangements.

   The results satisfied me at the time but since then I've wanted to see
a place where new people can work. Françoise and I want to see a place
for new themes to develop, new possibilities for what comics can deal

with. It's funny because things are now going full circle: underground comics were responsible for a certain kind of comic happening in France, the Netherlands, Spain and other countries. They took the lead from underground comics, which then indicated that comics could be done for adults. They could be a lot freer. It was permuted in France, for instance, to something exciting in its own right. Now it's our turn to accept that there's something happening over there. Let's bring it over here again and take it one *more* step.

We'd like to present the kind of possibilities that the European audience has and made possible, and make that available here. In *RAW*, 25–30% of the material is European art. Another percentage of the magazine is work by new cartoonists, people who have been active in animated cartooning, the world of so-called "high art"—painting and performance art—and illustrators doing comics. These are other inputs. We'll be using underground cartoonists and even overground cartoonists, if we find work that fits the sensibility of the magazine.

Feature: I notice that the first issue you're not using any of the well-known underground cartoonists. Is this because you don't want to be typed as an underground comic?

Spiegelman: There's two reasons: one is that I'm 3,000 miles away and while I keep in fairly close contact with a handful of my cronies, it was a little hard to explain what we wanted the magazine to be. We had a vision of what this would be as an entity as well as what the specific strips could be. Rather than try to do that, it was easier to just put it together and show people what we want to do. There've been commitments on the part of underground cartoonists who want to do work for it, and we'll have their work in future issues. Kim Deitch will be doing something with us, Bill Griffith . . . I'm hoping that Justin Green will do something with us, as well. I don't think we'll use everybody from *Arcade* in any given issue, but some of that stuff will filter in because those are the exciting artists who are working in America right now. The main thing with the first issue was to set a tone. We thought that was an easier way to set a tone. We didn't want to build up an expectation for an *Arcade* that happened to have three more inches in height and two more inches in width. I guess our distance from San Francisco is an asset because we wanted to do something that *wasn't* underground comics. This could have turned out to be just a big underground comics book and that's not as exciting as *RAW.*

Poster advertising *RAW* (vol. 1, no. 1, July 1980).

Mouly: At the beginning we were just trying to explain to people what we were trying to do. Then we gave up. We started looking at work from different people. Most of the work we looked at was European work because we could reprint it. A few people looked at what we were selecting and we looked at their portfolios—the people who were in New York. I'm sure that if any of the [San Francisco cartoonists] had been around . . .

Spiegelman: Yeah. Gary Hallgren, for example, is now living in New York and did some illos in *RAW* and also wants to do strips with us. It was very difficult to communicate the specific kinds of things we wanted to see. One of the reasons there's so many relatively short pieces in the first issue is not because we have a commitment to things that are one or two pages long rather than ten-page comics stories, but just because we wanted to give more of a spectrum in one issue.

Feature: So whereas the undergrounds fit their time, *RAW* is the direction you think comics should get into now?

Spiegelman: It's a direction for *RAW* to go into. When I say this about underground comics, that's in general. There are specific books which have specific pieces that I like very much. It's just that we wanted to see a new context for the material. And that's *RAW*. I think that it exudes a certain kind of class and elegance. I think it's an interesting tension because comics, in America at least, are considered this real gutter medium. To have that tension between an elegant format and a medium we're used to thinking of as junk literature makes you look at the work in a different way. The risk it runs is seeming pretentious. The risk is worth it because it asks for an involvement on the part of an audience that's much more intense than the audience is used to giving a comic. That makes a different kind of work happen. It's one possibility of what we want to see happen to comics in the future, and we certainly want to explore it.

Feature: Do you think it's an important part of comics that rather than be cheap entertainment, it be something the audience can really get into and think about?

Mouly: I don't think it should be just one way or the other. What we're trying to present is an alternative. If somebody wants to do comics that are like the ongoing daily strips to keep people entertained, that's one attitude and it's certainly never going to be cancelled by *RAW*. It might die of its own or have a rebirth, but if somebody is interested in comics as a medium, which is pictures and words together but is not necessarily adventure or humor, *RAW* is one place in America which can print that work.

Spiegelman: "Comics" is a word that sometimes gives people problems. As a medium it's as flexible and has as much potential as, say film. It's

not cheap film; it's something else. But it has as much potential as a medium so that to say "Well, should film be the kind of film that Jean-Luc Godard makes or should it be the kind of film that Howard Hawks makes?" . . . It's just a medium and what that vessel is filled with is dependent on the artist's interests and needs, as well as the audience's.
Mouly: We're more aware of artists' needs for this magazine than an audience's need for it, but that may be because we are in contact with the artists, and the audience is not aware that it exists yet.

We've been talking to a number of people who have been involved with redefining comics just by trying to find another name for it. That means that those people and a number of others—people we've met and people we've seen work from—are disturbed by the ghetto. They're interested in doing something, but cannot relate to the current work they see. In a sense, one of the rewards of doing *RAW* was meeting artists who are used to working on paintings for gallery shows and so on. Usually if you ask these people to do comics, they'll do a little doodly thing, a little story with a gag as a punch line. But in *RAW* we had a number of people who are gallery artists, filmmakers and so on, who did things which combined word and picture. They weren't necessarily funny and they weren't a parody of comics. They were thoroughly involved with words and pictures and what that meant for them. That is what we're really interested in seeing.

Feature: In other words, you'd like to introduce to the comics medium artists who work in other media and see what their perspective can bring to comics?
Spiegelman: Yeah. This is a magazine of words and pictures. It's a literary magazine. It uses comics instead of seas of type as its way of communicating. Any artist who's capable of expressing himself would have a vehicle in which to travel and present that work.

There are things that are just graphics in here, there are things that are just text pieces. *RAW* is an attempt at redefining what a comic can be. It's not by doing polemical essays; it's just by presenting the kind of work we'd like to see. It's one of the reasons I got into doing the kind of comics I do: I wanted to read that kind of comic and nobody was making it for me.

It's also a place where we want to reprint some early material that should be resuscitated. I found that in teaching at the School of Visual Arts, the only comics the students are aware of are the Marvel comics,

so they don't even have an option. Marvel comics are pretty feeble if
you compare them to, let's say, the EC comics of the 1950s. And going
back further than that, the great comics of the 1920s and 1930s. And
beyond that, how about going back before 1900? There were wonderful
things that happened that were basically comics.

Mouly: We're not trying to say "Now we're going to show everything
that can be comics." We're just interested in saying "Don't follow the
usual rules, but play around, experiment and stretch things out." When
you go back, even before newspaper comics, there were a number of
people who were experimenting with the idea of combining words and
pictures. At the time they didn't have anybody to follow, so each one of
them created his own world and his own rules.

Spiegelman: Did you know that Gustave Doré started out by being
essentially a comic book artist? He did two or three books that are picture stories: ten little pictures on a page, and I think there's even balloons in some of them. There's text underneath the pictures and it flows
from unit of time to unit of time.

Mouly: The main thing that makes this interesting is that rather than just
doing illustrated stories, Doré had graphic ideas which were wonderful.
For example, he did a scene that repeats: there's an army coming in and
the first scene is a detailed drawing; in the second one it becomes more
simplified; by the fifth or sixth time the army comes in, it's just little
sticks, a simplification of his first picture.

Spiegelman: The book is called *The History of Holy Russia*. So there's all
this great stuff and people should be exposed to that, as well as to
contemporary work because it's really a wonderful continuum worth
plugging into.

Feature: It seems as though you're expanding the spectrum of what has
traditionally been labeled comics. Are you looking for a new audience for
this magazine?

Spiegelman: We'd like to reach those people within the comics community who are receptive to something other than what they're ordinarily
exposed to. We'd also like to find an audience that right now when they
hear the word "comics," reach for their guns: "Comics? That's junk." It's
a trigger reaction; there's no intrinsic reason for it, but the history [of
comics] has been such that junk is what one associates with comics.
Those people won't even look at an underground comic unless I put it in
front of their noses and say, "This is something else. It's not what you

think it is." Everybody who's interested in comics has had this experience, of trying to turn somebody on to the material and saying, "No, forget about the fact that it's on newsprint and it's junky looking. Read this story." One possible way of getting around it—certainly the tactic we're trying to pull off here—is that nobody has to be ashamed to look at this magazine. That just allows things to happen.

Mouly: Another thing was trying to design this as a magazine.

Spiegelman: So it isn't just a large collection of comics, but the magazine has a look, feel, and flavor all its own. You pointed out before that when you looked at the title logo and the cover design, it reminded you of the new music magazines, like *Wet* or *Interview*, *Slash*, and magazines like that. To me that's a fine connection because those magazines are graphically a lot more stimulating than most other magazines.

Mouly: It's also a new format so that people don't have too many set expectations.

Feature: There's no stigma attached to it yet, since it's new.

Spiegelman: Not yet. If anything, *Wet* magazine is a coffee table magazine for the new generation the way at one time, in 1971 or so, every self-respecting hippie had to have a few underground comics on his crate, along with a hash pipe and a couple of other accoutrements. We may be all wet about this [laughter] . . . we may be all *wrong* about this, but we figured that one nice thing about these new large size magazines is that there's not a glut of them. One problem we had with *Arcade* when we tried to get a distributor, was where the heck were they going to put it? They'd look at *Arcade* and say, "It's a little like the *National Lampoon*. Well, it's a little like *Creepy*? No, it's not like *Creepy*." [Laughter] They didn't know what to do with us. Besides, if they were willing to take us at all on a regular magazine stand, they'd just have to put it in with the men's magazines, or something. *RAW*, at least, will be in a context of other magazines that don't have much in common except their size. There's a handful of magazines in this format: there's one that's just devoted to architecture, there's one that's just devoted to photography, called *Picture*, there's a couple of artists' magazines, certainly a few music magazines, fashion magazines, magazines of advertising . . .

Feature: Do you think *RAW* will ever expand the audience into the masses?

Mouly: Getting it to the masses isn't what we're thinking about. We think that we have queer enough—strange enough—taste and we're

not in touch with the masses. If we look at television or read mass market magazines, they're not things we're interested in. So we assume that people who would be interested in the same things that we are . . .
Spiegelman: Or are as alienated from the mass culture as we are . . .
Mouly: . . . would be interested in *RAW*. We certainly don't expect that this magazine will ever have a mass audience.
Spiegelman: Are you familiar with the Goethe awards? Do you know why they're called the Goethe awards? This ties right in to what we're talking about. The very first comic strip artist was a guy named Rodolphe Töpffer, a Swiss school teacher who for his own amusement did these picture stories, with, like, six panels on a page that for the first time told an interwoven story with closely interrelated pictures. This was about 1830. Töpffer would print up thirty or forty copies of this thing on a cheap lithograph and disseminate them to his friends. One copy reached Goethe, who said "God, this is incredible stuff! What a great medium, these words and pictures together!" He passed it around to his friends, who were a lot more influential than Töpffer's friends. As a result of that, the book ended up going into other kinds of printings. It was very popular in Europe until the beginning of the twentieth century.

The stuff that Töpffer did didn't reach a mass audience, but it did reach the movers and shakers. By doing that, the next generation was affected by what he did. Even better than reaching the people who were reading the cheap novelizations that they had then, Töpffer reached other artists, reached other writers. You can trace it this way: Töpffer directly affected a German artist named Wilhelm Busch, who did *Max and Moritz* (a book that is available through Dover, in fact). And that created American comics, in a sense, because William Randolph Hearst, as a kid traveling in Europe, was exposed to *Max and Moritz* and thought it was great. When he came back here, he hired an artist to do something like *Max and Moritz* for an American paper, and that was *The Katzenjammer Kids*.

So Töpffer was responsible for American comics. Alfred Jarry, whom we write about and have a piece by in *RAW*, was very affected by reading Töpffer's books when he was a kid. When he was an adult, he dedicated a chapter of one of his books to Töpffer. Cocteau claims that Töpffer was a big influence on him. Doré was also very influenced by Töpffer's work. So he had a strong impact.

I don't know how things work in an electronic age, but that's the way in which we'd like to reach a mass audience. If we only had 5,000 readers but they're the right 5,000, that's great.

Feature: You think, then, that *RAW*'s influence will be on other artists?
Spiegelman: Other artists, other art directors, other writers, other people involved in media. An important part of the equation that's usually left out is that the audience is as important as the artist. The audience determines what's possible, and right now the audience expects and receives this stuff that you're supposed to lean back and let hit you for a second, and then go away somewhere else. Nothing is asked of you as an audience; you're not asked to participate in a piece of work and give it your attention, give it your energy and thereby reap a far richer reward than you would from the kind of material that doesn't require any effort. Hopefully, we'll find that kind of an audience. We'd like to do real art that has an audience. That's why we're so betwixt and between: one of the things that attracts me to comics is that there is some life there; I find very little life when I wander into the Soho galleries—it just leaves me blank. We want to do art *with* an audience.
Mouly: Which doesn't mean that the artist has to play up to the audience. It just means that we have to find an audience which will respond to what the artist is doing.
Spiegelman: The impetus comes from the artist, but obviously if there's no audience, *RAW* magazine will come out two or three times and wave bye-bye. We assume, and hope, that there are other people like us.
Mouly: If we get letters saying "Well, this shouldn't have been like this," we're not going to chastise our artists.

Feature: In other words, you won't sell out.
Spiegelman: There's nothing to sell out. There's so little money involved here [laughter].

Feature: You mentioned before about looking for material which fits in with the sensibility of *RAW*. What exactly do you mean by that?
Mouly: It's very hard for us to define what we're doing because it's much more a matter of taste, rather than a commercial approach or an intellectual approach. It's just things that Art and I have been looking at that we want to pass along.
Spiegelman: We have certain antipathies. We don't have a predisposition towards science fiction and fantasy, possibly because that's where most of the action has been in the recent past. Anyone who's wanted to do so-called "adult comics" has been moving in the direction of the kind of things you might find in *Heavy Metal* or *Epic*. What that does is keep all the baggage that you associate with children's comics and move it

into adolescence. We're interested in going even further than that. I doubt if a superhero will find his way into our magazine. There are places for that to appear; there's no place for our kind of stuff to appear.

Feature: Would you say you're shooting more for literary material?
Spiegelman: And graphically exciting material—things with real content and things with a strong visual approach. Most comics material feeds in from relatively few stylistic sources. There's the so-called "Big-Foot" style, which we can take back to Bud Fisher and trace down to Crumb and Crumb's fifth generation clones. There are people we can trace back to the Caniff school, there's people we can trace back to the Raymond school, people we can trace back to the Howard Pyle school. . . . The world of graphics and illustration is even broader than that. What about tracing comics back to Dada artists, German expressionists, Constructivists? One thing we found out that is exciting: the Constructivist painters right after the Russian Revolution, like Mayakovsky and Lissitzky, had this great opportunity. They became artists of the Revolution. They wanted to revolutionize what art was. They didn't only do easel painting; they designed buildings, match book covers, film posters, cups, plates. They were trying to bring high art principles to the masses. It didn't work, but they tried. It lasted until Stalin said "Get these clowns out of here and let's get something that looks like Corben drew it!" [Laughter] One of the things Lissitzky and a few other people did that was so terrific was that they would do a daily comic strip. They took over the newspaper building. It was this big building with windows all across the front. Every morning they had these giant panels which they hand painted, that would be put one panel in each window and would relate the news. That would be the comic strip of the day. The one or two people in the crowd who were literate would read it to the rest of the people. Isn't that a wonderful thing? Much more interesting than the Times Square lit-up news bulletin.
Mouly: And that's our next magazine! [Laughter]
Spiegelman: [Laughter] That may be a tangential thought, but what I'm saying is that there are other traditions on which to draw, as well as the comics traditions. We're not rejecting the comics traditions; we just want to expand on what's possible.

Feature: You showed me the color insert you're working on for the first issue. Will there be inserts in future issues?

Spiegelman: I always liked Crackerjacks when I was a kid [Laughter]. Every issue will have a crackerjack in it. The first issue will have the twelve-page full-color, 5″ × 7″ comic book stapled into the center that I'm drawing. In future issues we'll have color comic booklets by other artists, we'll have paper dolls, we'll have bubble gum cards one issue, hopefully . . . whatever we can work out that's intriguing.

Feature: The hand-separated color insert plays around with color, a process of the medium which is not usually explored in stories. What are your thoughts about the relationship between art and printing?
Spiegelman: One of the things that is wonderful about comics is that comics are a printed medium. What that means is that there's no original. I like that fact. As I've been doing this strip, I've shown my work to my friends. It's a real problem because if I show them the original black-and-white drawings, I'll say "Well, that's not it. Try to imagine this with red over here, and then there's this blue streak . . ." and nobody's going to be able to follow my thoughts. The next stage is my color sketched-in thing and even that isn't it, because there are things that can only happen in printing. That's exciting to me, the fact that the printed version is the real object. Art to me isn't necessarily an oil painting just because an oil painting is done by hand and is precious. It's precious because of the thought and the energy of the artist which happens to manifest itself on an easel. What's great about comics is that the thought manifests itself on the printed page, which leaves it affordable. You don't have to be a millionaire to buy a comic book. If it's good enough, it's as good as any painting. It's just different.
Mouly: That's a problem with fine art: it is made in limited editions of one or prints in limited numbers. This limitation seems to me to be absurd. There's no reason if a piece of work is good that it would be any more valuable if it's unique.
Spiegelman: It's only too bad you only have one original painting.
Mouly: We ask the people who work for the magazine to be aware of the fact that it is going to be printed, for someone to think in terms of a reproducible image. One thing we don't want to do: we've been looking at another magazine that came out which had a few comics and they asked an artist to do a page and he did a painting. A grayish photograph of that painting was printed in the magazine. We're not going to print grayish photographs of a painting as an artist's contribution to the magazine. That's just absurd.

Feature: Do you feel that artists working in comics should be aware of the technical aspects of comics printing, color separation, etc.? For example, you're doing hand color separations for the insert in *RAW*. Is that an important part of being an artist in a medium which is printed?
Spiegelman: I think that a rudimentary understanding is essential. Otherwise it just doesn't look good when it's printed. Beyond that, it depends on the artist's interests. I certainly wouldn't want to say that every artist should have my specific set of interests in the printing process. The fact that I have that set of interests affects my work in a certain way.

Feature: Do you feel that knowledge allows you to go further than an artist who doesn't necessarily have that interest?
Spiegelman: It lets me do stuff that's different. I couldn't be doing the kind of work I'm doing if I didn't understand the process. I'd be doing something else. Printing is one of my interests. Another interest is the phenomenon of looking at a page and how you read. You tend to read left to right. Sometimes I'm interested in bursting that so that you have to find your way around a page. I'm also interested in some of the more traditional aspects of comics. I am interested in storytelling. Whatever else we may say, comics seem to be a storytelling medium. It's basic to it. I'm working on a book called *Maus*, which is a two-hundred-fifty-page comics novel about my father's and mother's experiences in Hitler's Europe. In that particular instance, I'm not that involved with formal experiment. I'm involved in the most traditional thing. I don't want to get in the way of the story. Some stories are so important that you want to get out of their way, and let them get told as fast as they can, as clearly as they can. Most stories, however, are just an excuse to spend a few minutes with somebody doing their riff. When that's the case, my riff isn't to do the story one more time because everybody knows the stories already. What's more interesting is finding a new way of presenting it so that the story's a coat hanger on which one's ideas can be hung.

Feature: You draw in a few different styles. Is that, as in doing straight-forward storytelling for *Maus*, your way of adjusting the art style to what you want to say in one particular story?
Spiegelman: Yeah, since I don't have one way in which the drawing always comes out of my hand, I've tried to turn what could have been a liability for me—the fact that I keep drawing differently—into some kind

of an asset: try to choose a way of drawing that seems appropriate to the material at hand.

An analogy, which I'm sure I've used before, is thinking of myself as an actor rather than a star. Like, Marilyn Monroe: whatever movie she was in, that's Marilyn Monroe. That's a star. And there's these people who you may not remember their names, then but they inhabit the character that they're portraying. What I want to do is put myself at the service of whatever material I'm involved with and bring it out the best I can.

Feature: How long have you been working on *RAW?*

Spiegelman: January is when we first decided, "To hell with it, we're going to do it ourselves. We're not going to wait for someone else to give us the magazine we want to read." [Laughter] After that there were two or three months of just muttering about what a magazine would be. And there has been about three months of actual work bringing the first issue out. What our hopes are is to come out between two and four times a year, depending upon the amount of good material we find, and on what audience interest there is.

Slaughter on Greene Street: Art Spiegelman and Françoise Mouly Talk about RAW

GARY GROTH, KIM THOMPSON, AND
JOEY CAVALIERI / 1982

From the *Comics Journal* #74, August
1982, pp. 70–82. Reprinted by permission
of Gary Groth, Kim Thompson, and Joey
Cavalieri.

Few artists care as deeply about comics as Art Spiegelman. He's as seriously dedicated to the medium as anyone I know, and it's his dedication,
knowledge, and passion that make his observations so relevant and
provocative and alive. Through *RAW* Spiegelman and Françoise Mouly
have opened our eyes to the broader and richer possibilities of comics;
I'm grateful for being introduced to the superior talents of Jacques Tardi,
Munoz & Sampayo, and the masterful Swiss artist introduced in the latest *RAW*, Francis Masse. And we all ought to be thankful to Spiegelman
for bringing subtlety, reflection, and maturity to the form with *Maus*.

    This conversation-debate among Spiegelman, Mouly, Kim Thompson,
Joey Cavalieri, and myself is actually a slightly demented tangent from

our earlier interview with them (*Journal* #65). The exchange occurred toward the end of a long interview and we decided to excise it completely from that issue and save it for a rainy day. The rainy day is upon us, made a little less bleak by a lovely X-Men cover. (The weather, as you know, can be tricky.) When we showed the transcript to Spiegelman, he was so horrified that he immediately dubbed it "Slaughter on Greene Street." (The interview was taped in Spiegelman's studio on Greene Street in Greenwich Village.) The title stuck. For those who think the editors of the Magazine of News & Criticism and the Graphix Magazine for Damned Intellectuals don't have senses of humor: surprise!—Gary Groth

Groth: What value do you see in publishing avant-garde material, outside of simply acting in opposition to the status quo?

Spiegelman: Okay. Now we're going to come into problems, although I've been bandying the word "avant-garde" around also, and I'm as guilty as you are of it in your question. I don't think the reason for the material is that it is avant-garde per se, the reason for the material is that it's interesting comics. And once you use that as your definition your question falls apart, because the reason to print interesting comics is because it's interesting.

Groth: But your interesting comics have a point of view different from the conservative approach?

Spiegelman In a way, *Maus* is a very conservative comic strip, you know.

Groth: Compared to what?

Mouly: Compared to some of the other material in *RAW*.

Spiegelman: Right, even compared to pages by Patricia Caire, say, or the page by Ben [Katchor]. In terms of narrative structure, I'm trying to do it as well as I can, but very firmly within the tradition of what you've come to know just by reading Carl Barks or something. Compared to some of my own work, compared to stuff that I've had in *Breakdowns*, it's a conservative strip. It's narrative in every sense of the word, it doesn't even stretch the boundaries of what narrative means, it just has a different story to tell.

Groth: Well, compared to what is available in the comics form, it stretches the boundaries of comics as art.

Page 1 of Spiegelman's "Ace Hole, Midget Detective" (1974).

Mouly: But it doesn't do anything to change the definition of the medium.

Spiegelman: It does in its scope, in a way, just in doing something that's this long and this intense, and—in light of its subject matter. But that's different from changing . . .

Page 1 of Spiegelman's "Nervous Rex: The Malpractice Suite" (1976).

Mouly: The way the words and pictures are used on a page.

Spiegelman: Right. The way those combinations of elements work. I found something interesting happening—I don't know if we talked about this in the past interview or not—which is that for several years I'd gotten very interested in deconstruction, in how there are certain narrative devices that you become used to and as soon as those crutches are removed you find yourself having the experience to work a different way. "Ace Hole" makes some use of that, the way the story starts swimming at a certain point. Other strips like this collage thing I did with Rex Morgan ["Malpractice Suite"]. Now, in order to reason my way into those situations, it's the same reasoning to do *Maus*, it's just to a different end. The thought process is the same, it's just instead of trying to make things more difficult, it's trying to make things easier. Reading *Maus*, in some sense I want to make my presence invisible. I want you to read and forget that it was drawn even, it just takes place in the brain, which is the way comics have always tried to work it.

Groth: Well, in a very real sense I got the impression that *Maus* was more difficult to the reader, because there was so much there, which is sort revolutionary in terms of comics.

Thompson: In *Maus*, there seems to be more emphasis on content than on form.

Mouly: Are you talking about the density on a page . . . ?

Groth: No, no no, my response as a reader was that you chose to emphasize, instead of immediacy, a greater resonance of feeling, which comics have traditionally not done. So in those terms it seems to me almost revolutionary.

Mouly: I think what he's talking about is, the usual way to read a comics page is to kind of glance at it and not even know . . .

Groth: Yeah, essentially that's it. In an average comic book, there's nothing really to focus your attention on. With *Maus* there is. That seems to be the most revolutionary aspect of the strip. And even of *RAW*.

Spiegelman: That's probably true, although on occasion—I can look back at certain stories that have appeared over the years in various comic books where that's happened. "Corpse on the Imjin" by Kurtzman is one example for me. "Master Race," not because it's on the same subject, but for whatever reason. Justin Green's work certainly. I guess what Kim interjected is pretty much the point I was trying to make in this kind of windbaggy, long, roundabout fashion, which was just that it emphasizes content over form, and up until recently . . .

Thompson: Doesn't that make *Maus* sort of an anomaly in *RAW*?

Mouly: Yeah.

Spiegelman: That's why it's in this small size. *Maus* wouldn't make sense blown up to fill a *RAW*-sized page. It requires the intimacy of a smaller size.

Thompson: Much of the other work in *RAW* seems interested in tinkering with the structures and the relationships between panels and less involved in actual content.

Spiegelman: Mm-hm. Which is why it was necessary to have something like *Maus* in *RAW* to keep the book balanced in terms of what possibilities are open for comics.

Mouly: In the third issue we have a twenty-page narrative strip, so again—it's funny, actually, because *Maus* in the third issue is not as separate from the rest of *RAW* as it is in the second issue. In the second issue, it's like when you finish a book you have another book you start, while in the third issue, it's almost in the middle though not quite. A small part of the magazine.

Thompson: Yes, because each of the first two issues has had only one classically structured narrative. In the first issue "Manhattan," in the second issue *Maus*. It struck me that since the third issue will contain that long, twenty-page strip . . .

Spiegelman: And more *Maus*.

Thompson: And more *Maus*, that will make it swerve more in that direction. Is this a permanent change in direction, or . . . ?

Mouly: We keep going back and forth. The strip by Joost [Swarte] in #2, as nice as it was, did not anchor the rest of the material. We've started feeling it now. We weren't aware of it at the time. It is very hard for us to find good narrative stories that develop over the course of ten to twenty pages.

Spiegelman: One problem is also finding stories that are worth telling. One of the reasons for that dabbling with the form, messing around with the way stories are told is because, most stories, you've heard 'em before. So what becomes interesting is the way the story is told rather than the story itself.

Thompson: One thing that bothers me a little and might bother other people more is that *RAW* fiddles a lot with the intellectual aspects of it, but very little actually touches on the emotions.

Spiegelman: Hm. I guess I would just disagree.

Groth: I would agree with that.

Spiegelman: You'd agree with disagreeing, or . . . ?

Thompson: He's agreeing with me.

Groth: Yeah.

Spiegelman: It's not emotional? I'd have to know what emotional would be. An example. What would be an example of some emotional comic?

Groth & Thompson in unison: I think *Maus* . . .

Thompson: . . . touches one because it concerns human relationships and human emotions.

Cavalieri: I think most of *RAW* #1 is pretty emotional. I went through that long harangue with you [Spiegelman] and I think it's really on the edge.

Mouly: It might be more intellectual emotions than are usually presented in comics . . . ?

Spiegelman: What would be a good example of an emotional comic strip? Certainly not a love comic.

Groth: I think Kurtzman's war comics had a certain human quality.

Thompson: In the sense of being able to relate—not necessarily identify with, but relate to—a human character within it.

Mouly: In the kind of stuff you're talking about, there is a certain element of manipulating the reader, trying to wrestle certain emotions out of him. I think this might come out this way to you mainly because the artists that we're printing in *RAW* are working more for themselves than for an audience.

Spiegelman: I'm not sure I understand the distinction. I'm just sitting here letting one word waft through the screen and then another one, like "emotional," "intellectual," trying to find out what you mean. I find Mariscal's work very emotional.

Mouly: But he's not out to direct you . . .

Spiegelman: You're talking about manipulative, or human interest, or . . . ?

Mouly: No, inner-directed vs. outer-directed.

Spiegelman: Inner-directed vs. outer-directed. I can't turn pages and look at it and say, "Oh, that's an intellectual page! That's an emotional page!" Do you find Mariscal's work emotional? Is that what you mean?

Thompson: Not really. It's one of the ones I can't quite get involved in. I look at it and it just doesn't register.

Groth: Much of the work in *RAW* I find very detached and coldly intellectual and simply experimental without embodying any human qualities.

Cavalieri: I find the general tone of the whole magazine pretty detached.

Thompson (responding to Groth): I wouldn't reproach the individual artists for that, understand, because I think it's an interesting thing to do and it interests me as a reader. It's just that *RAW* seems to lean preponderantly in that direction.

Groth: But that sort of thing doesn't seem to me to be artistically satisfying.

Spiegelman: It's funny, because the artists are more involved in satisfying themselves than in trying to satisfy a reader. So the idea of adjectives like "detached" . . . To me, "detached" is—even the Kurtzman war books. I thought [John] Benson's essay in *Panels* #2 was an interesting essay because it made something clear that I was trying to figure out when I was reading these reprints [of *Two-Fisted Tales*], which is, yeah, [Kurtzman] wavers around both sides of what is a very important concern and the only way he can do that is by being detached, by seeing it as, "This is a book that has to sell to x number of people and has to sell at a lot of PXs and while if this makes a good story it's fine, if the opposite point of view makes a good story that's fine." That to me is detachment.

Groth: That's opportunism. But that's not what I'm referring to.

Spiegelman: Maybe the reason you feel it is a lack is because you're actually talking about something that is so foreign to my way of understanding. You may be absolutely right. Since I don't understand what you mean, it obviously can't be expressed in a magazine if neither

Françoise nor I have experienced that part of the human spectrum that way. That's why I'd like a good example of what an emotional comic would be. If it's *Maus*, well, *Maus* is part of *RAW*.

Thompson: That's true, but as I was saying, *Maus* is exceptional in more ways than one. I think you said the story was more important than the drawings . . . ?

Spiegelman: Not more important, but that the drawing is subservient to the story.

Thompson: Right. And that strikes me as being exceptional within *RAW*.

Spiegelman: Yeah. Which is why I was talking about the preciousness of the paper. I guess I was talking about some of the same things when I was talking about emphasizing graphics rather than text. But "emotional,"—to me, a line is emotional. I'm not trying to take some weird stance, but drawings are emotional and to me, Mark Beyer's drawings are nothing if not raw nerve screaming.

Thompson: That's probably true. Beyer I have trouble with. I'm still working on him [laughter]. But I see your point there.

Groth: One of the problems I find in *RAW* which might help to articulate this is that so many of the drawings are so abstracted, and that's one of the problems I find in Beyer.

Spiegelman: Abstracted from the content, do you mean, or . . . ?

Groth: Well, no, they're abstracted from a naturalistic or realistic . . .

Spiegelman: Oh, representational.

Groth: Representational, right. Exactly.

Thompson: They're alienating.

Groth: They seem to represent the values of modern art. Abstraction.

Spiegelman: You know, "modern art" is like a hundred years old, so it's hard to think of it as too modern.

Groth: Right. I'm talking of modern art in terms of Gauguin on.

Spiegelman: One of the interesting things to me about comics is one of the last bastions, one of the things that remained figurative throughout.

Always. It's actually more likely to come to be accepted as an artform now that there's all this return to representational painting.

Groth: Then again, comics have only been around a hundred years, and when modern art came into . . .

Spiegelman: About the same time.

Groth: Well, my point is that art had gone through centuries of gestation and comics have only been around for ninety years. And comics, it doesn't seem to me, have even mastered representational drawing, much less abstracted drawing.

Spiegelman: To me, comics don't have that much to do with representational art. They have to do with representation in the sense that one of those universal symbols for "man" on a bathroom door has to do with representation, but it doesn't have that much to do with illustration to me, so I don't know why you're talking about illustration specifically. To me Hal Foster is rotten comics. Okay illustration. But it ain't as good comics as Chester Gould, which is more direct and has more to do with what comics are, picture-writing. And it seems reasonable that artists would be more interested in work that strays from the illustrative-figurative drawing, would be more prone to be interested in that, than your basic lay reader, who is primarily interested in whatever depth charge a story carries and finds—the less difficulty he encounters the happier he is. And that has to do with what we were talking about before, which is comics as something you read as a kid and you want to keep getting that specific thing.

Groth: When I was talking about representational art I wasn't talking strictly in terms of illustrations like Foster, which could be interpreted as being representational art, so much as comics being a reflection of life. I think this is best realized in something like *Maus*, which isn't accurate representational illustration, but it still reflects some aspect of life through the story and through the illustrations.

Spiegelman: But that's just as true of Mark Beyer's work. Everything you just said . . . it represents something actual about life through story and pictures, perhaps what it's representing is a specific person's pain, but that's as real as any kind of artifice that gives you the same information. If you talk about modern art, one of the things . . .

Groth: I see a greater sensitivity in your work than in Beyer's work. It's simply so abstracted and so divorced from any aspect of reality.

Spiegelman: But it's not. It's real basic reality, like AAAAAAAAAARGH-HHH! is basic reality.

Groth: Primitive art you mean.

Spiegelman: Yeah, primitive . . . I'm trying to avoid that word. It's a whole other can of worms.

Groth: And on top of that it doesn't seem to have the narrative structure of quality that *Maus* does.

Spiegelman: No. I'm very involved in the architecting of the time and space in *Maus*. It's very complicated in that sense. But that's what I mean by it being very traditional. It's much more traditional than Mark's work. I don't know how he became our sole example, but he's an easy one.

Thompson: The point, I think, that Gary and I are arguing is not against actual pictorial abstraction, because I for instance find Guy Colwell's work extremely emotional.

Spiegelman: [shudders]

Thompson: And that's not representational.

Spiegelman: Wait. Guy Colwell is not representational? Jeez, one of the most . . .

Groth: He really is. But he's a bad draftsman.

Spiegelman: More than most. But someone like Mariscal is more abstract than that.

Thompson: Okay. It has to do with abstraction of the narrative structure more than the—if indeed there is a narrative structure at all.

Spiegelman: Where? In Mariscal?

Thompson: In any of the strips Gary and I are inveighing against [laughter].

[Spiegelman, flipping through *RAW* 2, reaches Cathy Millet's strip in that issue.]

Thompson: I think that would be an example.

Spiegelman: What more do you need than that? It's got a surface cold-ness that is intentional. It's got this very angular, flat space. It's a person wandering through this apartment for days, not being able to find a pack of cigarettes, finally finding cigarettes and needing a lighter. It's got a story, and it's got art that is in keeping with its story. The story as such is not one that has all these . . . You see, usually when you read a story what you're going for is this roller coaster ride, and you want these little complications and twists and curves in it. But sometimes those twists and curves take place on another plane, so what you're getting is not a com-plicated story—Well, John almost got together with Mary, but then Elaine came over and as a result of that Murray—well, you know, that kind of complication—but there are other kinds of complications that involve gaps—for instance, that the date changes so much between one second in time and another—it's in the form of a diary, right?—is another kind of narrative movement. It just chooses to operate else-where, but it's just as rich. It's just something else, that's all.

One thing that's really germane here, I have to read you something. One of my favorite authors is a guy named Woodford, who wrote a best-selling book on writing in the '30s, called *Trial and Error: The Art of Writing and Selling* and followed it up with *Plotting: How to Have a Brainchild*. He's a terrible writer, but a great writer about writing, and the first chapter starts with this great thing, which is, "Why Plot?" (Chapter One): "There is only one reason for plotting a short story, play, novel, or radio program. Let's face it: We plot them because the general public demands that we do so. Everyone dreams. Life, because it has become unnatural, has been formulated by the politicians, priests, ministers, rabbis, and money-lenders who exploit us, is naturally unsatisfactory. To escape it, all of us dream. Among those of us who dream are a few who can dream better than others. These few sell their dreams to the many who cannot dream with unusual facility. Among those of us who dream with unusual facility there is no need for plot. We like to take off into the empyrean chartless, plotless, and unfettered. But the general public is so accustomed to the fetters of politicians, priests, ministers, rabbis, and money-lenders that the general public cannot even dream without a conventional formula. So we who write provide such a for-mula and call it, with macabre exactitude, 'a plot.'"

And to me, when you're talking about the specific kind of human-interest thing, what you're asking for is this very comfortable matrix that you've been brought up with on the TV and in certain kinds of movies and certain kinds of novels, that can be fine—that structure is useful sometimes, but sometimes it ain't. There are certain things you just can't do if you're stuck doing that instead.

Mouly: He's asking for manipulation. You want to be led somewhere.

Groth: That's not true.

Thompson: Well, certainly Millet's strip is just as manipulative.

Groth: You can't be saying that anything with a plot is manipulative.

Mouly: No . . . I think . . .

Spiegelman: By his definition. I'm saying that people have this very specific grid which is the only way in which they can follow something.

Groth: But that simply isn't true.

Spiegelman: It's been exploded more since 1930. It was more true when Woodford wrote it than it is now. See, one of the interesting things in *Maus* even is . . . , let me ask you this, what can you tell me about Willie as a person from the chapter you read?

Groth: All right. Something that I liked and that I didn't quite understand—I expect that I will understand it in the future—is that his set of values is not immediately, recognizably pure. He dropped the one girl and he took up with the woman who later became his wife. And I can't say exactly where, but there did seem to be some sort of cultural reason as opposed to say reasons of pure unadulterated love. That's one of my responses to it.

Cavalieri: I noticed that too, when he was checking the medicine cabinet in the apartment to see what kind of medicine she had.

Groth: Exactly. That was the scene that struck me. And he had to check that out—instead of going to her or approaching her directly—I thought that ambiguity was absolutely terrific. And I assume this will be explored further and perhaps clarified.

Spiegelman: Okay. This is the kind of thing I'm trying to get into. See, I had this amazing revelation by showing the first chapter of *Maus* to my class a couple of weeks ago. And boy, what a bunch of chowderheads!

[General laughter]

Spiegelman: To them Willie was this great guy, because he was the Dad. Hell, Dad, great guy, father knows best . . .

Cavalieri: Or even because he's the hero, because he's cast in the role of the protagonist. He's the square-jawed guy.

Mouly: He's the narrator also.

Spiegelman: And people are just going to follow him along through this story. Whatever he does you can identify with someone in the story, so it's gotta be him.

Groth: That seemed exactly the point, that he wasn't 100% good, he wasn't the Good Guy.

Spiegelman: Yeah. But I'm not trying to get into one of these *Young Lions* kind of stories where there's a little bit of good in the Nazis and a little bit of bad in the Jews. I'm not trying to deal with that kind of crap either. The only point that I was trying to make by bringing that up is that certain kinds of story approaches lead into this trap where you come with a whole baggage of expectations and a lot of the work in *RAW* and a lot of my other work is involved in directly trying to explode those expectations by just attacking them frontally.

Mouly: But you can't ignore them. You have to work against them.

Spiegelman: In the other strips?

Mouly: Even in *Maus*. Like you have to stress beyond what you need to stress . . .

Spiegelman: Yeah, but with *Maus* I'm trying to take it as a given that— I'm assuming that the 101 course is *Breakdowns*, the specifics of the approach to the material is already a given. And now I'm doing a narrative and it's not necessary to hit you over the head with this information, nor am I trying to feed you a story that has—it certainly ain't "Sgt. Fury attacks Treblinka."

Groth: To jump on something Kim said, I'd be interested in hearing you talk about this story [still the Millet story] in terms of manipulation, because this seems to me to be very manipulative in an almost Hitchcockian sense, in that you have to follow it very closely . . .

Spiegelman: But it's not following, it's filling in the interstices. And that's very different from being manipulated. Being manipulated, the way

I think Françoise is using the phrase and the way I would use it, is to be led around by the nose through a story . . .

Mouly: Through the wringing of your emotional capability.

Spiegelman: It's almost as if "applause" signs were held up: applaud, cry . . .

Mouly: Also, in a manipulative conventional plot you'll be made to identify with someone you'll wind up endorsing and loving and that person will be hurt and you'll feel the hurt that is happening to him, he'll be saved, you'll feel relieved that he was saved, and so on. There will be a number of devices, a certain wringing out of your emotions.

Groth: I see what you mean. But surely there must be enough there in the first place to evoke some kind of response.

Spiegelman: Hopefully there is. I find enough there for myself. Again, like I said, we're editing this magazine for ourselves. This is the stuff we like. I find looking at that interesting. I find things in it, but it requires me giving something of myself. It's the difference between asking something to come at you and being willing to go into it and find out what's there. Most of the work that I end up living with for a long time is not this thing that just lifts its skirt and it's already there. You have to really work your way in and find out what's going on and—I think I shifted out of my metaphor somewhere along the line.

Cavalieri: In that sense it's kind of like a print ratio in that you run the other part of it and you have to work with it.

Spiegelman: But all real art does that.

Mouly: But it gives different things to different people, because the component of what you have to put into it is so great, that each person's response will be entirely different.

Spiegelman: People don't understand how important the audience part of the ratio is in art. The usual cliche is that the artist has this messianic message from on high that he's splattering all over a canvas. But in a real work of art your involvement has to be as great as the artist's.

Thompson: In a sense, the work of art just primes you to your own insights.

Spiegelman: Yeah. And certainly there's a map there, it's not just like holding up something and asking you to hallucinate on it. But it does ask for your engagement. And that's what hopefully the material we'd like to have in the magazine asks for. And it ain't for people who are lazy. There's TV for that.

Mouly: There's TV magazines and cheap novels.

Spiegelman: It's [Judith Krantz's] *Princess Daisy* as opposed to some real lit.

Groth: Italo Calvino said that the writer and the reader become One. But couldn't that argument be used to defend "art" in which there's really nothing there?

Spiegelman: Well, you're taking a risk. What I end up doing is, I test the mattress before falling. I try to see if I can trust this guy enough to fall into his arms without him stepping away. Because there is fraud in every field of human endeavor. When you can feel, intuit one way or another the honesty in a piece of work I think it's safe to follow it along and see what's going on inside it. And . . .

Groth: Of course, a work requires more than honesty.

Mouly: Yeah. Definitely.

Spiegelman: Yeah. But what you were talking about specifically was something dishonest trying to pass itself off as art. Isn't that what you meant?

Thompson: I think we were arguing that it was manipulative, weren't we?

Groth: That's what we were arguing earlier. I think we got into a new argument here. I'm not saying this is dishonest. I think something can be manipulative and honest too, if it's by someone who doesn't have the wherewithal to transcend the manipulative.

Mouly: Oh, I agree with you.

Groth: So I'm not arguing that it's dishonest.

Spiegelman: I think here we're just talking about structure rather than manipulation.

Mouly: No, but the main thing that Gary is saying and with which I agree is that honesty does not make a work . . .

Spiegelman: Oh no, we get lots of submissions that are very honest but using up their return postage quick.

Thompson: I think what the point came back to was that we were arguing for emotional involvement in the work.

Spiegelman: And what I was saying was that this work does ask for your emotional involvement.

Mouly: But together with an intellectual labor and there is a part of having to work at it and having to put some of yourself into it. In that sense, since we do—all the material that is in *RAW* is things that have gotten response from us. I mean, there are things that we haven't printed that we had a first response to but weren't able to go deeper into it, and remained on the surface, and that's stuff which isn't being put in *RAW*. That explains partly why our editing has to do with our "taste," that the stuff we can get involved with for a long period of time, that we can live with around the house for six months . . .

Spiegelman: Yeah, when you see a page twelve times you really want it to hold up. And there are pages that don't. But the platonic form of the *RAW* page, the ultimate form of the *RAW* page would be something that you'd be able to spend a lot of time with, and that hopefully you'd get more out of when you go back to it.

Thompson: A blank page and a pencil [laughter].

Spiegelman: There's room for that.

Groth: For example, to stretch this out [laughter], this is another strip [by Kaz, *RAW* #2] that does not involve me in any substantial or meaningful way although it's very cleverly done. I guess you would disagree with that.

Spiegelman: To me it's like a nice piece of '20s jazz. It's like these various riffs. It's this little pinball machine that's been set up for your eye to ricochet through. It's hitting one note and there's other stuff in the book that hopefully hits other notes. But I guess in terms of your desire for human interest . . .

Thompson: I think our point is—you said it hits one note and there is other stuff that hits other notes. Our personal taste is such that we would probably like other notes hit more frequently and others not so frequently. It may just boil down to that.

Mouly: Mm-hm . . .

Spiegelman: Yes, but the notes you would like to see hit, are you getting that from other sources? Like, what gives you that?

Groth: I think you can find it in novels, films . . . , most every other art-form but comics, I suppose [laughter].

Spiegelman: Which films?

Groth: *Breaker Morant,* which we just saw.

Spiegelman: Which I didn't see.

Thompson: *Oblomov.*

Groth: *Oblomov. The Great Santini.*

Mouly: Which we never saw [laughter].

Spiegelman: Yeah, there's a problem: we don't see most films as they come out. We can talk about films eight years old and older.

Thompson: Well, certainly, I cannot think of any emotionally involving comics currently being published. Except perhaps for *Gen of Hiroshima.*

Groth: Jaxon's stuff, *Comanche Moon,* I think is involving.

Spiegelman: But in that sense you're asking for stuff that could almost translate into any medium, right? And one of the things we're interested in is things that are peculiar to comics. Some of the best novels, for me . . .

Groth: I don't think *Maus* could translate into other media.

Spiegelman: I don't think it can either. But the qualities that you're talking about probably could and in fact were translated into a film.

Groth: True. Then again, these are certain universal qualities that make most art art.

Spiegelman: Yes and no, because every medium has its own possibilities, and there's a reason why painters started doing these things that weren't seen through a window.

Mouly: I think the stuff you're looking at is very rooted in certain nineteenth-century ideas of entertainment and art. At that time there wasn't that much differentiation between entertainment and art, but . . .

Spiegelman: Let's leave that one. I don't know if I agree with you on that.

Thompson: Good. Let's let them fight [laughter].

Groth: I was interested in the point you were making. Even if Art does disagree with you.

Spiegelman: I think there's still a pretty great dividing line between entertainment and art. Go ahead, finish. I'm sorry.

Mouly: I think that in the past seventy to eighty years this number of things that have happened that went on a whole other tangent and they have been confined to the visual arts to an extent, and . . .

Groth: What has been confined to the visual arts?

Mouly: The other approaches to what you can get out of a piece of work besides human interest.

Groth: But isn't that because visual art is a sensory art and the verbal arts are conceptual?

Spiegelman: What about Gertrude Stein? What about James Joyce?

Mouly: Yeah, exactly, that's what I'm saying. You tend to think of writing or literature as this one thing as it was a century ago, but a number of things happened since in writing that took it into a whole other realm, and might be closer to the visual arts.

Groth: But was this other realm successful?

Spiegelman: Well, there are great works that have come out of—successful meaning what? Yes, they're successful works.

Mouly: They don't provide the same thing as novels do, but they provide a whole other input that can be very successful to whoever gets it, and I guess personally, to me, I'm a lot more interested in getting that kind of input than in getting one of story, or getting moved one way or getting to cry on somebody's unhappiness. I just don't get that moved by most human-interest stories, whether in films, comics, whatever.

Groth: Why do you think that is?

Mouly: Well, to me it's very repetitive. I just feel myself going through the same thing over and over again, whatever the novel or film is, and I just feel myself manipulated into it. I guess I'm just too aware of what's being done to me to get that sucked into it. And I try to keep some distance from it and therefore I'm not. I don't feel I'm getting that much more from one more novel or one more narrative film.

Spiegelman: Well, it depends on which. There's great books in every idiom. You like Philip K. Dick.

Mouly: Yeah, of course. This is not meant as a complete . . .

Spiegelman: It's hard not to get polarized when you're having this kind of conversation. But to come back to this one idea, that there are other possibilities. There are artists who explore those possibilities. Painting doesn't have to have a handsome man and a pretty girl in the picture to be interesting. It doesn't even have to have an ugly man and an ugly girl. It doesn't even have to have a human. It doesn't even have to have an apple.

Mouly: But that's accepted in visual arts a lot easier. That was accepted in visual arts a lot easier than it was accepted in literature.

Spiegelman: I don't know. That had to struggle in the early part of the century as painting also. It got laughed out of all these exhibitions, right?

Mouly: I know, but by now, in 1980 . . .

Spiegelman: It's been accepted. People accept Joyce as a great writer. Everybody will nod and say, "He's great."

Mouly: No, but when I'm talking to Gary, I think he accepts that as a fact, that he can be interested in modern paintings, ranging from cubism to things that happened before or after that, and they do not provide the human-interest narrative fulfillment that you get from other media. On the other hand I suspect that your response to works that use film or literature or video—although video is not something I really respond to myself—would be a lot more removed. You could be ready to accept this input from painting a lot more readily than you would from comics or from literature and film.

Spiegelman: You don't ask for a story from music.

Groth: No.

Thompson: But literature, comics, and film are all narrative arts.

Mouly: Well, no, that's where I disagree. That's how you see it.

Spiegelman: Well . . .

Mouly: You see that as solely a narrative art.

Spiegelman: I'll take a position firmly in the middle on that one.

Mouly: I think that they can be narrative art, but they can be something else.

Spiegelman: I don't think comics can be non-narrative. I kept trying. I think there's a narrative component that's essential to comics. Otherwise it's graphics.

Mouly: I guess you would have to call independent experimental film "narrative" because it happens in time, therefore it's narrative. But that's not the same meaning of the narrative that he's using. Inasmuch as the film is narrative.

Spiegelman: All right. Comics is a temporal medium.

Mouly: So is film.

Groth: Whoops. Can you define that?

Spiegelman: Yeah. It exists in time. Each panel represents a different moment.

Thompson: A painting is instantaneous [snaps fingers].

Mouly: No, it's not instantaneous, but you make the time for it. You decide what you will look at first and you make the movement on the page. In comics, the artist ends up mapping out your movement and your reading of the piece a lot more temporally than in a painting.

Thompson: I'm not sure I'd draw the distinction there, because by that token—

Mouly: Well, let's go to film, for example. In film, somebody working with the medium of film is stuck with the fact that one image comes after the other. And he has . . .

Spiegelman: I can see all these *Comics Journal* readers saying, "Where the hell's the X-Men material?"

[General laughter]

Cavalieri: She was rolling there.

Thompson: But when you read prose you make your own time, so that would put prose on the other side of the fence.

Mouly: Yeah, but poetry is something else again.

[Somewhat bewildered pause; everyone breaks into laughter]

Groth: What was this?

Mouly: Unfortunately, I don't know too many examples in American literature, but I know examples in French literature of people that have worked against that concept and wrote things that can be read forward and backward and in different moments of time, who were trying to get out of that straitjacket of imposing the continuity and succession of the book. I don't know if I should get into this. Should I?

Spiegelman: Yeah, sure. It's all right with me. It's their tape.

Mouly: [laughter] There is a "poem" called "Ten Thousand Billion Poems" that was "written" by Raymond Queneau, and the way he did it is, he wrote each line on a strip of paper and it was printed and cut so that with a book that's made up of little strips one after the other you can take the first one, the third one, the tenth one, the ninth one—it's ten thousand billion combinations, ten thousand billion poems in that book that exist, and he worked this whole thing out—he worked every single combination out.

Thompson: Every single one?

Mouly: Yeah.

Thompson: That would take a long time.

Spiegelman: At least they all work. I guess the main thing is that there are some things that are common to—just to loop it all back together—there are some things that are common to all art. On the other hand there are certain things that are specific to each individual medium, certain possibilities, and in some ways those are the most thrilling because those are really the ones where you're most engaged in what you're looking at or listening to. And there are certain things that can only exist when words are put together because words have a certain kind of imprecision that makes those kinds of possibilities fly off between sets of words. There are certain things that will happen in a picture that have nothing to do with what it's a picture of. It would have to do with the way the balances work, the way the color comes at you . . .

Mouly: Those are visual emotions.

Spiegelman: And those are as emotional in their own way, once you understand the medium that you're involved with, they're thrilling. And I think the medium that's gotten the least attention as to what these possibilities might be, is comics. And possibly that's why this work may seem alien to you, because it's trying to find out what these things are. The best way to find out is to do that. We're limited by what people are doing.

Mouly: But personally our response is very emotional in the sense that you were using it. When you're saying this is very intellectual and not emotional, that's just not the way we see it.

Groth: Yeah, I know. I gather that.

[General laughter]

Mouly: It's not like we sit around and try to think very hard of what the meaning, the content, the structure, whatever, is. It's not the way we react to it. Whatever we get out of it we might be able to express later on.

Spiegelman: And also, I keep getting confused, because when you said something like Kurtzman's war books' being emotional, to me Kurtzman's a very intellectual artist.

Groth: Oh, yeah, yeah. Emotion doesn't exclude intellectuality.

Spiegelman: As opposed to someone like Milt Gross, who was an emotional artist.

Groth: I think both elements have to be present in art, intellect and emotion. But my point is that the material in RAW—

Spiegelman: See, on the one hand I understand perfectly what you're saying, because on one hand Maus is in a sense a response to the problem I ran into with my own work, which is that I found myself talking to a smaller and smaller audience. I'm enough of an extrovert, or enough outer-directed, to have some notion of how other people respond to what I'm doing, and I was aware that certain things I was doing were just invisible. The things I was most interested in were invisible to people looking at the work. And the more I made those things my primary focus, the more I was talking to myself. Or at least to a very small group of people, although I worked them out and objectified them as clearly as I could, I was still talking to a very small group. *Maus* was an attempt to try to figure out, "Okay, people want stories, I'll find a story worth telling."

Cavalieri: Let me toss out a couple of things, and then you can react to them. First of all, when you said "Comics need a narrative, otherwise it's not comics," you sound as though you're talking from experience . . .

Spiegelman: Yeah, except Françoise said something and I ended up having to retract that. She threw in this idea of comics really being temporal rather than narrative. There's a difference. And I think that much is for sure. They definitely exist in time. If "narrative" means plot, no, comics don't have to have a plot, obviously.

Cavalieri: What I was trying to say was that a lot of the times as other artists try and perfect their narrative skills your work has been concerned with using those devices to disrupt the story instead of using them to tell the story. Trying to chop it up, using the same devices, only using them in an upside-down manner. Insofar as getting a smaller and smaller audience, I've noticed that you're not alone [laughter]. I think you quoted Picasso once in one of the interviews. "When I first started painting a few people understood it, and now I'm famous, I'm in galleries and millions of people pass my work every day, and now a few people understand my work." I've noticed that in a lot of artists: You, Picasso . . .

[General laughter]

Spiegelman: James Joyce . . .

Cavalieri: No, no, if you let me quote—all right, fine, the Beatles, the Firesign Theater . . . the more involved they got the more introspective they got, the more in tune they got with their own concerns, the smaller the group of people who understand their work.

Groth: This is a relatively modern phenomenon.

Cavalieri: Yeah.

Spiegelman: No. Wrong.

Cavalieri: You don't think so?

Spiegelman: A really great example is Vermeer.

Cavalieri: Really?

Spiegelman: Yeah. Because Vermeer painted very few paintings in his entire life. He was just one more of these Dutch genre boys, and these burghers would say, "We want our portrait painted." And they'd go, "Hey, you ought to go to Vanderhootch, because Vanderhootch, he can do it in about three days and it looks great, and this fuck-off Vermeer is going to take a year to get the damn thing painted, and it's all right, but it's no better than Vanderhootch's." In that sense, both of them were painting to fulfill a specific need by the audience. But Vermeer's own needs had something to do with something there was no real audience for.

Groth: But my point was that when he finished his work it was still understandable.

Spiegelman: No, what was understandable was the same thing that was understandable in Vanderhootch's work. The content was understandable.

Groth: Right. We're living in a time now where works of art have no meaning whatsoever to the general audience.

Mouly: I guess what you're saying is that in Vermeer there's still a surface thing that's recognizable to general audiences, whereas now that's been gotten rid of.

Groth: Well, you don't find people looking at it and shaking their heads in bewilderment.

Thompson: It works on more than one level.

Cavalieri: There was the intermediate of that with Rembrandt. *The Night Watch* was a daytime scene, it was supposed to be a scene of a group of burghers who wanted their portrait painted, and he took forever with it, and it wasn't what they wanted at all, but he was happy with it. So that was the intermediate between turning it into incoherency.

Spiegelman: So the secret language of the painting had nothing to do with what people were taking from it.

Cavalieri: Exactly.

Spiegelman: But it did have that other operative. I actually am most interested in work that exists at a certain point, which is right where things are flipping over. I'm more interested in Seurat than I am in Jackson Pollock. And it's because Seurat is this real hinge, this real lynchpin, you can still see that there are people hanging out on this beach, but it diffuses into being this field on a canvas, and I'm interested in that. But it's sort of like being interested in puns. I find personally for me they're the easiest kinds of paintings to get into. I'm more interested in that than in paintings that have a smoother surface—like older paintings—that we have to work harder to get into the paintings where there is less of a road map. Maybe that's just because of some failing or impatience on my part. Like when I find my way and I like those paintings, but it takes longer to find your way. And so I guess I do know what you're saying. I'm emotionally responsive to work that exists in the same way, that has that entrance. But it's just to use it as an entrance to find your way into the picture. There are rhythms in language as well as pictures, and those kinds of rhythms are pleasurable. There's a whole branch of literature called poetry, and it's all about that.

Groth: Yes. But unfortunately words mean something. They have a connotation and a denotation in and of themselves that you have to worry about.

Spiegelman: Yeah. And those denotations can be played off fairly abstractly. I guess the person who went furthest in that direction is Gertrude Stein, where she would just repeat words until they lost any sense of meaning and you were just left with . . .

Groth: Gibberish.

Spiegelman: Gibberish. But organized gibberish. Organized stuttering.

Groth: Gibberish devoid of meaning.

Spiegelman: Well, no. That's what gibberish means, doesn't it. Gibberish means "without meaning." [laughter] This is gibberish with meaning.

[General laughter]

Groth: Then indeed I was clarifying something.

[General laughter]

Groth: Mine was a redundancy or yours was a contradiction.

Thompson: An oxymoron.

Spiegelman: And one of the interesting things in comics is that it's such a bastard thing: the pictures and the words have different resonances and you can play off of those.

Groth: One thing struck me as interesting in *Maus*. You don't see a lot of movies?

Spiegelman: No, I see a lot of movies. I don't see a lot of movies when they all come out. They're too expensive. It's either do *RAW* or go to movies.

Groth: All right. Because it was my understanding that you weren't very involved in films.

Spiegelman: Oh no. I'm very interested in them.

Groth: I was going to say that I thought the *Maus* strip had a very cine-matic quality to it. I was wondering why. Apparently [laughter] now I can figure that out.

Spiegelman: No, I'm very interested in movies. The problem is just that I don't see a lot of things as they first happen. Doing *Maus* is a great edu-cation for me. I'm gaining new respect for artists I always sort of liked but never followed that carefully, like Carl Barks, somebody that I found more interesting as I continue to work on *Maus*.

Mouly: You can clearly see the influence of Carl Barks.

Spiegelman: Well, yeah, you can see those little Uncle Scrooge glasses on the father that help you figure out who he is. And in a sense certain artists were more important to me before. Maybe I've just absorbed whatever lessons I wanted to learn from them. Like Kurtzman, even. There are things that I've gotten from looking at that stuff. But I don't find myself studying his work right now, because in some ways it's more schematic than I'm trying to be.

Mouly: But you're using some of those things . . .

Spiegelman: But I've absorbed those lessons. The lessons that are there that I'm interested in I think I've already absorbed. Certain very rigid approaches to panel breakdown, like dividing a row into two, three, or four, trying to keep an equal ratio.

Mouly: Also dividing a page into sentences.

Spiegelman: Yeah, that's something from Kurtzman, I would say—each page being a unit of information and each row being a sub-unit of infor-mation as an organizational device.

Groth: One thing I found interesting in *Maus'* visual storytelling is that it was cinematic in the sense that the way you composed every panel, and the angle you drew the characters at always heightened the dramatic values of the story. And I mean "cinematic" in that sense as opposed to the sense that someone working at Marvel or DC might think, which is that they try to make the panels move, so they draw twenty panels across the top of a page and try to make it have the quality of an animated feature, which is what I suppose Steranko did and what someone like Frank Miller is doing now. And I think yours is much more at the service of the story.

Spiegelman: Part of that is since I'm dealing with a given narrative, which is my father's story, it's actually part of the reason I used mice instead of humans. In order to propel the story forward and not make up whole new work—like it might be interesting to me, for instance, to focus on a tabletop in Poland 1938 while this other stuff is going on, but it would be such a major act of hubris on my part to do that that I have to let myself come in through quieter methods. I think that one of the things that's important to me in *Maus* is that it's using this fairly complicated narrative technique, which is two first-person narrators—me and Willie—and in a sense it's all me and not Willie at all, once it's all out on a piece of paper. And trying to keep that separation is difficult in a sense. And the only way I can do it is to stay in service of these tapes that I'm working from, and trying to translate them, and let my own opinions about what he's saying exist, but not come into the forefront of it. And yet they're very emphatically there. That's why I think in order to really understand the story it's going to be necessary for people to slow down their reading time. Even after I've spent my eight-ten years on this whole thing in a three-hour sitting . . . I've seen people read a chapter, the first chapter, in eight to ten minutes maximum, and that's possible to get the narrative flow of it, but I think in order to figure out what the heck is going on, it's going to require a slower reading time. Because to me it only becomes interesting once you realize that I had to make certain decisions about having to do with my father's information. Because it's on that level that the interplay between me and my father takes place. And at least as much as it's a story about whatever you want to call it, genocide, holocaust, whatever, it's also a story about my relationship with my father, and that has to remain more or less as a subtext, but to me it's a more interesting one.

Groth: There was something I wanted to ask Françoise. You seemed to imply earlier that you found plot or structure itself repetitious or boring.

Mouly: No, I wouldn't dissociate plot and structure. I find structure fascinating and conventional plot . . .

Groth: Well, how would you define a conventional plot as opposed to a conventional structure?

Mouly: Well, a conventional structure can be a plot, but it can be something different. Structure is just the way a work is built, and in 99% of the conventional work it's going to be a plot, but it's not the same thing. A plot is very specifically like the part of the story that moves you through it and makes you want to read further and find out what is going to happen and plays on your emotions and so on to make you go on so that you don't get bored and close it.

Spiegelman: If you mention Klaus Wyborny's things I think you'll make it clear.

Mouly: You do it.

Spiegelman: Okay. There's a filmmaker in Germany named Klaus Wyborny who did this great series of lectures on movie structure and what he did was, part of his way of making it clear in these lectures was, he would take movies ranging from *Citizen Kane* to Fritz Lang and D. W. Griffith and he would refilm them, and what I think he would do—I may be wrong about this—two seconds for every shot, so any time the camera moved that was two seconds. And then he would give you these collapsed films where you would see *Citizen Kane* in about three minutes, and from that started talking about his way of understanding how movies are structured. This is why Françoise says plot and structure are different. The basic structure—it's a way of looking at plot, even—the basic structure is, characters exist in one space, move through various spaces, and come together at the end.

Mouly: They start up in a common space, they exist within the same space, they branch out, they are separated by circumstances . . .

Spiegelman: This is a whole other way of saying, "Boy meets, loses, and gets girl."

Groth: Right; I don't see that quite as a plot, though [laughter].

Spiegelman: Well, "Boy meets, loses, and gets girl" is one of the basic plots. But the structure of that is that figures exist in a common space, are separated in space, and struggle to find their way into the same space.

Mouly: And sometimes they meet again but it's not the final meeting because one of the characters is missing or whatever so there's some branching, but this happy ending is basically everybody getting back together within the same space.

Groth: You're talking about one very limited plot. Can't plots be structured in such a way as to be fascinating and complex?

Mouly: Well, keep it in mind and look at the next movie you see, the next book you read.

Groth: But on top of that, a plot is only one aspect of it. It's also how the plot is executed.

Spiegelman: The storytelling. That's what we were saying, most stories not being interesting, what one's left being interested in is the storytelling.

Groth: It's not just the storytelling, though, it's the point of the story, the meaning that is imbued in the story. In other words, Camus's *The Stranger* has a relatively simple plot but it's a very complex story. It seems to me that should . . .

Spiegelman: No, there's no argument there.

Mouly: No, none whatsoever.

Thompson: By the same token, the basic plot of *Moby Dick* could be applied to, say, a *Hulk* story. Which, in fact, it has.

Groth: My point is, it isn't simply a plot, which is in and of itself boring, but what a gifted artist does with this plot, or how he structures it and how he uses it.

Thompson: A plot is only a means to an end.

Mouly: It's only the structure, the bones.

Spiegelman: The coathanger.

Mouly: No, I definitely agree with you. I'm not saying that there's none of those stories that are interesting. I'm just saying that in the stuff that comes out, I find very little of interest, and mainly because it keeps repeating the same usual story in the same usual way, and I just find very little that . . .

Spiegelman: I find myself interested in that stuff too though.

Groth: Don't you see artists doing the same story in a very different way?

Mouly: I may be looking at the wrong stuff. I tend to be more drawn to things that are taking the basic components somewhere else and it's true that that is the attraction to books that deal with the structure of the work directly more than with the decorations of it.

Groth: Do you think there might be a danger that you become obsessed with form over content?

Mouly: As long as I'm enjoying it, that's fine with me.

Thompson & Groth: [laughter]

Spiegelman: Yes, folks, it's no accident that it's called the "Magazine for Damned Intellectuals." But we keep finding ourselves trying to dichotomize, this over that, I think that there's a lot of work that's involved in structure that is boring as all get-out.

Groth: See, I can't conceive finding structure in and of itself boring. I can't divorce that from content. I guess that's why I can't . . .

Spiegelman: I guess I'm trying to say the same thing, which is that this is such an artificial break that it's possible for a work to have as its main accent one element.

Mouly: Also, most work has an element of everything.

Spiegelman: Yeah, that's what we're all saying.

Groth: Does that mean we all agree?

Mouly: [laughter] Hell, no. We're supposed to—

Spiegelman: No, we have different interests. I think we all agree that there is no way of separating out each of these components we've been talking about aren't easily taken out and put on a table somewhere—

like the things you find interesting in a piece of work may be very different than what Françoise or I find interesting. But probably to one degree or another every piece of work has those elements and it's not something you can argue with. We were talking about the responses to *RAW* in the previous interview [*Journal* #65]. We found one thing—with the first issue, we were told by several people that the magazine's too depressing. And the second issue we were told that the magazine's too intellectual.

Mouly: The third issue, we will be told that it's too nihilistic.

Spiegelman: Because our subtitle for the third issue is "The Graphic Magazine That Lost Its Faith in Nihilism."

Mouly: Our interpretation of that is that some people didn't quite know how they felt and how to respond and how to take the material, and then had a very hard time articulating their own appreciation of it, and looked back on what we put onto it as a tagline, and it's like, "Well, if *they* say it's the Magazine of Postponed Suicides, the fact that they're being uneasy with this material must be because it's too depressing." Or if they say it's intellectual, it must be because it's *too* intellectual.

Groth: That seems to me to be a fairly shallow response to that.

Spiegelman: Oh yeah. I think so too. But I think what it is, is people groping to find out what it is. Because *RAW* is different from anything else. It's also different from European comics magazines.

Mouly: And it also stresses the fact that again, we're not trying to give any definition of what's inside this, inside the covers.

Spiegelman: It's people grasping at any kind of handle they can find.

Groth: These are probably all X-Men freaks.

[General laughter]

Groth: I'll have to excise that.

Mouly: Even though we edit the magazine very strongly we try to remove ourselves from any editorial stance. One thing that we very consciously do not do is say, "Hey folks, here is this great strip for you that we'll lead you through this and give you all this stuff." That would seem condescending. Let each person find whatever he wants within that material. It's up to him.

Spiegelman: Okay? Phew.

Thompson: God.

Spiegelman: Is that it? Why don't you turn the tape off?

Cavalieri: What?

Groth: There's the temptation to start jabbering again.

[General laughter]

[Click]

Art's Father,
Vladek's Son

LAWRENCE WESCHLER / 1986

From *Shapinsky's Karma, Boggs's Bills, and Other True-Life Tales*, North Point Press, 1988, pp. 53–68. Reprinted by permission of Lawrence Weschler.

A good way to study the many possible furrowings of the human brow is by telling a succession of friends and strangers, as I've taken to doing lately, that the best book you've read in a long time is a comic-strip history of the Holocaust. Brows positively curdle, foreheads arch, faces blanch and stiffen as if to say, "If this is one of your jokes, it's not very funny." Only it's not one of my jokes—it's the truth. The book is *Maus* (published by Pantheon), and its author—the perpetrator of my perplex—is Art Spiegelman.

Actually, the fans of *Maus* have been following its development for some time in installment form. Each new episode has been tucked inside successive issues of *RAW*, the semiannual journal of avant-garde

cartooning (THE GRAPHIX MAGAZINE OF ABSTRACT DEPRESSION-
ISM, as its cover once proclaimed) that Spiegelman and his wife,
Françoise Mouly, have been editing and publishing out of their Soho loft,
in New York City, since 1980. Jules Feiffer has described *Maus* as "a
remarkable work, awesome in its conception and execution," and David
Levine has characterized its effect on the reader as "on a par with
Kafka" and its mastery of tone as "reminiscent of Balzac."

   "A comic-strip history of the Holocaust" isn't quite right: such a char-
acterization is begging for trouble—or for misunderstanding, anyway.
This is no Classics Illustrated/Cliffs Notes digest of the despicable schem-
ings of Hitler and Himmler and their whole nefarious crew. Hitler and
Himmler hardly appear at all. Rather, *Maus* is at once a novel, a documentary, a memoir, an intimate retelling of the Holocaust story as it was
experienced by a single family—Spiegelman's own. Or rather, as it was
experienced by Spiegelman's father, Vladek, who recounts the story to
his son, Art, who was born in 1948, after the war was over, after everything was over, including the possibility of any sort of normal upbring-
ing. The conditions of survivorship skew everything: Vladek's first son, a
brother Art never knew, was an early victim of the Final Solution; Vladek
and his wife, Art's mother, Anja, somehow survived their separate fates
in concentration camps, emerging hollowed out and cratered; years later,
Anja would take her own life, just as Art was leaving the nest. Art's
relationship with his father is a continual torment, a mutual purgatory of
disappointment, guilt, and recrimination. This relationship is as much the
focus of Art's story as is his father's reminiscence. The elegant back
jacket of the Pantheon edition features a map of World War II Poland
and, inset, a street map of the Rego Park, Queens, neighborhood where
that war continued into the present in the mangled graspings and
grapplings of father and son. *Maus* is subtitled *A Survivor's Tale*, but the
question of *which* survivor is left to hover.

   Maus is all this—and then again, it's just an animal story. For
Spiegelman has recast his tale in the eerily familiar visual language of the
traditional comic book—animals in human clothing and in a distinctly
human environment—thereby playing off all our childhood associations
and expectations. Art, Vladek, Anja, Art's stepmother, Mala, and all the
other Jews are mice. The Germans are cats, the Poles pigs, the
Americans dogs. Spiegelman's draftsmanship is clean and direct, his
characterizations are charming and disarming—the imagery leads us on,
invitingly, reassuringly, until suddenly the horrible story has us gripped

and pinioned. Midway through, we hardly notice how strange it is for us to be having such strong reactions to these animal doings.

And then, midway through, it all stops: the volume is truncated in mid-tale. Vladek and Anja's desperate progress from prosperity into the ghetto and beyond, from one hiding hovel to the next, ends abruptly with their arrival at Mauschwitz. To learn what happened to them there, how on earth they survived—and whether or not this father and his son ever do achieve a measure of reconciliation—we are invited to await the second volume.

The man greeting me at the entrance to the fourth-story walk-up apartment in Soho looked far younger than his almost forty years. He also looked considerably more clean-cut and less threatening than the intense, long-haired, mustachioed, scrungy Zappaesque character he had contrived as his own stand-in in some of the existentialist underground comic strips he'd produced during the seventies.

The apartment, too, was more spacious than I was expecting, and it was bustling. In fact, the Spiegelmans occupy the entire floor, which they've divided in two: the front half consists of the staging area for *RAW*, while the back half provides them with living quarters. After seeing me in, Spiegelman excused himself to go confer with Françoise, a strikingly lovely French woman with high cheekbones and a luxuriant overflow of wavy brown hair. The next issue of *RAW* was about to go to press, and Françoise was on her way out to consult with the printers. The production values of *RAW* are exceptionally high—"neurotically precious" is how R. Crumb, the legendary underground-comics master and an occasional contributor to the magazine, once described them to me.

Spiegelman and Mouly launched *RAW* with the twin intentions of raising the status of cartoon graphics to an art form and introducing an American audience to the sort of high-level comic-strip art that has thrived for many years in Europe and Japan. Mouly, as the publisher, is famous for the painstaking attention she lavishes on all technical aspects of the production process.

The two of them had a certain amount to discuss before she left, and they stood together for a few moments huddled over the proof sheets, chain-smoking filtered Camels. Meanwhile, several assistants sat hunched over flatbed tables, monkeying with galleys. The room was surrounded on all sides by bookshelves, sagging under the weight of the most extensive library of comic books and anthologies I could ever have imagined. After a while, Mouly took off, and Spiegelman invited me into the back half of his loft, the living quarters.

"The whole next issue is ready," Spiegelman confessed anxiously. "Everything's now waiting on me, because I still have to finish the next installment of *Maus*. And it's taking forever." He escorted me to the far back of the loft, to his Maushole, as he calls it, where a worktable was covered with a neat clutter. Notebooks bulging with transcripts and preliminary sketches were piled to one side; dozens of little packets of papers were scattered about on the other—each bundle representing the successive workings and reworkings of a single panel. "Comics offer a very concentrated and efficient medium for telling a story," he said. "And in this case it's like trying to tell an epic novel in telegraph form. In a way, it's a lot more challenging than trying to simply tell a story. In a prose story, I could just write, 'Then they dragged my father through the gate and into the camp.' But here I have to live those words, to assimilate them, to turn them into finished business—so that I end up *seeing* them and am then able to convey that vision. Were there tufts of grass, ruts in the path, puddles in the ruts? How tall were the buildings, how many windows, any bars, any lights in the windows, any people? What time of day was it? What was the horizon like? Every panel requires that I interrogate my material like that over and over again. And it's terribly time-consuming.

"It's strange," he continues. "The parts of my father's story which I've finished drawing are clear to me. The parts I haven't gotten to yet are still a blur—even though I know the story, know the words. I've got everything blocked out in abstract, except the ending. In Part Two, the question of my father's veracity starts coming into play. Not so much whether he was telling the truth, but rather, just what had he actually lived through—what did he understand of what he experienced, what did he tell of what he understood, what did I understand of what he told, and what do I tell? The layers begin to multiply, like pane upon pane of glass.

"I still don't know how I'm going to end it," he said, pointing over at the notebooks. "But I don't *see* most of it yet. I'm only just beginning to see Mauschwitz."

I asked him why he'd decided to publish the book version of *Maus* in its current truncated form.

"Funny you should ask," he replied. He suggested we go up on the roof, where he'd installed a rudimentary sun deck. We sat on some garden furniture and surveyed the Soho skyline, the tar-roof line. He lit up a Camel, took a deep drag and resumed: "I'd never really had any intention of publishing the book version in two parts. But then, about a year ago, I read in an interview with Steven Spielberg that he was producing an animated feature film entitled *An American Tail*, involving a family of Jewish mice living in Russia a hundred years ago named the Mousekawitzes, who were being persecuted by Katsacks, and how eventually they fled to America for shelter. He was planning to have it out in time for the Statue of Liberty centennial celebrations.

"I was appalled, shattered," Spiegelman continued with a shudder. "For about a month I went into a frenzy. I'd spent my life on this, and now here, along was coming this Goliath, the most powerful man in Hollywood, just casually trampling everything underfoot. I dashed off a letter, which was returned, unopened. I went sleepless for nights on end, and then, when I finally did sleep, I began confusing our names in my dreams: Spiegelberg, Spielman. . . . I contacted lawyers. I mean, the similarities were so obvious, right down to the title—their *American Tale* simply being a more blatant, pandering-to-the-mob version of my *Survivor's Tale* subtitle. Their lawyers argued that the idea of anthropomorphizing mice wasn't unique to either of us, and they, of course, cited Mickey Mouse and other Disney creations. But no one was denying that—indeed, I'd self-consciously been playing off Disney all the while. If you wanted to get technical about it, the idea of anthropomorphizing animals goes all the way back to Aesop. No, what I was saying was that the specific use of mice to sympathetically portray Jews combined with the concept of cats as anti-Semitic oppressors in a story that compares life in the Old World of Europe with life in America *was* unique—and it was called *Maus: A Survivor's Tale.*

"I didn't want any money from them—I just wanted them to cease and desist. What made me so angry was that when *Maus* was eventually going to be completed, people were naturally going to see my version as a slightly psychotic recasting of Spielberg's idea instead of the way it was—Spielberg's being an utter domestication and trivialization of *Maus.* And then there was a further infuriating irony: theirs supposedly took place in 1886, and what with the Statue of Liberty tie-in, they were going to be swathing the story in all this mindless, fashionable, self-congratulatory patriotic fervor—whereas, if you were being true to the initial metaphor, in depicting the way things actually were in 1940, you would have had to strand my mice people off the coast of Cuba, *drowning*, because it is precisely the case that at that point, the time of their greatest need, mice people were being denied entry into the U.S."

Spiegelman started to calm down. His cigarette had gone out; he lit up another. "Well, anyway, it's over for the time being. My lawyers told me that while I had a very strong moral case, my legal one wasn't so hot. It'd be hard to prove anything one way or the other, certainly not enough to justify a prior injunction against release of the movie, which is the only thing I really wanted. Some of my friends couldn't understand why I was getting so worked up. One editor told me 'Look, all the guy stole was your concept, and frankly, it's a terrible concept.'" (The redoubtable R. Crumb was likewise bemused by Spiegelman's desperate churnings. "He's such an egomaniac," Crumb told me, laughing. "I mean, who the hell cares? I've seen some of the previews for Spielberg's film. Those mice are cute." R. Crumb has the most devastatingly prurient way of pronouncing the word *cute*.)

Spiegelman may have been calming down, but he was still obsessing: "I mean, if Samuel Beckett had stolen the idea, I'd be depressed, but I'd be *impressed* as well. But Steven Spielberg! Oy! I just read where they've now licensed off the *doll rights* for the Mousekawitzes to Sears, and McDonald's is going to get the beverage-cup rights!"

So, Spiegelman continued, he decided that if he couldn't stop Spielberg, he might nevertheless beat him to the turnstiles, immediately publishing as much of the story as he'd already completed (he explained how all along he'd seen the arrival at Mauschwitz as the narrative's halfway point) and thereby at least establishing primacy. Pantheon was happy to go along, and Spielberg's production company obliged by running into difficulties and having to delay the film's release until around Thanksgiving. As Spiegelman observed, "It was actually a great idea. You see, in Europe there's a real tradition, in serious cartooning as well as in high literature, of multivolume projects—just think of that supreme mouse writer, Proust, and all the volumes he was able to generate from that initial whiff of Camembert!"

When Art Spiegelman was about ten years old, in 1958 in Rego Park, Queens, he fell one day while roller-skating with some friends, who then skated on without him. Whimpering, he walked home to his father, who was out in the yard doing some carpentry repairs. Vladek inquired why his Artie was crying, and when Art told him about the fall and his friends, Vladek stopped his sawing, looked down at his son and said gruffly, "Friends? Your *friends*? If you lock them together in a room with no food for a week, then you could see what it is, friends!"

Spiegelman places this incident as the first episode in the book version of *Maus*, and it serves as a sort of overture, an intimation of one of the book's principal themes. For, at one level, Artie was an all-American boy, roller-skating, out goofing with his gang. Back home, though, life was haunted, darkly freighted with overcharged parental concern.

Actually, Artie had been born in Stockholm in 1948, three years after his parents' miraculous reunion at the end of their separate camp fates. Two years after Artie's birth, the family was finally permitted to immigrate to America. Back in the old country, in Poland between the wars, Vladek had been a wealthy man, or rather Anja's father had been a wealthy man, and Vladek had married into that wealth. Art seems to leave intentionally ambiguous (although here, as elsewhere in *Maus*, the ambiguity is of an almost crystalline precision) whether or not he thinks Vladek initially married Anja for her money and her station. At any rate, Vladek managed important aspects of her family's textile business and attained substantial financial security for himself, his wife, and their beloved baby son, Richieu—until the war, that is, when both the wealth and the beloved son were snatched away. In America, in New York, Vladek worked in the garment trade and later in the diamond district, but he never recaptured the security of his earlier life. Though the Spiegelmans were basically middle-class, they lived below their means. Raising his first son, Vladek had been a young father with a buoyant sense of his future. Raising his second son—his second "only child"—he was an old man, fretting over his insecure present when he wasn't fixated on his desolate past. Art's parents *were* old. There were really two generations separating them from this American boy; on top of that, they were old-world; and on top of that, they'd aged well beyond their years owing to their experiences during the war. As Artie grew into young adulthood in America of the sixties, he would be facing generation gaps compounded one upon another.

And yet, for all that, Art remembers his childhood as remarkably normal. "I really didn't encounter serious problems," he recalled that afternoon on his sun deck, "until I went away to college and was able to match my experiences against those of others. I mean, for instance, the fact that my parents used to wake up in the middle of the night screaming didn't seem especially strange to me. I suppose I thought everybody's parents did. Or the fact that in the Spiegelman household, the regular birthday gift for my mother, year in and year out, was some sort of wide bracelet, so that she could cover over the number tattooed on her forearm. Sometimes when neighbor kids would come over and ask her what that stuff on her arm was, she'd say it was a telephone number she was trying not to forget.

"No," he continued, "I was a pretty normal kid, except that I was reading a lot too much Kafka for a fourteen-year-old. I knew I'd grow up to be neurotic, the way today I know I'll soon be losing my hair." He brushed back a thinning, brown wisp, further revealing his precipitously receding hairline. "It didn't, it doesn't bother me."

"By fourteen, too, I knew I'd be a cartoonist: I was obsessed with comics. I spent hours copying from comic books, especially the satirical ones, like *Mad* magazine, which was a terrific influence."

I asked Spiegelman whether any of that bothered his parents. "They encouraged me up to a point," he replied, "up to the point where it became clear that I was serious. A kind of panic set in as I turned fifteen and was still doing it. They were terribly upset because clearly there was no way one could make a living at cartooning, and my father especially was, perhaps understandably, obsessed about money. They wanted me to become a dentist. For them, dentist was halfway to doctor, I guess. And we'd have these long talks. They'd point out how if I became a dentist, I could always do the drawing on the side, whereas if I became a cartoonist, I couldn't very well pull people's teeth during my off hours. Their logic was impeccable, just irrelevant. I was hooked."

Young Spiegelman knew he wanted to be a cartoonist, but he wasn't sure what kind, so he tried everything. When he was twelve, he approached the editors of the Long Island *Post*, a local paper, seeking employment as a staff cartoonist. The *Post* ran a story about the incident, headlined, BUDDING ARTIST WANTS ATTENTION. When he was fifteen, he was in fact appointed staff cartoonist of the *Post*, an unpaid position. Meanwhile he commuted by subway to the mid-Manhattan campus of the High School of Art and Design, where he edited the school paper, hung out after (and sometimes during) school at the nearby offices of *Mad* magazine, and, inspired, began turning out his own cartoon digests, one called *Wild*, and another *Blasé*, which "was printed with a process even cheaper than mimeo." He contributed to a Cuban exile paper, and served a stint up in Harlem, disguised to the world as a hip black cartoonist ("Artie X").

In 1966, Art left home for Harpur College, the experimental subcampus of the State University of New York at Binghamton, and there things began to come seriously unmoored. The underlying conflicts with his

parents roiled to the surface now that he was no longer in their immediate presence. Furthermore, "Binghamton was one of the early capitals of
psychedelics," he says, "and the drug culture definitely accelerated my
decomposition beyond any containable point." His intensity became
increasingly manic. He was living off campus, in a forest cabin. "And I
made a strange discovery," he recalls. "I was just kind of holding court,
people were coming out to visit, and I found that if I just said whatever
came into my mind, the atmosphere would get incredibly charged—and
if I kept it up, within half an hour, either my guests would run out,
screaming, or else we'd approach this druglike high. It was like a primordial sensitivity session. And this was going on for days on end. I wasn't
eating, I was laughing a lot, I was beginning to suffer from acute sleep
deprivation. I was starting to experience these rampant delusions of
grandeur. I was sure I was onto something, and sure enough, I was—a
psychotic breakdown."

Eventually, they came to take him away (he informed the school
shrink that the top of his head looked like a penis); he was dispatched by
ambulance to a local mental ward (exaltedly he wailed in tune with the
siren); they sedated him (it took three full-bore shots) and threw him
into a padded cell ("Waking up, my first thought was that I was God
alone and that what I really needed to do now was invent me some
people. . . . Later, I began screaming for a nurse, and when this guy
came in, I said, no, I wanted a *nurse*. He said he was a nurse—I'd never
heard of such a thing as a male nurse—and I said, 'Gee, how do you
people reproduce here on this planet?'"). Gradually, they reeled him
back in—or he reeled himself back in; they didn't seem to be of much
help. One attendant, a conscientious objector doing alternative service,
befriended him and advised him on how to get out ("He told me to
drink less water—they seemed to think I thought my brain was over-
heating or something—to play Ping-Pong, *lots* of Ping-Pong, and to
blame it all on LSD, which was a category they could understand; all of
which I did, and within a month I was released").

He was released on two conditions: first, that he start seeing a psy-
chotherapist on the outside, and second, that he go back to living with
his parents. "Living at home was exactly the wrong prescription,"
Spiegelman said, "since it was home that was driving me crazy. I said
this quite emphatically to the shrink one day, and he asked me, 'So why
don't you move out?' I told him about the condition. And he said, 'You
really think they're going to throw you back in if you don't follow their

conditions?' I said, 'Gee, thanks,' and immediately left both home and psychotherapy.

"The wonderful thing about the whole episode, though, is that it cut off all expectations. I'd been locked in a life-and-death struggle with my parents. Anything short of the nut house would have left things insoluble. But now I could venture out on my own terms. Over the years, I have developed a terrific confidence in my own subconscious."

Art was out of the house, but the tormented Spiegelman family drama did not subside, and a few months after his release, his mother committed suicide.

Spiegelman becomes quiet and measured when he talks about this period. "The way she did it, I was the one who was supposed to discover the body, only I was late coming by, as usual, so that by the time I arrived there was already this whole scene. . . . Was my commitment to the mental ward the cause of her suicide? No. Was there a relation? Sure. After the war, she'd invested her whole life in me. I was more like a confidant to her than a son. She couldn't handle the separation. I didn't want to hurt her, to hurt them. But I had to break free."

He's silent for a moment, then resumes: "But talk about repression. For a while I had no feelings whatsoever. People would ask me, and I'd just say that she was a suicide, period. Nothing—I moved out to California, submerged myself in the underground-comics scene, which was thriving out there, imagined myself unscathed. And then one day, four years later, it all suddenly came flooding back, all the memories resurging. I threw myself into seclusion for a month, and in the end emerged with "Prisoner on the Hell Planet.""

The four-page strip, which first appeared in San Francisco as part of the *Short Order Comix* series in 1972, was an astonishment—one of the most lacerating breakthroughs yet in an extraordinarily active scene. The strip opens with a drawn hand holding an actual photograph portraying a swimsuit-clad middle-aged woman and her smiling T-shirted boy; the photo is captioned "Trojan Lake, N.Y., 1958" (that same year of the roller-skating incident with which *Maus* opens). In the next frame, the mustachioed narrator peers out, framed by a fierce spotlight and decked out in prison (or is it concentration-camp?) garb. "In 1968, my mother killed herself," the narrator declares simply. "She left no note."

There follow four pages of vertiginous, expressionist draftsmanship and writing—part Caligari, part Munch. The story of the suicide is recounted, and the strip concludes with the narrator locked away in a vast prison vault: "Well, Mom, if you're listening, congratulations! You've committed the perfect crime. . . . You put me here, shorted my circuits, cut my nerve endings, and crossed my wires. . . . You murdered me, Mommy, and you left me here to take the rap." A voice bubble intrudes from out of frame: "Pipe down, Mac, some of us are trying to sleep."

A few months before "Hell Planet," Spiegelman had composed an earlier version of *Maus*, a three-page rendition which he included as his contribution to an underground anthology called *Funny Aminals*. In that first version, the relationship between father and son is quieter, almost pastoral. The cozy Father Mouse is telling his little boy Mickey a bedtime story. It's an adorable, cuddly scene (there's a Mickey Mouse lamp on the bedside table)—only the story is ghastly. Several of the incidents that were to be amplified years later in the book-length version appear here in concentrated form. But by the strip's end—as Daddy and Mommy in the bedtime story are being herded into Mauschwitz—Daddy explains that that's all he can tell for now, he can tell no more, and Mickey has, in any case, already nodded off to sleep.

It's strange: Spiegelman's 1972 take on his parents—a warm, empathetic father and cruelly manipulative mother—was to undergo a complete reversal by the time he returned to these themes in the book version of *Maus*. As if to underscore this transformation, he contrived to include the entire "Hell Planet" strip within the body of the new *Maus's* text, drawing on a true episode in which his father accidentally comes upon a copy of "Hell Planet" his son never intended for him to see.

The 1972 "Maus" and "Hell Planet" strips were representative of one channel in the distinctly bifurcated artistic program that Spiegelman was pursuing now that he'd launched his underground cartooning career. On the one hand, he was trying to push the comic-strip medium as far as he could in terms of wrenchingly confessional content. Simultaneously, although usually separately, he was testing the limits of the comic strip's formal requirements. In high deconstructionist style, he was questioning such things as how people read a strip; how many of the usual expectations one might subtract from a strip before it began to resemble an inchoate jumble of images on the page; whether that mattered. By 1977, he managed to unite examples of both his tendencies in a single anthology of his work, which he titled, with considerable punning cleverness, *Breakdowns* (besides its obvious confessional connotation, the word *breakdown* refers to the preliminary sketches that precede and block out a finished comic strip).

"*Breakdowns* came out as I was turning thirty," Spiegelman recalls, lighting up another cigarette, "and with some of the strips there, it was really like I'd taken things, particularly the formal questions, pretty much to the limit. So I was faced with a dilemma, 'Now what?' And after all my experiments, it was as if I finally said, 'All right, I give up, comics are there to tell a *story.*' But what story? Drawing really comes hard to me. I sweat these things out—one or two panels a day, a page maybe a week. And I was damned if I was going to put in all that work for a few chuckles. I hesitated for a while, but finally I decided that I had to go back and confront the thing that in a way I'd known all along I'd eventually have to face—this presence that had been hanging over my family's life, Auschwitz and what it had done to us."

With the first installment of that second version of *Maus*, which appeared in the December 1980 issue of *RAW*, Mickey, the little pajama-clad mouse boy of the initial version, had grown up. He was now a chain-smoking, somewhat alienated, somewhat disheveled, urban cartoonist mouse named Art. His father, too, had aged, become more stooped and crotchety, and their relationship had become far more complicated. "I went out to see my father in Rego Park," says Art, the narrator mouse, introducing his tale. "I hadn't seen him in a long time—we weren't that close."

"After I'd left home to go to college," Art, the real-life cartoonist, recalls, lighting up another cigarette, "my father and I could hardly get together without fighting, a situation that only worsened after Anja's suicide. Vladek remarried, this time to a kind woman named Mala, another camp survivor who'd been a childhood friend of Anja's back in her old town of Sosnowiec, but it was a sorry mismatch, and that relationship too seemed to devolve into endless kvetching and bickering. It was a classic case of victims victimizing each other—and I couldn't stand being around. And yet now, if I was going to tell the story, I knew I'd have to start visiting my father again, to get him to tell me his tale one more time. I'd heard everything countless times before, but it had all been background noise, part of the ambient blur; precisely because I'd been subjected to all of it so often before, I could barely recall any of it. So now I asked him if he'd allow me to tape-record his stories, and he was willing. So I began heading back out to Rego Park."

"From the book," Spiegelman continues after a pause, "a reader might get the impression that the conversations depicted in the narrative were just one small part, a facet of my relationship with my father. In fact, however, they *were* my relationship with my father. I was doing them *to have a relationship with my father.* Outside of them, we were still continually at loggerheads."

The Vladek portrayed in the present-tense sequences of *Maus* is petty, cheap, maddeningly manipulative, self-pitying, witheringly abusive to his second wife, neurotic as hell. But when he settles in and starts retelling his life story, you realize that, yes, precisely, he is a survivor of hell, a mangled and warped survivor. The present Vladek imbues his former self with life, but that former Vladek illuminates the present one as well. Spiegelman develops this theme overtly but then, too, in the subtlest details. At one point, for example, Vladek is recounting how when he was a Polish soldier in a Nazi POW camp, early on in the war, he and some fellow soldiers were billeted into a filthy stable which they were ordered to render "spotlessly clean within an hour," a manifestly impossible task, the failure at which cost them their day's soup ration, "you lousy bastards." Suddenly Vladek interrupts his story and the scene shifts to the present, with Artie seated on the floor before his father, taking it all in. "But look, Artie, what you do!" Vladek cries. "Huh?" asks the absorbed Artie. "You're dropping on the carpet. You want it should be like a stable *here?*" Artie apologizes and hurries to pick up the cigarette ashes. "Clean it, yes?" Vladek will not relent. "Otherwise I have to do it. Mala could let it sit like this for a week and never touch it." And so forth: kvetch, kvetch, kvetch. And then, just as suddenly, we're back in Poland: "So, we lived and worked a few weeks in the stable . . ."

While many of the ways Vladek grates on his son amount to minor foibles and misdemeanors, he is capable of more substantial outrages as well. Perhaps the most mortifying (and unforgivable) of these atrocities emerges only gradually as the story unfolds—the fact that Vladek didn't just misplace the life history that Anja had written out years earlier to be given someday to their son, a folio Artie even remembers having seen somewhere around when he was growing up . . . that, actually, he destroyed it. "Murderer!" cries a flabbergasted Artie when Vladek finally confesses the callous immolation at the climax of Book I. "Murderer," he mutters, walking away. Curtain falls.

"The fact the he'd destroyed that autobiographical journal of hers," Spiegelman says, "meant that the story forcibly became increasingly *his* story, which at first seemed like a terrible, almost fatal, problem. The absence of my mother left me with—well, not with an antihero, but at any rate not a pure hero. But in retrospect that now seems to me one of the strengths of *Maus*. If only admirable people were shown to have survived, then the implicit moral would have been that only admirable people deserved to survive, as opposed to the fact that people deserved to survive as people. Anyway, I'm left with the story I've got, my shoehorn with which to squeeze myself back into history.

"I've tried to achieve an evenness of tone, a certain objectivity," Spiegelman continues, "because that made the story work better. But it also proved helpful—*is* proving helpful—in my coming to terms with my father. Rereading it, I marvel at how my father comes across, finally, as a sympathetic character—people keep telling me what a sympathetic portrait I've drawn. As I was actually drawing it, let me tell you, I was raging, boiling over with anger. But there must have been a deeper sympathy for him which I wasn't even aware of as I was doing it, an understanding I was getting in contact with. It's as if all his damn cantankerousness finally melted away."

I asked Spiegelman about the mouse metaphor, the very notion of telling the story in this animal-fabulist mode. It seems to me one of the most effective things about the book. There have been hundreds of Holocaust memoirs—horribly, we've become inured to the horror. People being gassed in showers and shoveled into ovens—it's a story we've already heard. But mice? The Mickey Mice of our childhood reveries? Having the story thus retold, with animals as the principals, freshly recaptures its terrible immediacy, its palpable urgency.

I asked Spiegelman how he'd hit upon the idea. "It goes back to that *Funny Aminals* comic anthology I told you about before," he explained. "Along with several of the other underground-comics people out in California, I had been invited to contribute a strip to this anthology of warped, revisionist animal comics. Initially, I was trying to do some sort of Grand Guignol horror strip, but it wasn't working. Then I remembered something an avant-garde-filmmaker friend, Ken Jacobs, had pointed out back at Binghamton, how in the early animated cartoons, blacks and mice were often represented similarly. Early animated cartoon mice had 'darkie' rhythms and body language, and vice versa. So for a while I thought about doing an animal strip about the black experience in America—for about forty minutes. Because what did I know about the black experience in America? And then suddenly the idea of Jews as mice just hit me full force, full-blown. Almost as soon as it hit me, I began to recognize the obvious historical antecedents—how Nazis had spoken of Jews as 'vermin,' for example, and plotted their 'extermination.'

And before that back to Kafka, whose story 'Josephine the Singer, or the Mouse Folk' was one of my favorites from back when I was a teenager and has always struck me as a dark parable and prophecy about the situation of the Jews and Jewishness.

"Having hit upon the metaphor, though, I wanted to subvert it, too," continued Spiegelman, the veteran deconstructionist, lighting up again. "I wanted it to become problematic, to have it confound and implicate the reader. I included all sorts of paradoxes in the text—for instance, the way in which Artie, the mouse cartoonist, draws the story of his mother's suicide, and in his strip (my own "Hell Planet" strip), all the characters are *human*. Or the moment when the mother and father are shown hiding in a cramped cellar and the mother shrieks with terror because there are 'Rats!' All those moments are meant to rupture the metaphor, to render its absurdity conspicuous, to force a kind of free fall. I always savored that sort of confusion when I was a child reading comic books: how, for instance, Donald would go over to Grandma Duck's for Thanksgiving and they'd be having turkey for dinner!

"But it's funny," Spiegelman continues. "A lot of those subtleties just pass people by. In fact, I remember how I was over at my father's one evening soon after I'd published the three-page version of 'Maus.' As usual, he had several of his card-playing buddies over—all fellow camp survivors—and at one point he passed the strip around. They all read it, and then they immediately set to trading anecdotes: 'Ah, yes, I remember that, only with me it happened like this,' and so forth. Not one of them seemed the least bit fazed by the mouse metaphor—not one of them even seemed to have noticed it! A few days later, I happened to be making a presentation of some of my work at this magazine. I was sitting out in the art editor's waiting room with a couple other cartoonists, old fellows, and I pulled out 'Maus' and showed it to them. They looked it over for a while and began conferring: 'Kid's a good mouse man,' one of them said. 'Yeah, not bad on cats, either,' said the other. Utterly oblivious to the Holocaust subject matter."

I asked Spiegelman what his father had thought of the newer installments of *Maus*, as they began appearing in *RAW*. "He never really saw them," Art replied, snuffing out his cigarette. "Early in 1981 he and Mala moved down to Florida, and within a few months of that he was already beginning to lose it. He was past seventy-five years old, and he was pretty much incoherent throughout the last year before his death. We had to put him in an old-age home. He died on August 18, 1982."

Art paused for a moment, then continued: "I was less affected by his death than I thought I'd be, perhaps because he'd been a long time going, maybe because there was no room for that relationship to change. I went to his funeral, almost like a reporter trying to see how his story was going to end up. But my feelings were more inchoate than anything that would make a good anecdote.

"I'd already finished all my taping sessions with him before he'd begun to go senile, and I had the story pretty well blocked out, chapter by chapter, except for the ending. As I say, I still don't know how I'm going to end it. The last time I saw him, he was sitting there propped up in the nursing home. He may or may not have recognized me. The nurses were trying to stroke any last vestiges of memory in him. They were showing him these "Romper Room" flashcards, you know, 'Dog,' 'Cat,' 'Dog,' 'Cat'. . . 'Cat.'" Spiegelman's voice trailed off. It seemed he might have come up with his ending after all.

Postscript (1988)
As things turned out, Spiegelman need not have worried about Spielberg's film. The film opened to middling reviews and middling suc-cess—no one, at any rate, was confusing it with *Maus*, which, for its part, was greeted with overwhelming critical acclaim and proved an unexpected best-seller. During its first year and a half, Spiegelman's book sold almost one hundred thousand copies in the United States, and arrangements were under way for no less than twelve foreign editions (including German, French, Hebrew, Finnish, and Japanese translations). Meanwhile, Spiegelman continued to eke out the subsequent chapters, slowly laboriously. . . . And a new character made a brief appearance in the eighth chapter, in a momentary flash-forward to the present: a baby girl mouse named Nadja, Vladek's sudden granddaughter.

From Mickey to *Maus*: Recalling the Genocide through Cartoon

GRAHAM SMITH / 1987

From *Oral History Journal* Spring 1987,
pp. 26–34. Reprinted by permission of
the Oral History Society.

Dundee, where I live, was once a city whose comic industry dominated the British market. Indeed Dundee still produces a huge number of comic papers which include the *Hotspur, Beezer, Warlord, Twinkle, Victor, Suzy, Hornet, Bunty, Beano, Commando, Judy*. Having misspent my childhood on the sort of material that makes liberals cringe, I grew into a youth and forgot Korky's japes and dying Japs in favour of the imported comix from the United States. These comix were more sophisticated in style and content, more subversive and outrageous, than anything produced in Britain. Drawn by people like Robert Crumb and other Underground artists, they were usually well hidden under my bed so that the prying parental eyes were not offended. Amongst the Freak

Brothers and Fat Freddie's Cat, Gurus and Yetis, there was the cartoon work of the young Art Spiegelman who was quoted in *The Apex Treasury of Underground Comics* (1974), as saying that 'As an art form the comic strip is barely past its infancy. So am I. Maybe we'll grow up together.'

Art Spiegelman returned to my life a couple of years ago when a friend lent me a copy of *RAW*, 'the graphix magazine of abstract depressionism', published yearly in New York, and edited by Françoise Mouly and Art Spiegelman. Inserted in the magazine was a booklet which turned out to be a chapter of Spiegelman's *Maus*, the comic strip story of his father's life in Nazi occupied Poland.

Maus is an incredible use of cartoon, but what impressed me even more was that the strip explicitly stated that the story was based upon oral interviews made by Spiegelman with his father. Two great loves in my life were combined: interviewing and cartooning. Determined to find out more I wrote to the artist and asked him what he thought of oral history. Never expecting a reply I was excited when through my door came a bundle with a New York post mark. It contained several chapters of *Maus* and a cassette on which were some extracts of the original interviews with his father, and, on the other side, Spiegelman's answers to my questions. Thanks Art.

Here is an edited version of an interview conducted between Dundee and New York which perhaps proves that cartoons and cassettes can bridge the Atlantic and through which something important can be told.

Could you describe the historical methods used in creating *Maus*?
I have no background per se in oral history. Long after the interviews I did with my father I found a book on oral history, read it, and found out that maybe I have gone about it in an unorthodox way—I don't know. But since it was my father the situation was very unspecific, and was so laden with psychological undercurrents I don't know if I could have perceived it in any other way than I had.

Maus, the book I'm working on, grew out of a comic strip I did in 1971 for an Underground comic book. A three-page strip that was based on stories of my father's and mother's that I recalled being told in childhood. When I finished the 1971 strip, I was pretty much estranged from my father, I went back to him and showed him the strip as an excuse to renew contact with him. Some of the information he gave me at that point actually made me go back and rework the three-page strip. And that led me to tape his experiences in more full detail, and I spent about four days with him talking into a reel-to-reel clunky tape recorder.

I pretty much just let him put his story forward in which ever way he chose to do, and I did not do much cross-examining or pushing for more detail. I just wanted to have some record, not specifically at that point to use for another strip, but just out of interest to have some record of what my father had gone through.

And that turned out to be about nine hours of tape. Well after that I again went into a period of not spending much time speaking with my father. Anyway in 1977 I decided to do this longer work that I've been working on ever since. At that point I set up an arrangement to go see my father more often and talk to him about his experiences. And this was a way for me to have a relationship with my father as much as it was to get the information. When we focused on talking about his past it was something that I was interested in and eh we would spend time without getting into heavy water where we'd just start arguing or whatever.

When I went back to him I'd be taking notes, knowing at that point that I was going to do a book. And found of course that was not the best way for me to get information down so I gotta tape recorder and came back and taped whatever was possible. So one way or another most of it's on tape.

At the beginning my father was kind of self-conscious about me putting a microphone to his muzzle, but by the end of it he seemed totally unaware of that. So much so that I thought that he didn't realize that I was taping him, but at the very very end he'd grab the microphone from me and gave some sort of coda saying, 'I hope people will never forget the six million' and whatever—very out of character. He had somehow retained the idea that this was for posterity.

I would ask questions of him that I would ask over and over again, because often he just wouldn't answer the question, not meaning to evade I don't think, but it would trigger some associational response and he'd get off on that. And I'd hear the same stories maybe four, five, six, seven, times. I'd have to sort of trick him by finding other questions—other ways of asking—t'get a little bit more information. When I've gone back over his several times retold story I find discrepancies either in dates or in the duration of time that something took.

How important was the accuracy not only of your father's story, but also how he recalled the story, to the final version?

Well, looking back at these various versions of the story I have t'kind of figure out what probably happened, and that's sometimes based on using some reference books about the period including one very specific work that was about Jews of his home town. It was published in Polish after the war and I've had it translated as some kind of objective guide post of dates. And to a degree I've been able to get correlating information from a cousin of mine named Lolek Spiegelman, who's mentioned in *Maus*, or from my stepmother, or from other friends of the family that I talked to. I've done that to corroborate his story, on the other hand most of the story I can't corroborate.

Although I set about in doing *Maus* to do a history of sorts I'm all too aware that ultimately what I'm creating is a realistic fiction. The experiences my father actually went through, there's what he's able to remember and what he's able to articulate of these experiences. Then there's what A'm able to understand of what he articulated, and what A'm able to put down on paper. And then of course there's what the reader can make of that. *Maus* is so many steps removed from the actual experience, they're so distant from each other that all I can do is hint at, intimate, and try for something that feels real to me.

Were there problems of using transcribed language in the cartoons?

One moment I'm going to put you on pause while I gather my thoughts. O.K., so I was making these tapes and taking these notes, and I spent a long time organizing that information as best I could—chronologically. Nd from that began to break the material down into chapter form and then into comic strip panels, which is the language A'm comfortable with. Nd this breaking down did involve *not* using his exact language, that is spoken language when transcribed. Transcription is not the easiest language to understand and it also fills a lotta space ye know. In a comic strip one has to be efficient to be uh able to get ideas across in a small number of words so that they will fit into a caption and a balloon. So there is a kind of reduction going on to get to the essence of something. In the captions I've tried to capture my father's cadences and speech pattern, and eh his specific kind of language if not always his exact phrases. That's based on having spent many years listening to his language while I was growing up and therefore feeling comfortable enough with it to be able to make a facsimile of it or even a caricature of it.

I was able to use his exact words in the captions whenever that particular phrasing was felicitous. Sometimes where that was the most beautiful way to say something, although obviously it was not necessarily the grammatically correct way to say it.

I decided not to use my father's broken language for the balloons in the past. Sometimes when telling me his story he would make up dialogue for various people he'd been in contact with as if these were direct quotes, which he didn't remember word for word, obviously. When I came t'put the words in their mouths I felt very uncomfortable, because that was based on not being present and not knowing how people spoke. So I tried a fairly neutral kind of dialogue. In other words if I'd been writing a true fiction piece I'd probably would have taken a lot more liberties with the dialogue in order to give certain kind of cadences and to specify character. Here I felt I could use it as a way of conveying information and moving the narrative along, but not to hallucinate what I'd like that character to be like and make them too specific.

Also I didn't want to put the dialogue balloons in my father's broken English, like it was in his captions, in that in the captions I wanted t'use my father's difficulties with th'language as a pointer toward his situation in America where English is not his first language. I didn't want to impose that broken English on the characters in the past where they were speaking their native tongue and therefore spoke as fluently as one would in that circumstance.

Why did you choose to tell your parents' story in cartoon?
It's important to me that *Maus* is done in comic strip form, because it's the form A'm most comfortable shaping and working with. *Maus* for me in part is a way of telling my parents' life and therefore coming to terms with it.

That's important to me. It's not a matter of choice in the sense that I don't feel I could deal with this material as prose, or as a series of paintings, or as a film, or as poetry.

The methods you use produce a distancing effect. Why was this effect sought?
Yeh, yeh, uhm that was nice of you to say it that way, 'cause that was a phrase that was in my mind when I was working on the material. Uh again I don't just feel that I had that much choice about the way I've approached this material. Obviously I could have chosen to do commercial art comic strips, which I was doing when I started *Maus*, and not

dealt with the material at all. But once I started on *Maus* I can't really imagine having done the comic strip for instance with people rather than with animals. And using the animals is one way that this distancing effect is achieved. If I'd tried to do a comic strip about my parents' experiences with human characters in which I tried to get likenesses of everyone I would be involved in a rather different endeavor. I'd be a kind of counterfeiting reality, in that I would be making the pretense of being a camera wandering through the ghettoes of Europe. That would be something far enough away from my own direct experiences that any attempt to do so would be doomed in failure.

By using these mask-like faces, where characters look more or less the same, a sketchier drawing style, I am able to focus one's attention on the narrative while still telling it in comic strip form. So that distancing device actually brings one closer to the heart of the material than a true comix approach.

Another thing I suppose is the fact that I've chosen to use a very sedate comic strip format. If one compares the panel layout in *Maus* to say a Marvel or Japanese comic it's rather quiet. Most of the boxes are nice rectilinear forms, and even rows—not very chaotic. It creates a kind of quietness and it makes you enter in, rather than it aggressively coming out and grabbing your eyeballs. I've done other comic strip work in the past, and probably will do others in the future, that have a stronger, more overt, visual component. In this instance I wanted it to be quiet in that it would force the reader into a relationship with the strip.

In looking at other art and literature that's been shaped from the holocaust—a histrionic term I find problematic—that material is often very high pitched, very histrionic. And I've always been put off it a bit; in that the material's so horribly strong. That pitching for a tear or for an emotional response seems redundant. I felt a need for a more subdued approach, which would incorporate these distancing devices like using these animal mask faces.

Another aspect of the way I've chosen to use this material is that I've entered myself into the story. So the way the story got told and who the story was told to is as important if not a more important part of the story than solely my father's narrative. To me that's at the heart of the work. I suppose that's a distancing device in that one is constantly brought back to how the story is being told. And of course being brought back to who's telling the story and to whom they're telling the story and how that colors the information. It leaves more in the control of the reader to understand, to apply the reader's intelligence, and to pull out of the material what the reader will.

Some critics might complain that you've trivialized the treatment of the Jews, how would you reply?

Well, Graham, if it was somebody else asking I'd tell them t'go fuck themselves—frankly. Uhm, obviously I wouldn't put the kind of effort into this project if it was to trivialize anything.

I suppose that someone saying that would probably believe that comix are intrinsically trivial. It is my conviction that comix are a medium. They can be used to do something trivial or used to do something else. Same is true for novels that range from absolute pornography to James Joyce and William Faulkner. I believe that it's true that comix haven't been used that way for the most part. But there are occasional, beautiful, achievements in comic strips that aren't at all trivial. As a medium it has certain advantages and disadvantages. Among the advantages I would include a certain kind of accessibility, an immediacy, a certain kind of intimacy that is to do with the interplay of one's own handwriting, as expressed in writing out the balloons and the drawn signs that represents characters. It's immediate in that it appears one step closer to uh the way the mind works than pure language. It also doesn't require the high finance, and working with large groups of people that making a movie would entail. It allows one to carry more narrative content than painting. It just has its own rules that's maybe too complex to go into now. But to work with an interaction of words and pictures is nothing intrinsically trivial.

Uh, using the animals allowed me a handle on the material. It wasn't meant t'turn it into a funny animal story. On the other hand it was intended to allow me to make reference to and use cartoon conventions, of ideas that have to do with cat and mouse chases. I suppose one of the original inspirations to do the story this way was from seeing old animated cartoons in which cats and mice are portrayed. Mice are kinda seen as "happy darkies," if you'll pardon the expression. The way blacks were portrayed in these early cartoons and the way mice are portrayed are almost identical: uh, singing and dancing, playing, not being adults with responsibilities.

At first, the genesis of that first-three page "Maus" strip was that I was asked to take part in an "Underground Comic" that Robert Crumb was part of, and a few other Underground cartoonists who were based in San Francisco were part of. The only editorial premise was one used anthropomorphized creatures rather than people. At first I wanted to do comic strips about black oppression in America using cats and mice. As I started I realized that this was a ridiculous thought in that I just didn't know enough about the situation to be anything other than a liberal wimp with good intentions, but not enough underlying knowledge about the situation to do uhm any meaningful work. I realized that my own background included material of oppression which could be more directly applied.

As soon as the idea hit I realized that there's all too much justification for it. The rhetoric of the genocide that the Nazis used had to do with the extermination of vermin; it wasn't murdering people, it was squash-ing parasites, lice, rats. In fact there's a movie—a propaganda film—uh by a guy named Hitler, called *The Eternal Jew*.

That was made under Goebbels during World War Two. In the movie there is a scene of Jews milling around a ghetto and then it cuts to rats milling around a hole. And the intertitle is very germane if I kind of find it—I'll read it into the microphone here, one moment—let's see—yeh, O.K. "wherever rats turn up they spread annihilation throughout the land, destroying property and food supplies. This is how they dissemi-nate disease, pestilence, leprosy, typhus, cholera, dysentery. Just like the Jews among mankind; rats represent the very essence of subterranean destruction." Uh I've a number of other quotes from the Nazi period that also uh cover the same kind of ground.

And I then would find references to the fact that, in one history of comix Hitler banned Mickey Mouse from Germany, 'cause he thought they were a Jewish art-form and he hated them as such.

I understand that the metaphor I'm using is just that. It's a metaphor and can't be carried very far before it cracks. See on the hand A'm using these mice as Jews, cats as Nazis, Poles as pigs, umh dogs as Americans, and so on, in an ironic fashion, in that on the surface at least this tends to, uh, verify the Nazi racial theories, and of course that can't hold up as a—tsshh, *can't* hold up even as a metaphor. And as a result the metaphor cracks a number of times in the book. There's a point where my father's traveling from prisoner of war camp, sneaking across the border to his own part of Poland, the Poles feeling rather antipathetic towards the Germans, although they also bore no love t'the Jews. My father never mentioned he was Jewish, he was just wearing a Polish army uniform and said he'd escaped from a prisoner of war camp and was trying to sneak back and some Poles helped him. Now in my comic book if I did that straight I would have been in a bind in that the Pole pig looking at the mouse in uniform would be aware that he was a mouse. So I had my father wearing a pig mask, that's a mask on top of a mask, and it's obviously there as a way of calling attention to the fact that this metaphor can't hold.

Um also in the course of the book there's a number of places where this thing, this dynamic, operates, including in chapter five where I include an earlier strip I'd done about my mother. There's this mouse cartoonist who draws a comic strip about his mother committing suicide, and uh 'an there's the cartoonist drawing about real humanoid-types, which is a reversal of the situation that exists in the rest of the book. There is also incorporated somewhere in that strip a photograph of my mother and me. Later in the book there'll be a photograph of my father incorporated in the book. All these things are meant to call attention to the fact that A'm making use of a set of ideas that I'm not expecting anyone to take literally. I think that as one reads the book one forgets of course that you're reading about anything other than people, and this dynamic pulls you up short, makes you think about the ideas I'm playing with.

What did your family and father think of *Maus*?
My father really wanted to put the War behind him as best he could and start his life over. Uh at best he couldn't do that all that well, he would wake up with nightmares almost every night—couldn't sleep well—and had many psychological and physical ailments that stemmed directly from his experiences in concentration camps. Nevertheless he never really wanted t'talk about it all that much. My father was never one of the Jews that felt the need t'bear witness the same way that many other survivors had felt that need.

Uhm o.k. my father by growing up in Poland 19 circa—you know being a child in the early part of the twentieth century—did not have much exposure to comic strips and never really learned to read them or to understand them. As a result he never had a very clear idea of what it is I do. Sometimes it would sort of slip his mind that I was doing anything other than taping, and even that wasn't that clear to him. In chapter six I relate the experience of reading a bit of the work in progress to him and he responded. What I'll try to do is getta xerox of that—that's the chapter I'm working on now—so you can take a look at that.

My mother kept like diaries of her experiences and after the war she reconstructed those diaries and I remember seeing notebooks around the house when I was a kid, that were written in Polish. I didn't have much interest, but of course when I wanted to do this project I tried to find them—they were important. And as it is related in *Maus* my father at some point after her suicide destroyed the diaries, something I don't think I can ever forgive him for.

My stepmother seems to have had a much clearer idea of what it is I'm doing, and seems to be quite supportive. It was she that translated the document on the history on Sosnowiec Jews from Polish to English for me, and has tried t'help in whatever way she could think.

The only member of the family that A'm in touch with is Lolek, who figures in chapter five of the book—my mother's nephew. I didn't interview him and his vantage point on the book is "well why dwell on all this stuff?" And, "this is a hopeless project in that it's fraught with the impossibility of saying anything real or accurate." All of his responses reflect his background and his orientation as an engineer for concrete things—someone who doesn't have all that much use for the humanities.

Since this interview was completed Art Spiegelman has published *Maus* in the United States where it has sold 45,000 copies and has been a critical success. Penguin and Deutsch were sold the British and Commonwealth rights, however when Spiegelman signed the contract he deleted South Africa. In a letter to his London agent, he wrote that he would not "compromise with fascism" and wished to uphold the ANC boycott of all works of art. This stand led him into conflict with the publishers. In correspondence with Tom Rosenthal, Deutsch's co-director, he explained: "Though I have faith in *Maus*' message, books are commercial as well as political artefacts of culture. I feel that I must respect the ANC's request for *total* cultural boycott . . . since the ANC represents the best hope for change there. I'm in the odd position of only wanting the book to get into South African bookstores if it is banned by the Government. . . ." Both Deutsch and Penguin argued that refusing to publish in South Africa amounted to self-censorship, however Spiegelman maintained his position. "They're talking about business as usual, with criminals, and that's a problem for me. I just can't allow my book to be sold by distributors and bookstore owners who, one way or another, have made their peace with the regime." With the publishers refusing a deal which excluded South Africa it looked like the British edition of *Maus* was doomed. However when Spiegelman approached the ANC in New York for advice they offered a way out of the deadlock: "To my surprise and pleasure, the ANC do see the significance of *Maus* and its relationship to their battle with racist oppression. They are currently arranging for a movement publisher within South Africa to publish it and make it available there. All profits would go to the ANC." This has left Deutsch and Penguin with no option, but to allow the striking out of South Africa in the contract. *Maus* will be published in Britain this spring.

Interview with Art Spiegelman

Roger Sabin / 1989

Transcribed from the original audiotape
by Joseph Witek and published by
permission of Roger Sabin.

This previously unseen interview was for the London magazine *City Limits*, and took place on 1 November 1989 at the Basil Street Hotel in the swanky Knightsbridge district of London. I believe it was Spiegelman's first trip to London, and in my memory he was a wide-eyed tourist, eager to see the entire city in the space of a few hours.

The focus for the trip was the new Penguin *RAW*, which in the U.K. (and the U.S., I'd imagine) introduced *RAW* to a whole new audience because it was stocked in the book stores. As a result, book reviewers for the major daily papers were occasionally tempted to offer an opinion, and their response was far from uniformly positive. On 24 October 1989 the *Sunday Times* wrote: *"RAW* is not even funny . . . *Beano* and *Dandy* have nothing to fear."

The hipper magazines were more sympathetic, and in 1989 *City Limits* was perceived to be hipper than most. It was the most politically radical of the London magazines and included such stars of the "intellectual left" as Judith Williamson and Suzanne Moore. However, hip can also often mean shambolic, and the magazine was notorious for its screw-ups. Thus, when a new Books Editor was appointed in November 1989, it was no surprise to discover that page space had been double-booked, and that anything commissioned by the previous incumbent of the post over the past few weeks would have to be scrapped. That's why the Spiegelman interview never saw the light of day. *City Limits* went bust a few years later.

So here it is, the "lost" Spiegelman interview, straight from the tape . . .

Roger Sabin

RS: The first thing I was going to ask you was for a bit of biographical information. I was reading your introduction to Harvey Kurtzman's *Jungle Book*, and I didn't understand whether you actually got published by Kurtzman or not.

AS: No, I didn't. What happened was that he got my cartoons just as *Help!* magazine was going out of business. He sent me a letter back, which was more than I could have hoped for, telling me that he really liked my stuff and that he was going to work for *Playboy*, and that Hefner should see my stuff. I was about—I don't know, fourteen, fifteen years old at the time. If I had just sent these things in six months earlier I could have been in *Help!*, because he liked the material I sent. So I missed my chance.

RS: And *Help* was one of his follow-ups to *Mad?*

AS: He did first *Mad*, then a magazine called *Trump*, and then *Help!* was his real low-budget magazine, and even in this low-budget context he managed to pull off some amazing things. He introduced Terry Gilliam to the world, introduced Robert Crumb to the world, introduced Jay Lynch to the world, started what eventually devolved into *Little Annie Fanny*—it was a more interesting strip called *Goodman Beaver* at the time. Just with no budget at all, he invented photo-balloon-caption format things, did some of the most elaborate *fumettis* that had been done to date, with big-star celebrities in them. It was an amazing thing. But when that went under, I think he just sort of threw up the white flag and grabbed for safety with *Playboy*.

RS: Then there was your involvement with the undergrounds. When did you start writing for the undergrounds?

AS: I was working for the *East Village Other* back in '66, '67. Maybe a year after it started. I think I mentioned this anecdote somewhere: I went to Walter Bowart when he had just started *EVO*, and he said, "These are good, but could you have more stuff about sex and drugs?" I was a kid, I was just turning eighteen, and I didn't know that much about sex and drugs. I had comics about masturbating, and I had comics about hallucinations, and whatever my life was like at the time. So I went to college, learned about sex and drugs, came back and worked for the *East Village Other* about '67.

Somewhere in there around that time, maybe even before the *East Village Other*, I invented this other format. It was the days of the invention of instant printing, where you could bring something in and get 500 copies for two dollars, or whatever it was at the time, so I would do one-page comic strips that had no specific message, then get 500 printed and go out on the street leafletting, as if it was for a cause or something. So around this time I was doing these leaflets, and they're comic strips, and it seemed like a nice way to distribute, and get to choose your audience on the street, on the basis of whether she was pretty or not, or whether it was somebody you thought was interesting, or somebody who would be put uptight by your strips, or whatever. They were unsigned. Those strips ended up being reprinted in just about every underground newspaper, because they were unsigned and they were available. So that was the beginnings.

RS: Are we talking about the East Coast scene? Were you ever involved in the other side?

AS: Well, first of all, the network was pretty tight in those days; somehow if something happened in New York you knew about it in Chicago, and then you knew about it on the West Coast, and you knew about it in Atlanta. So the strips were reprinted in all the underground papers around the country. I made my first trip to San Francisco in about '67 and got involved with the underground comic books there, shortly after they just started, and then I moved out there in 1971, I think, moved out there for about four or five years. That was when underground comix were really blossoming, so I was involved with that world around that time.

In 1974, when it stopped blossoming, and indeed began wilting, I, together with another cartoonist named Bill Griffith, who does *Zippy the Pinhead*, started a magazine with one of the comix publishers, Print Mint, called *Arcade*, and that was kind of a life raft for the underground cartoonists who were watching all of the underground comix not selling. We would make one glorious comic that wouldn't sell, and come out regularly, which we actually did for a couple of years.

RS: And then *RAW* was, what, 1980?
AS: That was after [*Arcade*] had all burst.

RS: *Maus* [was] '86 in book form?
AS: It started in 1978.

RS: I also hear that you lecture in New York, and I wondered where and about what exactly?
AS: Oh, about the homeless, about going on to the metric system, on street corners, and when I'm not doing that, comics, usually. [laughter] That had been for a long time at the School of Visual Arts in New York, which is an accredited art college. I've taught the history of comics and a studio class about comics. I stopped doing that a couple of years back; I just didn't have time anymore. I just couldn't afford to do it—the pay was ridiculous. Now I lecture individual lecture dates, sometimes on *Maus*, sometimes on the Holocaust, sometimes on comics, sometimes on recent comics, sometimes on the history of comics, and that will be at universities around the country or at museums, lecture venues, things like that.

RS: I'm writing a book at the moment as well, an introductory book on comics for an academic market.
AS: There's one thing I did that you might want to take a look at. I gave one lecture at Yale, and in the audience were the editors of *Print* magazine.

RS: I've got that at home. I haven't read it yet; I got it this morning. It looks good.
AS: There are problems with the issue. The dream was different than the reality, but nevertheless it's pretty good, and in any case that introductory article is a reworking of the speech that I gave that sort of inspired them to do an issue on comics.

RS: You're here to push *RAW*.
AS: Yes, buy *RAW*, buy *RAW*, please.

RS: The thing people coming to this might say is that it has this arty image and reputation. It seems to me this was very much sought after in the early days of *RAW*, but I'm wondering if you regret that now.

AS: Well, it wasn't ever really "arty," and I resent the word, because arty is different than art. "Arty" is like lah-de-dah, lifted finger, "artistic," which is the enemy of art. I don't know if this is even as much of a problem here in the U.K.; maybe it is since you're asking the question. In America it's a terrible label, because it means it's intellectual, and anything that's intellectual is suspect. Maybe that's true here too. To me it's all on one continuum, and it's all the same stuff. I'm equally interested in paintings and Bazooka Joe comics, let's say. To me it's just one continuum of stuff, and all this thing about high art, low art, it's nonsense. On the other hand, when we started *RAW*, there was a conscious strategy, which was—"people don't look at comics, we're going to have to clobber them over the head and make them look at what we're doing." It seemed to me that one reasonable way to do it was to go to this large format, where the reader would have to literally take its measure. And it worked—people stopped and looked.

RS: Was that an imitation of *Interview* magazine? Was that an influence?

AS: Well, *Interview* was one of about a dozen—I don't know whether they all got over here, but at that time large-format magazines were quite popular. There was something called *Wet* magazine, there was a magazine called *Fetish*. *Wet* magazine was the magazine of gourmet bathing; *Fetish* magazine was about getting and spending; there was one called *Skyline* about architecture, there were about twenty music ones, there was *Interview*. What was interesting about them was that they had nothing in common except their size and the notion that somehow these appealed to, I don't know, someplace between a punk and New Wave audience.

This was part of the strategy. When we had done *Arcade*, *Arcade* was an 8½ by 11 magazine with really good comics inside. We tried to get a magazine distributor interested, because the problem we had—real-world business stuff—was that underground comix just weren't equipped to distribute a magazine that came out every three months, which is what our goal was. And we actually made it, and with this group of people it's insane that we made it—it's almost impossible to get a magazine out every three months with the San Francisco underground cartoonist community as your resource. But we did it. And then we found out when the second one came out, because of the way underground comix were distributed, the second one came out and stood next to the first one. When the third one came out it stood next to the first and second one, when the fourth one came out it stood next to the first, second, and third one, and when the fifth one came out the bookstores started pleading with us not to put out a sixth one, because the way this thing usually worked was that somebody put out a *Zap* and then a year or two later somebody put out another *Zap* and they could sit comfortably with each other. But our rate of speed wasn't allowing this stuff to get digested through that particular conduit.

We had gone to magazine distributors, and they would look at it and say, "Well where does this belong?" "I don't know, put it next to the *National Lampoon.*" "It doesn't look like the *National Lampoon!*" "Well, put it next to *Mad.*" "Nah, it's not like *Mad!*" So there was no place for them to put it. And when I saw that these big magazines were beginning to happen, it was like, "OK, so there's a New Wave architecture magazine and a New Wave magazine for gourmet bathing, why not a magazine of comics?" And that seemed like a reasonable strategy at the time. These things eventually all went away; it was kind of a fad, and *RAW* was maybe the last surviving large-size magazine for a while. It was a wonderful, luxurious format.

But to return to the point of what you were talking about, this reputation as being "artistic" and "arty," I think when anybody does something in comics that's not superheroes or goofy humor, then it's going to be suspect. And yet there's a lot of people who are doing that work, and I believe that there's a lot of people who can dig it if they get it in their hands. So then how do you get it in their hands? That's always the difficulty. Maybe I'm not the best person to judge, but I don't think of it as especially "lah-de-dah" or artistic; I just think of it as a bunch of vital nuts who are doing comics.

RS: So anybody could enjoy *RAW*?
AS: I think anybody who has ever had a moment of angst; maybe there's that prerequisite. It's not for people who are thoroughly satisfied with things as they are, because they've got their *Garfield Treasuries* and they don't need us. On the other hand, I believe it would appeal to people who are capable of reading something other than a *Racing Form*, people who go to a movie other than *Batman*, people who will go to a theater once in a while, will listen to something other than what's playing on the

top charts. It's not mass-market in that sense, and comics are expected to be mass-market. What I figure is that for poetry it's selling *real* well. [laughter] I don't think of it as requiring some kind of special expertise. I've even seen some reviews in the States, where it's gone over fairly well, where people say, "Ah, yes, this is post-modern blatta-blatta blather whatever, and the joke is that there is no joke," and I don't know what they're talking about. I really don't know what they're talking about.

RS: Well, it's just words like "avant-garde" . . .
AS: We totally riff off that—the current issue is called "Open Wounds from the Cutting Edge of Commix."

RS: Like "A Comic Book for Damned Intellectuals," stuff like this. This actually put me off the comic for years, and then when I finally looked at it, it wasn't that difficult. I could get into it.
AS: It doesn't require special training. That's the whole point of comics— it's a popular medium. The idea is not to exclude people. I figure that, in a world where people don't read anymore, this is a literary magazine. It's meant to allow people to experience something, and that experience hopefully is a pleasurable one on some level. I don't know—I'm stuck. I don't really want to do *Backstreet Boys Comics*, and I don't really want to do *Garfield*, and I don't really want to do *The Incredible Teen Titans Meet the X-Men*.

RS: The new small format of *RAW* should draw people in to read it.
AS: I hope so. It's certainly more inviting to read. Comics actually have different properties at different sizes. It's an interesting thing to me. For years we did *RAW* big-sized, and people talked about an artist like, say, Charles Burns, and said, "Wow, that stuff's really weird looking!" I never heard anything about the story. Now we have this thing out and people are talking about "Teen Plague," and they're talking about the content of the story. That's an interesting thing to me. Somehow small equals "read comics," big equals "look at comics," and comics are actually involved in this mixture of looking and reading. It seems to work that way. Ultimately, I'm beginning to think that the best size for comics is probably 8½ by 11 or something, where it's sort of a mix between look-ing and reading that's very easy to arrive at.

This to me is a very interesting thing to work on, and ironically, I've heard it said in some comics circles, at least, "Oh, now *RAW* has to

make this horrible compromise as a result of going with Penguin Books."
That's bullshit, because we changed the format before we went with
Penguin. What happened is that we were tired of doing *RAW*, period.
There's not any real money involved in doing *RAW*; it's even more lucrative to teach comics at the School of Visual Arts, and it's more lucrative
than either of those things to drive a cab. We just were letting it lie fal-
low because we just didn't have the energy to do it again, and then on
the other hand we had material accumulating, and then we started to
think about changing format. And then it got interesting again. Every
issue something's had to happen to ignite it, to make us interested.
Partially it was, "Oh, look at this stuff! It's great!," and then we wanted
to put it out, and partially it was some notion, usually some weird
notion, like "Let's rip the cover corner off or something, and do that on
8000 copies and see what that's like." This time it was, "Hey, let's make
it like a literary magazine, and make it small-sized and see what the work
is that way." Partially it was because we had a number of strips that
were very good that were quite long, and to even remotely try put them
together in one issue was impossible, because *RAW* in its former incarnation only allowed for maybe one or at the most two longish things,
and longish had to mean about sixteen pages, certainly not thirty pages,
for one piece. We found that if you make it smaller you save on the
paper cost and it all comes out that you get more pages of comics for
the same price. So that's what got us moving toward that, and then I
met somebody from Penguin and showed them what we wanted to do,
and they said, "Sounds good." The other one didn't sound good to
them anyway, because it's so hard to display. Ironically, they're also
going to be selling this large-size *RAW* anthology at the same time.

RS: You can read it on the tube.
AS: You can take it with you; that's a definite advantage.

RS: I think it works quite well, actually. The last big American comics person I got to speak with was Will Eisner. He had just compressed *The
Spirit* down to paperback size, and he was talking about that. There's a
lot to bringing a comic down; it raises lots and lots of issues.
AS: Every format is interesting. What I would really like is to have pages
one through twenty-three be 6 by 9, and pages thirty-three through
fifty be 9 by 12, and then some the size of the *Guardian*. I don't know
how you bind it, but that would be nice.

RS: Next question, how are Brits going to take a story like the Kim Deitch story ["Karla in Commieland"]? Some of the stuff is culturally as difficult to get into as some of the European comics.

AS: I guess so. You'd be in a better position to tell me than I would to tell you about how Brits are going to respond to this. From the outside, it seems to me that if anything England has been infected with the same anti-commie virus that America has. The dynamic is the same; probably some of the cultural references are different, but I don't think they're that hard to figure out.

RS: The Drew Friedman thing, are they supposed to be characters that I should recognize?

AS: That's one of the more obscure things. That's a bar that they [Friedman and Mark Newgarden] know about.

RS: Oh, is it? Because he sometimes draws famous people, and I was just wondering whether I was supposed to recognize the people.

AS: This was like some bar that they know. I didn't get it either the first time, but I liked it. It was like some anecdote that made them laugh over and over again whenever they thought of it. They wanted to draw it up, and it seemed all right. It was a short piece in the book, and I figured, let them do their thing.

But as far as the Kim Deitch one goes, I don't know that his stuff is that hard to get into, finally. You're saying it's as hard as the European stuff, but is the European stuff that hard to get into?

RS: Some of it is, with cultural references and so on.

AS: I like that stuff. I like some of the European stuff and some of the Japanese stuff, and the stuff that I like the best is the stuff that's not the most homogenized. I mean, how am I going to find out about these other cultures; am I going to go there and live there for ten years? I think that this is a way in.

RS: Can you tell me more about the international material?

AS: Next issue we have a twenty-four-page story by a Japanese artist. Did you see the issue of *RAW* that had the torn cover, by any chance? There was a special section called "Tokyo Raw," and there's one comic strip we used called "Red Flowers" about a girl's first menstruation by a Japanese artist, Yoshiharu Tsuge. He occupies an absolutely unique slot in Japanese comics culture, which is—all this stuff is mass-culture manga, or bizarro crazy guys who just make doodles of some kind or other,

some of which we also published in that issue of *RAW*—and then there's
this guy, who does something else that they don't have a word for, I don't
think, that's just comics literature, and he's the only one of that kind. In a
country where everybody reads comics, he's the one that people read even
if they didn't read comics. This was heavyweight stuff. Whenever I would
go into a bookshop with people, they'd say, "Oh, do you know this guy
Tsuge?" I'd go, "No." "Oh, you have to take this!" So I came back with
about two boxes of books, and I didn't like the Tsuge stuff especially,
because when I first looked through it, they had these big eyes and. . . .
But it wasn't robot mutants, or samurais, or things like that. I put it on
the shelf without thinking about it, and a Japanese friend came over and
was pulling stuff off the shelf, looking through stuff, and said, "Ah, what
good taste! You got this!" I said, "Um, yeah." She said, "No, you don't
understand!" I said, "No, I guess I don't." She says, "I'll translate." And
she just did this literal translation, then she and all the other Japanese
people said, "This is great, but it can't be translated *well*, because there's
too many cultural specifics." So we read it and I went, "Yeah, I guess
there are, on the other hand, *I* get it, and I think it's great."

RS: There has to come a point where you say if people don't get it they
don't get it, and if they do they do.
AS: For this one we actually put footnotes in for the things that they
wouldn't get. The second story we're publishing by him is in the second
of the small-format *RAW*s and doesn't require footnotes, but it's very
culturally specific. But that's what's *interesting*. In some ways it's much
better than going to see a foreign film where you've got to sit there
reading subtitles through the whole thing or hear somebody talking out
of sync on the soundtrack. It's a dipping into another culture.
      I hadn't thought much about the Kim Deitch thing one way or another.

RS: It's just one off the top of my head. At the moment Britain's going
through a phase of being deluged with American comics. With the direct
sales boom, we have American comics as the glamour comics.
AS: I'm sometimes on the other side of it, because there's a comic that a
lot of my British friends recommend and I've always found it a bit
opaque, and which is something that's called *Alex*. I don't get it.

RS: Well, it makes me laugh. You wait 'til you see *Viz*, you won't get that!
AS: I've been buying *Viz* and I kind of like it, and I get some of it. But I
don't think the Kim Deitch story is in the same [category], because that's

dealing with more-or-less shared cultural phenomena, and all it really requires is that you have some sense of who Joe McCarthy is, some sense.

RS: I think Brits do have that. I don't think anti-communism ever was as strong here as it was in the States. There are other examples in *RAW*; the Charles Burns story refers back to drive-in movies and '50s horror comics and so forth, so you have to have some knowledge to get into it.
AS: Maybe this is just being chauvinistic, but aren't those specific aspects of American culture like part of the Roman empire that's kind of stomped through the rest of the Western world?

RS: You mean the same thing happened here?
AS: Not necessarily that it happened here, but at this point, it's a cultural reference, because so much American culture has seeped through into France and England and the rest of Europe.

RS: I think it has to a degree. My standard is that if my mom can understand the comic, then it's understandable, [laughs] but that's not always the right way to look at things. I think people are culturally literate, generally.
AS: I don't think your mother would not understand it any more than she would not understand any other comic, but she probably wouldn't be that interested in reading a comic, right?

RS: Yeah, that's true as well. I've shown her *Maus*, and she thought that was great, but that's different.
AS: *Maus* actually has managed to cut through generational barriers that I wasn't aware it would do.

RS: The last few years there's been a lot of articles written about the history of comics, but when people write about the history of comics they write about the history of American comics, which is fair enough, but there's the European tradition and there's a British tradition—people seem to forget the British tradition—in this country it's much more coming out of children's comics. The best children's comics in this country were very anarchic, and that carried on into *2000 AD*. This is my reading of the history anyway.
AS: That's interesting. Certainly the American underground comix grew out of that kid-comic tradition as well, and really rooted itself back into the best of kid's comics which were killed with the Comics Code of the 1950s. But the underground comix represent an important plateau in the history of comics, all through Europe and England as well. It made a big

difference; it made a change because it was the first time comics didn't have to be for kids.

RS: Would you class things at the turn of the century as adult comics? They used to call them the "penny horribles" or penny dreadfuls in this country, and I know America had some too.
AS: You mean pulp magazines?

RS: They were like pulps, but they were illustrated pamphlets with fiction stories, sometimes nonfiction as well—I've seen one about Jack the Ripper.
AS: Those things go back to the Middle Ages, some of that stuff, like the woodcuts—those things are proto-comics.

RS: When does a comic become a comic? [laughter]
AS: I've always been interested in that—quite seriously. One semester I was teaching the history of comics and I never got up to 1940 because I spent the first third of the semester on comics before 1910, mostly medieval cuts and a lot of nineteenth-century stuff, because that was what I was just drinking in. In some sense maybe Dickens's stuff was comics—I guess—it was co-mixing words and pictures to one degree or another. Traditionally where most people launch from is the American newspaper comics of the turn of the century, and anything that's before that is proto-comics. I don't know if there's any good case to be made for that, because there's always something that came before. I kept digging my way back until I was talking about cave paintings.

RS: That's the danger, isn't it?
AS: For practical purposes, the modern comic as the man on the street who couldn't care less about comics knows it, is this thing for kids, and that's something that really started happening around the turn of the century and entrenched further and further. Even then it's just not true. In newspaper surveys, all the adults read newspaper strips, and when comic books were at their strongest in America lots of GIs were reading them, and they were at least of drinking age by then.

RS: You mean the EC comics or the superhero comics?
AS: The superheroes maybe not quite as much, but by the mid-'40s the superheroes were in eclipse; they weren't really the most popular comics anymore.

RS: So the ECs definitely had an older readership, then?

AS: And the war comics, not just the EC war comics, but the less aesthetically exciting ones—or maybe more aesthetically exciting, but different. Not as intelligently put together, perhaps. Also the love comics had an older readership, and the crime comics had an older readership. This was all kind of batted to hell when the Comics Code came down.

RS: And after that, I suppose *Mad* had an older readership as well. And the ones after that, the ones you mentioned earlier, *Trump* and so forth . . .

AS: They were aimed at adults.

RS: *RAW*'s big selling point is that it has *Maus* in it; that's because people know *Maus* from the book. Do you think that's unhealthy; do you think that overshadows what *RAW* is all about?

AS: I hope not. If it works, it works in such a way that people who at least heard of something will now hear of more things.

RS: So it's a foot in the door?

AS: It's at least a way to display one's wares. There's at least fifty interesting cartoonists in the world right now—at least—and we're trying to present as many of them as we can in any given issue. It's possible that somebody who has left comics behind for the last decade will find their way back in because they pick up *Maus* or hear about it. I don't think that's a liability; I suppose it would be if they say, "Well, I really like *Maus* but the rest of this stuff—why did they pad that book out? There are only like thirty pages that are worth anything," which I certainly don't believe. I figure once you plunk down your—whatever it is, fifteen bucks, I don't know what it is in England—you're probably going to read the rest of it even if you did pick it up for *Maus*, and you'll probably get hooked on some other artists in there.

RS: I think it would be a pity if people just saw this as the comic in which *Maus* runs.

AS: Well, if it is then it's rather short-lived, because eventually *Maus* is going to finish. It's not my notion that this should be . . . "And now in 1999, chapter ten! Chapter twenty! Chapter fifty!" It's a finite book, and afterward I'd like to do other things and hope that there will be an audience for these other things I do as well that don't necessarily look like *Maus*.

RS: It's been three years since the *Maus* book came out, and people have analyzed it to death; there's been some criticism of it—mostly praise, I'm glad to say—but the thing my friends who have read *Maus* generally say is, "You know, I really liked it, but I just wish he would draw them as ordinary people." I know you must have been asked that a hundred times, but I have to ask you that one for the magazine.

AS: A zillion times. It wouldn't work; it would be very flat. I actually tried. I haven't heard it as much as you have; it's been one quarter where I've been getting that criticism. I think it actually would have put the book into a different key, and the key that it would put the book in would have been flat. At that point, I would be trying to do an ersatz historical reconstruction, and I could never match the actuality. By putting these masks on, everything takes place in a netherworld where things exist as commentary. It allows one to go through the comic into looking at the event, as opposed to trying to replace the event with the comic. The faces are real blank, and that's really an important part of it. I suppose I could have drawn a circle with an X in it to represent faces or something, but this was a more direct way of doing that.

This is something where I don't quite have it worked out now, but I'm thinking about it, which is—there are many ways to do comics. I'm less sure of the ones that come closer to appearing to be storyboards for films, because I think there's some kind of distantiation thing that happens in comics, there's some kind of abstraction that's really necessary to comics. Even a comic that approaches being a storyboard for film, by which I mean, you could relatively easily imagine actors walking through the part and bringing it more to life than it happens in the comic. Even in those, it's not really true, because there is something very specific about comics language and the way you get information in a comic. Because comics by definition involve a kind of abstraction, I think one should go with it; that abstraction is part of the form. This animal metaphor (which ultimately is designed to blow up in your face; it's not something you're supposed to buy into totally) functions to give one that kind of distance, that degree of abstraction. Because comics are a way of putting id creatures on paper (I think all cartoonists start by drawing naked girls and blown-apart bodies and monsters on lined sheets of notebook paper when they should be doing their schoolwork), there's something about that energy that's basic to comics, and it shouldn't get lost.

That's why I bristled at this idea that comics are "arty," because what they are really is something else. They have a kind of directness because of that connection to the way people actually think. What I mean is (this is actually in that *Print* magazine article, to get it phrased more succinctly than I'll be able to do now), your brain is an abstracting device. When you leave here, mainly you'll remember that I wore a vest, that I had hair going that way, maybe, a couple of notions, and you'll have abstracted some sense of me; you won't be carrying a hologram of me, and vice-versa, and it's abstract enough that if I show up not wearing a vest, with hair parted another way, you'll still be able to superimpose that first image on the second image and still find me, but it'll have been through some kind of abstracting. It'll be through some kind of cartoon-making in your head. It seems to me that you think in a combination of short-hand images and words; that's how most thought happens. I don't think it's just me because I'm a cartoonist. When I've discussed it with people and read about it, this is how it works. That means that comics have a pipeline to something very basic about the way people think.

RS: Is *Maus* taken seriously as a work of Holocaust literature?
AS: Yes, it is. My publisher at the time was Pantheon Books in America, Penguin here, and the Pantheon editors were warning me at the time that I should go into hiding when the book comes out; I'm going to get a lot of heat for this, and they'll put it out, but hoo, boy. Instead, what happened was, to my surprise, it was very generously accepted, so that it received a National Book Critics Circle nomination for best biography and the Joel H. Cavior Present Tense Award for best work of Jewish fiction. Biography, fiction, who knows? And as a result it was accepted as, yes, this is one more way of telling a story and of dealing with the genuine problems that the so-called Holocaust brings up.

RS: In the recent chapter, it's obvious that it's taken some sort of personal toll on you to do it.
AS: It's been horrible.

RS: There's that famous phrase, "look not into the abyss lest the abyss look into you." It must have been quite difficult, and I just wanted to ask you about that; did it depress you to write that chapter?
AS: That chapter more than the others?

RS: Well, to continue. To continue doing *Maus*, to the bitter end.
AS: Well, I'd signed on many years earlier, and there I was at that point in the story, and I had to keep going. I had been dropping into that abyss stage-by-stage, just as my family did, in fact, and there was no

turning back at that point. I have the luxury of slowing it down. For my parents it lasted from 1939 to 1945; for me it lasted from 1978 to 1989 so far. So I'm doing it slow, a few hours a day.

RS: But it is a catharsis?

AS: I don't know. That was one of the weirdest questions I got in my fifteen minutes of fame where I was on the *Today* show. This had been thoroughly rehearsed before I went on, for like three days this interviewer was calling me up going, "OK, that's a good question—she'll ask you that question, and you say just what you said now." Everything was brought down to soundbites, and then they were going to have certain panels from *Maus* showing on the screen during certain moments, and it was as rehearsed as could be. The only thing that wasn't counted on was the fact that the woman—I don't know if it was the *Today* show, there are three of those in the morning in America that are like get up brush your teeth, watch television, get out of the house and go to work shows—so one of these women, they just didn't count on how big of a dork she actually was, basically. And she got it all wrong. She asked the questions out of order, and then she forgot a question, so I'm looking at these things on the monitor that have nothing to do with what I'm supposed to be saying, going, wow, this is a mess. [laughter] I did my best to match up my answer with those, and that worked well except, by messing it all up, what she did was she left us with about forty-five seconds or a minute and a half of blank air time where she had run out of questions because she had forgot one in the sequence, so then she's looking real uncomfortable, and then she says, "So how do you feel?" I was prepared for any question except how I felt. I was prepared for, "Why mice? Why the Holocaust? Why comics?" I wasn't prepared for "So how do you feel?" I guess she was asking whether it was cathartic or not. I don't even remember what I said; I think I got off the hook on that one by saying what a painful experience it was. Essentially I don't even know if it's cathartic. I'm just sort of traveling down this road because I don't see where else I can travel.

RS: One of my closest friends is the son of a survivor as well. Does there come a point where you have to confront this heritage, and you have to ask serious questions?

AS: It's either that or you have to keep ducking and covering for a long time and trying to suppress it, and then it just comes out and hits you from behind. So you've got to do it one way or another. I don't think it's possible—for me it wasn't possible, I shouldn't generalize, I shouldn't generalize—for me it wasn't possible to ignore it. It was too basic a part of my life. In that sense, I felt more sane and healthy when I was directly aiming at it, rather than letting it obliquely rattle me. Other people, perhaps, cannot do that, I don't know. One of the things that was puzzling to me was that I was being turned into a spokesman for the second-generation Holocaust kids, and I kept refusing it.

RS: It's kind of natural given the success of the book.
AS: Well, see what happened is that there were a number of taboos that were broken with *Maus*, and I wasn't trying to break any. For me this was really a natural process. One of the taboos is dealing with the Holocaust as a comic book using animals; that's the first layer of taboo. Then the other taboo, which hit a very strong nerve evidently for other kids who had been in similar, analogous situations, is the taboo of being angry at your parents. And I didn't realize that either one was such a big taboo until I came into contact with a lot of people who were trying their damnedest to be good little kids because their parents had gone through so much. It was cathartic for them, it seems, to find that wasn't the only avenue of behavior.

RS: Were you ever in contact with these children of survivors groups that kind of emerged a few years ago?
AS: Yeah, a little bit.

RS: It's interesting that your psychiatrist should be a survivor as well.
AS: That's why I chose him. I wanted specifically somebody to continue a dialogue that I couldn't have with my father anymore, and here I found somebody who is far more sensitive and articulate than my father was to what he had gone through, which wasn't the *same* as what my father had gone through, but there were some points of contact and similarity. I figure every session with him is tax deductible, because I'd spend an hour trying to find out, "Well, look, do they wear socks in the camps?" And then he'd explain not only that they did, which were rags, but exactly how you tie the rag around your foot. This was really great for me; it made it possible to make the book, because I needed that kind of minutia.

I'm sorry this interview is turning so much into a *Maus* interview, because we are talking about a small piece of another book right now. But doing a comic in some sense involves getting much more information than you need. If I was just writing this, and my father said, "So in the morning we marched past the gate," OK, so you type and write, "marched past the gate." Here you've got to find out what the weather was like, what were they wearing, how many of them were there, did they march three across, four across, five across, did the guards stand on the sides, at what points did they stand, which gate did they march through. There's a million things to solve, in that sense analogous to film, where you've got to concretely visualize every moment. In film, most Holocaust films are quite unsatisfactory because there's just something so goofy about seeing all these well-fed actors in this context, which just immediately shatters one's ability to see into it.

This is something about comics in general; it involves a certain kind of inhabiting a moment-to-moment space by one individual. One of the things I've cursed about, and this is not just true of *Maus*, I think all of the comics involved, you have to really inhabit that world in order to allow it to come to life again and to reconstruct it in the reader's head. One of the things that happens is, it's inhabiting it moment-by-moment, and it's an *individual* inhabiting it, so when I see these Holocaust movies on television I start cursing, because they have zillions of dollars and they have zillions of people all running around trying to get their facts straight, more or less, when they're even remotely conscientious, and so these things I would struggle for, really struggle for, like I went back to Poland and was really digging through archives to find out some information, I would then see some really rotten TV movie where they just have that as a scene in the film, and I thought, "Oh, *that's* how they got into those showers down those stairs." Somebody had to do the homework on a big budget.

I think that there are some comics that are good that are done by more than one person, but one of the real strengths of comics is that it can be a world made by one person for another person to read, so that it's just that individual's statement.

RS: You're saying you researched *Maus* very carefully?
AS: As best I can, although ultimately I do have this hedge where if I get a small detail wrong the whole thing doesn't collapse. That's another thing, if I was doing it with drawings of people and I just get one thing wrong, it shatters. For instance, before I went to Poland, my father would say, "So we walked down the street." I would picture 14th Street and 6th Avenue; I didn't picture these European streets, because my

concept of a street was different. Now, I've tried to steep myself as well as I can in trying to understand what did happen and what it must have seemed like and looked like. On the other hand, should I get a small thing wrong, the work doesn't then wither, because I've already set up this other situation which is, "Well, this is animals that are walking through this other thing." It actually does allow that space for something to operate in. It would be very different than pretending I've got it all down.

RS: Just out of interest, did your father used to watch plays on TV about the Holocaust?

AS: I watched one part of the 1978 series *The Holocaust* with my father. It was actually a three-night thing, and each night I watched it with a different group of people. One night was with my father, and I hardly saw that night because I was busy trying—he would say, "Oh, they were over there, I was over here, and I was . . . ," and I'm busily taking notes again. He just used it as a trigger. He certainly didn't have any distanced critical response. Mala, my stepmother, wouldn't watch it, because she just said, "I was there; I know it already—you watch it." The next night, I watched it with this Soho video artist at his loft. His wife and kids went shrieking from the room and didn't want to see it, and I was sitting with this filmmaker friend and this video artist, and they were analyzing it as film. Then the next night, I saw it with a bunch of underground cartoonists who were over at my house, one of whom was a houseguest of mine at the time who finally had his girlfriend coming to visit him after two weeks of being celibate, and so he was fucking in the other room during it and we just kept hearing these screams coming out of the other room, so it was a very strange way of getting each of the three nights of the *Holocaust* TV miniseries.

RS: My friend's father watches everything, so I didn't know if that was something that was common to many of the survivors.

AS: My father did not go out of his way to expose himself, whereas others find themselves ineluctably drawn to knowing what other people know. And I'm in the situation where I'm trying to monitor just about everything—here I am running off to [Joshua Sobol's play] *Ghetto* tonight, with only three days in London, of trying to steep myself in what other phenomena are happening as the Holocaust gets rewritten and mythologized. Most of this work is really pretty awful—I'm not saying this play is, I haven't seen it, it might be wonderful—but most of the things I've been seeing, like this TV movie have major problems.

RS: *Shoah* is the only thing I've seen lately that's been any good.
AS: Yeah, it's amazing.

RS: A couple general questions: Ron Mann's film, *Comic Book Confidential*, I wonder if you've seen the film, and if you thought it hit the mark?
AS: I thought the film sucked, but I'm glad to have an hour-and-a-half commercial for comics out in the world.

RS: That's a fairly heavy reaction; I wasn't expecting that.
AS: I think probably ultimately it's going to be better when people see it on TV, because you can walk out on the boring parts or fast-forward them or something. He's faced with this really insoluble problem, which is that comics aren't film, and then what do you do to keep it from being static. So then there's all this kind of Rumanian Third-World animation going on trying to keep the comics moving across the screen, where even the format of the screen is different than the format of the panels, and it's just one crazy gimmick after another to try to make it happen, and not trusting the artists, the people he's interested in, enough to just be a talking head. We were just talking about *Shoah*, and one of the amazing things there is that he just trusted his material. He knew what he was working with, and I don't think he was figuring out, "Well, we can't just stay here talking until dark, we're just going to have to show this line of people wandering into a gas chamber somewhere." So from the sublime to the ridiculous, with the comics stuff the one thing I really missed was seeing people draw. There's no just sitting around having somebody draw and having somebody talk to you about what they do, and then just show some pictures, and don't pretend that you can show a comic onscreen, because one of the great things about comics is you read them in the privacy of your own bathroom, train, home, whatever, and you read it at your own speed, and you provide the voices, you inhabit the world through the guideposts of the comic. That's what's great about comics, and that can't be translated directly to film. The best you can do is make something else, which is an animated cartoon. That's something else again, and then it would be *Animated Cartoons Confidential*. It's something else. I felt that was a problem.

I also felt that he fell in, very well-meaningly, way over his head. Like he started out not knowing that much about comics, got excited, but had to make a film before he had a year to let the whole thing steep and gestate and really find out what he thought. He did, I suppose, manage to communicate the excitement that he had, and that's on the plus side for the film. The other side is that I'm not sure that it really serves as a way to introduce people to the work. Better than nothing, certainly.

RS: Did he get it historically right, do you think? He had women in the interviews, which I was glad about, and he had some of the context.
AS: More or less. One other problem I have with his documentary is that, like all good contempo documentary filmmakers he's suspicious of the voiceover. I think it's crazy. He was trying to make several films at once. One of them was to do a history of comics, and to have to go into, "Meanwhile, back at the superhero ranch . . ." as a title card, and he had to work with whatever little scraps of footage he could get, and try to patch a history together from that. It probably would have been better served by having that "March of Time" omniscient voice in the background saying, "And then, in 1959, *Mad* was blatta-blatta . . . ," and just give the information straight out. It's not that what he had was so inaccurate, it's just that what he wasn't able to put in made for distortions just as an ineluctable result of the system he was using.

RS: I'm not sure I'm with you.
AS: I saw it a while back, so I can't remember the specific moment-to-moment thing. It's not like he got it wrong, it's just that there's lots of bits of history that he could have made smoother transitions between if he was just able to have a few sentences on a voice track explaining how this stuff actually happened, and it would have become a lot clearer what was going down, and who was doing what, and what was happening simultaneous to what, what was happening after what, what was happening because of what.

RS: It's every historian's problem.
AS: Yes, and the documentary filmmaker has worse problems, because ultimately you have the footage you shot, period. Unless you're able to patch together with some other system, like either title cards, which were less effective than just being able to say things, it's hard to get bits of the history across. The only people he was left with, for instance, for the early days of comics were a miserable interview with Jack Kirby,

William Gaines, who is an important figure, and Will Eisner. Yes, they are the key figures, but I'm not sure that what was said ultimately really gives one a clear sense of what was happening in comics in the late '30s into the '50s. That could only have been done, given the footage Ron had, with a kind of narration.

All that being said, I don't know who it's for. I suppose it's for people who don't know that much about it, and then if you don't know that much about it I'm not sure what it tells you. If you do know a lot about comics, then you can sit there thinking, "This film must be for people who don't know much about it, but it sure is interesting for me to see what Jaime Hernandez looks like."

RS: OK, then the future—where next for comics? The evolution in this country has been slightly different. What's happened recently here is that a lot of big book publishers are getting into comics. I don't know if that's happened so much in the States. I heard about Doubleday doing it a few years ago.

AS: And Pantheon, which we were involved with, and now Penguin in the States, and a couple of others. It sort of came and went. It was *Maus* and *The Dark Knight*, which had nothing in common except speech balloons, but since both of them happened the same year, and since both of them sold unconscionably large numbers of copies compared to what publishers' expectations were, the buzzword for a while was, "Graphic novels, graphic novels, graphic novels!" Unfortunately, as soon as that buzzword went around, yes, a number of publishers did put things out, and yes, some of the smaller comics publishers managed to repackage things and get them out in bookshops, and yes, Marvel and DC put out books, but because the editors of the large houses didn't know their way through what was a good comic and what was a bad comic, enough comics came out that did badly right off to kill this new genre on the vine. Now it's still sort of happening, witness *RAW*/Penguin in the U.S. and here, but I don't know what the long-range results of all this will be. I think—I *pray*—that it works, because right now one of the problems I'm going to have with *RAW* here, and to a degree in the States, is that there ain't no section in the bookstore that's appropriate. The best we can hope for is to be next to a book like *1001 Farts and What to Say When You Make Them*. There's this humor section, so they'll put the comics there because it's cartoon drawing. And that's not perfect, and on the other hand I'm not sure that it's the best thing for bookstores to

say, "Oh, this is a horror comic, we'll put it in the horror fiction section
and this is a detective comic, we'll put it in the detective story section,
this is a Holocaust book, we'll put it in the history section."

RS: Are you saying that's what you would like to see, or that that's a
bad idea?
AS: That's what I am seeing. I'm not sure which is worse and which is
better. I think that the ideal would be as it in French bookstores, there's
just a section for comics.

RS: They have the range. The thing is, if you had that here, you'd have a
shelf where you'd have *Maus*, but you'd also have *The Incredible Hulk*
in graphic-novel form on the same shelf.
AS: What I've been hoping for is a *sui generis* section: "This is the stuff
that doesn't belong anywhere else, so it's here." There's no good answer
to it. I figure if there's more books coming out, an audience can get
built, and a constituency that can support this stuff. That's certainly what
the publishers are hoping. On the other hand, I can just see the whole
thing dying on the vine and everybody having to go back to making
little leaflets and passing them out on the street to the pretty girls.
[laughter]

RS: But this isn't the end of the direct-sales shops, though.
AS: The direct-sales shops become less and less interesting every month
because, now that the large comics publishers have discovered what a
gold mine they indeed are, and since those comics shops are primarily
geared to an audience that thrives on what those two or three major
companies can offer, the other stuff is all marginal. So at least for what I
see as vital in comics, it can't really flourish in direct-sales shops either.
    It's a funny medium, because it's born of the urgency to do it; it's
born because certain people just need to make comics. For the most part
we're not making big bucks off of making comics. Those same skills are
far more lucratively applied to illustration or to screenplay writing, or
something else. I think that doing comics is born of some real love for
the medium. One friend said a devastating thing to me. He said, "Ah,
the audience for comics is just people who can't draw but would like
to." [laughter] I hope that's not the limit of it.

RS: Can you see more women getting interested in it if they're in the
bookshops?

AS: That is happening. I would say that the demographics, in quotes, for *RAW* is far, far different than Marvel comics demographics. It's at least 30 or 40 percent women based on letters we get and people we meet; it's not really gender-specific. Maybe it's even fifty-fifty—I have no way of knowing. I've heard that *Love & Rockets* also has a fairly sizable constituency among women. Plus there's more women beginning to do comics. For a while in the States, that was appearing as "women's comics," which I always thought was kind of deadly, sort of like baskets by the blind; it doesn't have to be a good basket, but isn't it amazing that they can make a basket at all? I hated seeing that. What's much more interesting to me is seeing women who make good comics and happen to be women, and that just mixes itself up with the other half of the population that makes comics. The problem is that for so long, at least in the States, there weren't that many comics for women to read, especially after love comics went bust in the '50s, it just wasn't something that developed as a passion for women. So it took a really peculiar woman to develop that passion and stay with it. It was a much smaller gene pool to draw from to make a woman cartoonist; there weren't that many women cartoonists. Since 90 percent of the male cartoonists, or more, stink, it makes sense that 90 percent of the women cartoonists would stink, except that only left you with one or two really decent women cartoonists. That's beginning to change. The next issue of *RAW*, the one that we're just working on now, that will be out, God willing if this one works its way through the marketplace and finds homes, has a lead story by Lynda Barry that's really great, and also has a very long feature which is at least a co-mix if not comics by Sue Coe. A large chunk of the issue is by artists who happen to be women.

RS: Any other thoughts on the future of the medium?

AS: It seems to that at least in the short long-term, comics have a future.

RS: The short long-term?

AS: In the long long-term I think we're moving toward video terminals and reading being a vestigial skill because it's not necessary anymore. At that point, comics might be the last print medium to go, but they too might suffer. On the other hand, every medium ends up finding its own space. Just looking at it abstractly, I would think, how come there's still theater? Why do people still go to the theater? In America they don't, actually. Most Americans don't live anywhere near the theater and if they do they can't afford to go there. It's about three times more for a ticket than it is here, or more. And yet there is still a theater, and I wouldn't think there should be anymore, and maybe in a hundred years there won't be. On the other hand, at one point it was *the* vital, tribal form. Something similar might be said of comics. They had a certain function and role in the culture that they still vestigially perform, i.e. to sell newspapers and keep the kids quiet for ten minutes. Now that's changing. I think that makes it a very exciting time. I think ultimately, and the other artists whose work excites me bears this out, this is probably the best time in the history of comics to be a cartoonist. *Maybe* barring the turn of the century, but maybe better. Aside from the economics of it.

RS: Do you see this as a more important time than the time of the undergrounds?

AS: I see it as an extension of the same time, because those people are still working. We're not dead yet. I don't see it as, "Well, Kim Deitch, Art Spiegelman, Robert Crumb, or Mark Beyer, those are the old farts," and then there's this crazy new crowd that does something in contradistinction to that. It's really a fluid thing that started sometime in the late '60s and has gone through various permutations and is still living off that particular burst of energy.

RS: So you wouldn't agree that New Wave is something distinct?

AS: If it is I've lost it; it's not really distinct. There's aspects of this where the edges get blurry. What has happened is that when I was teaching comics, I'd get kids in my classes who were serious about becoming cartoonists; they were going to that school to learn to draw comics, period, that's what they wanted to know how to do, but the only comics they'd seen were the comics they were growing up with, which were more or less boring newspaper strips and really more or less boring comic books. Not even Steve Ditko's *Spider-Man* but Johnny Romita's *Spider-Man*, and as a result, they didn't have much of a history to work from. And considering that, cave paintings aside, it's not that long a history; it's possible to get some fairly firm grasp of it in a finite period of time, it seems that having that base might be important to making work. As a result, some people are now coming to what I see as a continual thing that started sometime in the mid '60s really coming from the superhero comics tradition, which is a relatively bankrupt one. As a result, there are these things appearing in the comics shops that are not from Marvel or DC, but almost might as well be. That seems to be a dilution, and not exactly the same thing that I'm talking about when I say that comics are exciting right now.

RS: What titles do you mean?
AS: Even something like say *Cerebus the Aardvark* or *Elfquest* or God knows what all else.

RS: Or even something like *The Dark Knight*, which was a DC comic.
AS: Or *The Dark Knight*. Actually, Miller has a better grasp of the history than many artists do, but ultimately even *The Dark Knight*, sure. Those aren't the most vital areas that comics can move in. For one thing, it's just one narrow genre, and it's a genre that's been so thoroughly dug out that there's relatively little to find there. And it's a very narrow graphic tradition. When cartoonists come into comics and all they've ever looked at is other cartoonists, it's kind of hemophiliac bleeder comics. They don't even learn to draw from Jack Kirby; they learn to draw from somebody who learned to draw from somebody who learned to draw from Jack Kirby, and they never quite heard of Kirby, and they certainly never heard of Milton Caniff and so on, let alone talking about hearing about Picasso or George Grosz, or hearing about them as something more directly involved in their craft.

RS: I suppose that artwork and storytelling has been incredibly improved in the last few years.
AS: One of the things that is making it more interesting and vital, which is what I was getting to also, is now it seems like really recently, in the past few years, a lot of stuff is getting reprinted, even if it's by small publishers. So it becomes possible for somebody to really begin to get a sense of what did happen, where people did go.

RS: I might be wrong on this, but it seems like the first time that people have really experimented with not having sequential panels or having jump cuts each panel, it just seems an exciting time for experimentation. I don't know if that happened in the undergrounds so much.
AS: Yes, it did—different kinds of experimentation, but including absolutely non-linear comics.

RS: I've seen Crumb's acid-inspired comix.
AS: OK, or Moscoso, Rick Griffin. Also acid-inspired, I guess, but very non-linear. I don't know if you ever saw my work from those days—did you ever see something called "Ace Hole, Midget Detective"?

RS: Was that the anthropomorphics again, about the two dogs?

AS: No, that one was something from *Playboy*, that was commercial art. I was doing things that, from what I was told by Alan Moore, were very influential on him being able to do something like the *Watchmen*. They were definitely involved in separating the words from the pictures, having them move in different directions from each other, having non-sequitur images, apparent non-sequiturs. *Maus* is very linear compared to the kind of work I was doing before. If anything it's sort of working in reverse; all of the things I was trying to deconstruct for a decade, I was trying to reconstruct in *Maus*, to see if I could make things flow more fluidly.

RS: OK, I'll conclude it there, then. Thank you very much indeed.

Art Mimics Life in the Death Camps

MICHAEL FATHERS / 1992

From *Independent on Sunday*, 22 March 1992, p. 25. Copyright © 1992 Independent News and Media, Ltd. Reprinted by permission.

It was an unpleasant beginning. I went admiring the man and his books. His parents had survived Auschwitz; his mother committed suicide when he was twenty; his relationship with his father was difficult, to say the least. And out of this he had produced a masterpiece about the Holocaust, in comic book form, which was also a history of his family. I was in awe. But we became antagonists.

Art Spiegelman, forty-four, is the author of *Maus*, a story of survival that begins in Poland in the mid-1930s and ends with his father's death in the United States in 1982. It is no ordinary story because the characters are portrayed as animals. Jews are mice, the Germans are cats, Poles are pigs, Americans are dogs, the English fish. *Maus* is an adventure, a love story, a horror story, with incredible intensity of image and emotion.

It is, furthermore, the story of Spiegelman's relationship, or lack of one, with his father, who in his post-Auschwitz life in New York harasses and infuriates almost everyone he comes in contact with, including his second wife, his son, and his neighbors. He is a difficult man—made more so, it would seem, by his ingenious ability to survive.

Spiegelman was once an obscure comic-strip artist. He is now something of a celebrity. *Maus I*, which takes the story of his father and mother from their marriage to the gates of "Mauschwitz" in 1944, was a huge success when it was published in 1986. *Maus II*, which deals with their life in the death camp, their separation, the end of the war, their search for each other and reunion, arrives in British bookshops this week. In the United States it has been on the *New York Times* bestseller list for three months. An exhibition, "The Making of Maus," has just ended at the Museum of Modern Art. The two volumes are set texts at American universities for courses ranging from history to "dysfunctional family psychology."

I met Art Spiegelman twice last week, and the first time I offended him. The occasion was a publisher's supper at a London dining club. Conversation was strained, and to my despair hardly touched on Spiegelman's books. At last, seeking a response, I told him I liked his new book, but not as much as the first. I gave my reasons, which were that although we all knew what happened in Auschwitz, the period covered by the first volume, when the family was on the run in and outside the ghetto, was an extraordinary and vivid story.

Spiegelman said quietly that the "gathering up" of the Jews had been as well documented as the death camps. He worried in case my comment meant that the British reader could not understand—or, more likely, did not *want* to understand—Auschwitz, and preferred to focus on the adventure story rather than on the genocide.

The conversation moved on. Raymond Briggs, the artist-storyteller, said he was surprised at the coincidences in *Maus*—Spiegelman's father runs into friends, family, family contacts, former business colleagues at Auschwitz. Spiegelman said this was natural, because they came from nearby Polish towns. He explained how he had persuaded the *New York Times* to transfer *Maus II* from the fiction to the non-fiction bestseller list, and how he had visited a slaughterhouse in Poland to understand the routine indifference of mass killing.

We touched on the symbolism of animals. He chose pigs to represent Poles because they were non-Kosher, and because although they were outside the immediate "food chain" of the farmyard, where cats kill mice, they were destined to eventually die. The dinner ended amicably enough.

Next day, when I visited his hotel, he returned to my criticism of *Maus II*. He explained how difficult he found it to depict his parents' experiences in the concentration camp. He has spent long sessions of psychoanalysis trying to grasp what it was like there. "I couldn't visualize it," he told me angrily. "How was I to draw what happened to my father at Auschwitz? It is a separate universe. In the death camps there aren't any known laws. And lots of people died in the first week in the camps because they couldn't adjust to this universe. It was very difficult for me to understand in a detailed way what this universe was."

Spiegelman is carrying a huge burden. He still sees his shrink; they have spent hours talking about Auschwitz. "It's much easier to think people arrived and were just turned into soap," he said. "Yet there was a process of being alive in the death camps. For some it was an immediate journey to the showers and all that stuff. For others there was a day to day life amid the terror—bonding, momentary joys, and humor in a horrifying way."

My comments had touched a raw nerve. "I hear you saying that I have an inability to focus on the horrors of the death camps. To say that you *know* about those horrors I find hard to believe. You think you know about it, because you have a general outline about it. It's a way of not needing to understand it. We are dealing with a situation that is absolutely central not just to my family but to the twentieth century. You are keeping your distance. 'Oh it's not us,' you're saying, 'it's the Jews.'"

Spiegelman, who describes himself as a "frustrated Utopian," is a radical anti-Zionist. The Second World War should have ended with the dissolution of all nations, he said. Israel acts no better and no worse than any other government: they are all dominated by national self-interest. And it is nationalism that permits extreme violence, even genocide.

Spiegelman grew up an ordinary American kid with Elvis Presley and *Mad* comics, graduating to the anti-Vietnam movement, pot, and LSD. From time to time his mother told him about Auschwitz and the ghetto. His father did not want him to know, and held himself aloof. Spiegelman knew he wanted to be a cartoonist from adolescence, but his father wanted him to be a doctor or dentist—because they had a better chance of surviving. In the camps, professors and lawyers went right to the showers.

Was it a happy childhood? "It wasn't bad. There was a certain age when I realized, gee, I'm going to grow up being neurotic. As soon as I read what a neurotic was, I knew that was me." Did his father mind? "My father's reaction to everything was, 'don't stand in the first line.'"

"He didn't like me being a hippy but he was really upset when I bought a [German-made] Volkswagen van. My having a Volkswagen damaged our relationship beyond repair."

However, it improved in 1978, when Spiegelman got going with his tape recorder. "As an adult I never really had a relationship with my father outside interviewing him—that was the relationship. We found a common ground even though it meant keeping the microphone as a wall between us."

The barbed wire between Spiegelman and me, on the other hand, seemed to be coming down in places. Talking to him, you are sucked in by his obsession, and by his humor, just as once you have opened his books you cannot close them. His intensity is unnerving and exhausting. But if I left him feeling drained, how must he feel after all these years with *Maus* and Auschwitz on his back?

The Cultural Relief of Art Spiegelman: A Conversation with Michael Silverblatt

MICHAEL SILVERBLATT / 1992

From *Tampa Review* 5, 1992, pp. 31–36.
Reprinted by permission of University of
Tampa Press and Michael Silverblatt.

This conversation with Art Spiegelman took place in April 1992 on "Bookworm," a program produced by Michael Silverblatt for National Public Radio's affiliate station KCRW in Santa Monica, California.

Silverblatt: I wanted to start by talking about the way comic books usually defy gravity, offer super heroes, take off into space—whereas your books seem to be about powerlessness, and thereby are the antithesis of what most people look for in comic books.

Spiegelman: Yes, I suppose it's become a medium of escapist entertainment. And that's kind of moving in an opposite direction. Instead of making comics into a narcotic, I'm trying to make comics that can wake you up, like caffeine comics that get you back in touch with things that are happening around you. On the other hand, comics also have had a tradition of being used as barometers of moral behavior. There's a satirical tradition in comics that is involved not in fantasy super heroes, (or) Manichaean escape adventure. Like today, reading the newspaper, when asked about what to do about the economy, George Bush says, "Move 'Doonesbury' to the obituary page."

Silverblatt: Oh Boy. Well, you know, he knows! [Laughter.]
Spiegelman: They do have an impact.

Silverblatt: Well, sure. When I go back and look through those pornographic "Popeye" comics that were once—there are hundreds and hundreds of pages of them—and you know, the culture wanted to do something to this spinach-chewing super hero—or look at Fearless Fosdick in the Little Abner strip and you see that here was someone who was tired of Dick Tracy.
Spiegelman: But Dick Tracy is already a sinister and tense "Id" creature. Essentially, this is like cartoonists admiring each other and trying to inhabit each other's skins rather than just simply inventing antidotes. What's true in both cases is that there's an attempt in both Fearless Fosdick, and these Tijuana Bible comics, to get underneath the sanitized part of what comics can be. There's always been in our popular culture a kind of a tension between genteel and low-brow, and comics have always sort of resided in the low-brow, yet there've been attempts to kind of reel them back in. I mean, Dick Tracy and Popeye are about as sawdust and tinsel as it gets, and yet, even there—

Silverblatt: I wanted to start our talk about *Maus* in another area entirely by talking about Henry Darger and the obsessive, compulsive nature of comic fantasy. I first saw some of Darger's stuff in, I guess, *Wet Magazine*. He was, I think, a janitor in a girls' school who had composed book after book after book (it's a book I long to read) of what happened in an amusement park in a ten-second cyclone, is it? And on his walls when they went into his room after his death were vast frescoes of the girls in different battles being impaled. It seemed to me to represent, more than any way I could think of, that life of the person who has to protect himself by projecting images.
Spiegelman: Yes, I suppose it's a result of a brain that's trying to make itself known to itself and it functions somewhere between words and pictures, so that Darger kept all these notebooks that were the stories of

the Vivian sisters and then started illustrating these pictures, these stories, with notebook after notebook of images, trying to conjure up the world more clearly for himself.

Silverblatt: And I think of that cyclone, that cyclone in the amusement park—this was a prose project of his—as being the vision of a world of one in which permanent catastrophe occupies a playground. You know, there's a very bitter, excluded middle here.

Spiegelman: Yeah, but that actually wasn't the only thing he wrote. He was doing this other thing that was just this war between different races on different planets.

Silverblatt: Right, and there was this enormous journal in which he kept the weather for every single day for the last, what was it, the last twenty-five years?

Spiegelman: Yes, he was comparing the weather report with the actual weather, which was a way of proving the media wrong.

Silverblatt: So I wanted to begin by comparing you with Darger.

Spiegelman: OK, well, I think one difference would be that Darger wasn't aware that his work would ever be seen. It was all just discovered after his death—this was the work we published in *RAW*—and it's just because his landlord was an artist of sorts himself and knew that the stuff had a value. Otherwise, it would have all ended up in a dumpster. And, although I do work to make things clear for myself, there is an awareness that somebody, somewhere, is going to be looking over my shoulder. I don't think it acts so much as a censor, but it does act as a prod to bring things into a crystalline focus that can exist without my hand pointing.

Silverblatt: It seems to me, though, that for something to be so visceral, as simultaneously so cooled out and intense as *Maus* is, that there has to be so much more, as you call it, rawness, or intuition, or personal need. Art seems to be the subsequent factor, something that comes in almost by default. You need it. It's another ingredient, but the primary one seems to be the need to settle or organize.

Spiegelman: The motor is the need to clarify. But where the coolness comes in, I suppose, is that the organizing principle is the result of weighing possibilities, and it's nothing that's just accreted in a notebook like Darger's work. I mean, there are differences. I guess that's what I'm saying, though I certainly responded strongly enough in seeing these

Darger things to want to find a way to show some of it in *RAW*. But I suppose I knew I was making something, that I was working toward a specific narrative arc. When I started it I made an outline, so that I knew that I was going to get from A to B somehow, even though I didn't know it was going to take thirteen years to get there. And then I have to inhabit every moment to get from the first point to that last point. But I suppose just knowing that, knowing that you're aiming somewhere, already indicates a degree of artifice that is less true for Darger, let's say.

Silverblatt: I am not being fair, perhaps, to readers who I am supposing already know that *Maus* is the story of your father and the years that took him, prior to Auschwitz, to Auschwitz, and then eventually to the Catskills. And that this story is told via mice as the Jews, and cats as the Nazis, and your wife, a French woman, at one point was thought to be a frog, but she converted, and so she is a mouse, too. And yet whimsy is not a part of the ongoing procedures here. How did you exile it? I mean, it seems necessary to have taken whimsy and said that it will take a back seat, but was it of concern to you?

Spiegelman: Well, there were a number of things that were a concern to me, and whimsy was just one of several inappropriate methods to proceed with in order to avoid a kind of cheap cynicism that comes with the underground comics territory I tend to walk around in. I had to also steer clear of any kind of sentimentality or pathos so that I wouldn't be guilty of creating some kind of "Holokitsch" literature. And I also had to watch out for what aspects of the story can legitimately allow for laughter, without saying, "OK, now it's time for a good laugh, now it's time for a good cry." I really tried to stay clear of manipulating readers into an emotional response. I was trying to withhold emotional response long enough to allow for some kind of understanding. And yet within that there were things that happened between me and my father that can only be described as funny—there's a kind of cognitive dissonance between us that keeps creating odd collisions. And even on occasion, in the ghetto, my father, who was a rather good storyteller, tells me these anecdotes that were amusing.

Silverblatt: When one opens the book and sees the harsh blacks and whites, one thinks, not only of the graphic novels of [Frans] Masereel, but also in an odd way of the demented geometries of *Little Nemo*. There's that kind of intense organization of material into discrete bits, and because the concentration camp experience is, as has been said elsewhere, the experience of repetition—repetition with terror—there is the quality here that they imputed to Sade. They said ultimately the tendency of cruelty, when ordered, is that it results in geometry.

Spiegelman: Wow! OK. I came at it, I suppose, a little bit differently, which is, I thought of this thing as trying to structure and visualize something that was for me not visualizable. And the only way to do that was to sort of move toward an abstraction. And in terms of, let's take, since you mentioned him, Winsor McCay [*Little Nemo*]. What was important for me in his work didn't have to do so much with the ways of drawing as with the ways of structuring a page. So that at some point I was looking through a dictionary, and I sought "comics," comics means a narrative series of pictures; "narrative," narrative means a story; "story," story comes from the medieval Latin "historia," which is the medieval picture windows. Therefore the word "story" as narrative is the same as the word "story" as in stories of a building. And McCay was the architect of comics. I mean, he was somebody who dealt with this amazing fantasy architecture in *Little Nemo*, and his pages have a kind of architectonic rigor that I found necessary to understand to compose the pages of *Maus*.

Silverblatt: It seems to me that that is the thing—that there is a rigor *and* a squalor that are operating simultaneously in each page—the raw and the cooked. Well, let's talk about the "rawness," the necessary rawness of a text like this.

Spiegelman: Of *Maus*?

Silverblatt: Yes, of *Maus*.

Spiegelman: Well, unlike some other comics that I've done, this is one in service to a deposition—my father's text is driving it. Sometimes things that have grown up around an image that explodes in my head turn into other images surrounding it and eventually build themselves outward into enough boxes to be a comic. But here it was like trying to inhabit my father's words and not give the lie to them. And that was a very different way of having to proceed. So I had to go about it by trying to get everything very structured, and within that not allow it to become domesticated and die on me. I suppose there's a look in *Maus*—I like the phrase you just used—in that there's an incredible amount of underlying work before the final picture, and yet the final picture has to look casual enough to not be off-putting in the sense that "I am the artist, and therefore I have more skills than you, the reader, and I can keep you away from this just by the fact that I can draw circles around you and

you've got to respect it." And it was necessary for me to do all my drawing, but keep that drawing in check, because sometimes the drawing
would get too interesting and I'd have to kill it. I had this quote up
above the drawing table that said "Writing consists primarily of killing
your little darlings"—Faulkner. As a result I had to scrap things when
they got too finished.

Silverblatt: Some of my favorite work takes incompetence in the face of
extreme ability as its watch-cry, as its lantern. Beckett, for instance, or
Kafka. One senses the steely precision of what they do, and yet at the
same time they've thrown away all of the trappings, the beauty part.
Spiegelman: Which I have to do, in *Maus*, for instance. I don't know if
you've seen any comics originals. They tend to be quite large, compared
to what you see printed. It's a way for the artist to kind of minimize his
mistakes. His errors get reduced when they're printed small. But I did
Maus the same size. What you see when you look at my book is a one
to one relationship. That's the real reason: it's a one to one relationship.

Silverblatt: We're seeing the art full size, as you drew it.
Spiegelman: Yes, and if I make a mistake, I want you to have my mistake. There's an intimacy that is accorded that way. That was part of the
reason for drawing small. It keeps you from getting involved in a certain
kind of flourish and decoration in that if you only have, as I do, sometimes only have an inch and a half of space or less, by two inches or
three inches in which to draw thirty people, you're not going to get
involved in a lot of extraneous nonsense. You're going to go for the
immediacy and the urgent sign.

Silverblatt: Well, what struck me was that one's involvement with these
books—with the *Maus* books—has to be myopic. You hold them very
close to you because you are looking at them, you're interrogating them
in a peculiar way. And what's more, that myopic involvement precludes
distance in a text that you want to keep far away from you. These two
books, *Maus* and *Maus II*, are very much "lest we forget books," books
that want to prohibit forgetfulness, loss of memory—both the memory
of your father and the memory of the Holocaust. These are books that
are against repression. And I found the closeness with which you have to
handle them to be technically an embodiment of that.
Spiegelman: Hm! About memory: I've thought of these things as a
thirteen-year-long yahrzeit candle. You know it was a long act to have to

organize memory, and, oddly enough, because I've been drawing these tiny panels, my eyes have been going, so I have to hold things far away from me in order to see.

Silverblatt: In the course of doing this, I guess one operant phrase was how to prevent the banalization of evil about the concentration camps. These are very methodical comics. But there are surprises—as your psychoanalyst mouse says, the concentration camps were like a time when a lot of people were going around saying "Boo," all the time—and they're all unpleasant surprises, terrible surprises. Did you feel—since the cartoons in RAW are the most outlandish, surprising, visually amusing, and shocking—did you find yourself, how to put it, defining your work in contrast to that of your friends in RAW?
Spiegelman: Not at all. I was surprised to hear you, after being so sensitive with language, dumping together all these other artists into one category.

Silverblatt: No. No.
Spiegelman: Ultimately—well, what's interesting to me about RAW is that each of these artists inhabits a unique territory. There's very little of them using each other's premises of what a comic strip means. So that Lynda Barry's work is, in some sense, more conventional in its comics telling than an artist like Pascal Doury in France, whom we've used in RAW. So that I felt myself, while working in the early days of RAW, especially, as an equal moving in one territory where there were thirty other people moving into their own terrains.

Silverblatt: What I meant was not to group them all together. I meant that as an object, one finds that RAW enunciates itself as something wild. It has many different kinds of paper. Some of its texts are colored, some of them are tinted. There's every kind of line imaginable in it, so it's very variegated and the Maus text is strict. So I was just thinking about the spirit of the object.
Spiegelman: Well, I would say that the main thing is that—in that everybody has their own territory—Gary Panter's stuff you'd never even think of calling a graphic novel unless you were just taking it 'cause it was a word in the air. Graphic novels having this problem of "graphics are respectable; novels are respectable; graphic novels, double respectability." But his stuff, if anything could be, what—graphic paintings? And, on the other hand, out of all people that this curse could be laid onto, Maus comes closest to being a graphic novel—I don't like the term,

obviously—in that a novel has a very specific kind of literary structuring, ways of revealing information. And I indeed used a number of those models in trying to figure out how to make *Maus*—not how to make all my comics I've made in my life—but how to make *Maus*, in that, as I said before, this is a story that's motored by the word. And the pictures have to inhabit those words as opposed to different possible directions for the words and pictures to co-habit. As a result, novelistic structuring was necessary.

Silverblatt: What are some examples of novelistic structuring in *Maus*?
Spiegelman: Well, I suppose it's the kind of stuff that you learn in lit classes.

Silverblatt: The flashbacks?
Spiegelman: Well, foreshadowings of information. Being shown some-thing, then having it made more resonant by something that happens as many as sixty, seventy pages later. A simple example would be using this kind of introductory two-page comic strip about me and my father when I was ten years old. He's sawing. I fall down, my friends don't wait for me. I come back crying. I complain about the fact that my friends left me, and he says, "Well, come on, hold this while I'm sawing. Friends, I'll tell you what it is. Friends. Try to put them together in a room with no food for a week, and you'll see what it is, friends." Well, all of a sudden this kind of shadow falls across a kind of banal, non-historical moment, you know, just being a kid and playing. The shadow of a past time inter-weaving with a present time is one of the central themes of *Maus*, and it's introduced in that fashion, very kind of straight-forwardly. Later on there's a lot of other ways in which time interweaves, so that my father and I and my wife, Françoise, are driving together in a car in the Catskills, and as we get into the car and drive into the forest there are corpses hanging from the trees. It's one of the few moments where I allow time to visually intersect. But it's another way of showing these different times, and having the same space. In fact, if you don't mind a sentence that's running on forever, I would say that comics, in their essence, are about time made manifest spatially, in that you've got all these different chunks of time—each box being a different moment of time—and you see them all at once. As a result you're always, in comics, being made aware of different times inhabiting the same space. That's a theme of *Maus*. I would say that in volume one of *Maus* there's a comic strip within the comic strip called "Prisoner on the Hell Planet" that I'd

actually done years before doing the rest of the book. And that's entered into the story in a certain way. In the second volume there's a kind of balancing that might be novelistic which is to have a sequence that exists outside of the frame of the rest of the book, which is the one you were referring to, of me and the psychoanalyst, the therapist, sitting around together. There are correspondences in these two sequences, but they're not the same—they're not the same kind of sequence—but they definitely pull the narratives taut in different temporal and spatial directions. That's something I would think would be more easily understood in a novelistic kind of work, a work that was prose. The problem with the word novel here, of course, is that it implies fiction, and I've been very insistent that *Maus* is non-fiction with mice.

Silverblatt: This is kind of a tough question: Given the fact that, for better or worse, the primary audience for *RAW* and the underground comics is a kind of underground audience, and a couple of years back would have been a punk audience, and this was an audience that had taken swastikas as an article of fashion, were you concerned about the appropriation of this text to purposes very different from your own?

Spiegelman: Well, no, in that, although *Maus* was embraced within a punk scene, I always felt I was flying under false colors. I remember when, in the underground comics days, Bill Griffith and I were doing a magazine called *Arcade*, and at that point we got a letter from Charles Bukowski saying, "Ah, you guys are all ministers in Popeye suits." Essentially there's a great moral center to the work even though it appears on the surface to be nihilistic, or anarchistic, or something. Most of the artists in *RAW*—I won't say every single one of them—are moving forward from a moral center. As a result, it just seemed to me to be interesting to be able to make ethics hip.

Silverblatt: That puts it well. Your father was alive when the first sections came out. Had he seen them?

Spiegelman: Yes, but in so far as he had a response, it's included within the work. As part of this great self-referential process of trying to swallow everything that was happening there's a page within the book, in which I'm showing an earlier page, and that pretty much condenses his responses.

Silverblatt: I didn't really mean to ask what his response was so much as the way in which these books become him. By the end of the book, it's his tombstone that these books are—or his testament. And I guess I wondered—it's very unusual for this kind of art, this comic art, to become testamentary.

Spiegelman: No, I can't think of another example. Well, no, I can think of one other example which would be. It's a comic book for children, and it was called *Hiroshima Gen*. Do you know about this thing? It was done by a guy who was a kid in Hiroshima when the bomb fell.

Silverblatt: No, I don't know it.

Spiegelman: Then he became a professional cartoonist in Japan, where being a cartoonist meant you could make a living.

Silverblatt: A good living!

Spiegelman: Yes. You could become a "God King of Manga." And as an adult he started doing this story about a young boy who survived Hiroshima. It became a several-thousand-page work and it's very much engaged in bearing witness, although through a very different idiom, and for children. Yet, nevertheless, I saw it after I had already started *Maus*. Part of it had already been translated by the War Resisters' League. I found this a kind of chilling thing, even in a comic strip idiom that's much grosser than the one I've been using in *Maus*. You know, the eyes are all Walter Keane giant mirrors.

Silverblatt: Orphan eyes.

Spiegelman: Yes. And when the father wants to pat the kid on the head before the bomb falls, he sort of gives him a "noogie" on top of the head. It's like this big child abuse whack that gets the eyes to cross and the kid almost falls over. And it just means a sign of affection in Japanese comics. And yet, through all that exaggeration what comes through is so chilling and burns its way so far into your brain that I would say the descriptions of the Hiroshima bombing in *Hiroshima Gen* are more firmly etched inside me than many of the written or photographic testaments I've seen.

Silverblatt: I've been talking to Art Spiegelman. And I want to say that I am grateful for the existence of the *Maus* books. I can hardly look at them for more than a couple of pages without crying. But I've read the first one many times, and the second one twice, and it satisfies something in my heart or soul that the books exist, and that's a great cultural relief.

The Man Behind Maus: Art Spiegelman in His Own Words

CHRIS GOFFARD / 1992

From *Fish Rap Live!*, 1992 pp. 1 + 8.
Reprinted by permission of *Fish Rap Live!*

Art Spiegelman is a tired man. Having recently won a Pulitzer for
Maus—the story of his father's struggle for survival in Hitler's Europe—
the artist/writer describes his life as "a relentless game of beat-the-
clock." He is currently teaching a course entitled History and Aesthetics
of Comics at the University of California, Santa Cruz, which chronicles
the careers and achievements of seminal comic book artists such as Jack
Kirby, Robert Crumb, and Will Eisner, and traces the development of the
medium for which, with *Maus*, Spiegelman has himself become the
dominant figure. Spiegelman lectures with a slide-projector screen at
which he gestures with a pointer, drawing his students' attention to the
nuanced dynamics of comic book pages. Spiegelman is a chain-smoker,
and his insistence on smoking during lectures has caused a stir on
campus, where fire-safety regulations have forced him to move his

lectures out of a classroom and into a dorm-house recreation lounge. Spiegelman is now also at work supervising translations of his *Maus* books (Volume II is now on the stands), anthologizing out-of-print issues of *RAW* magazine, and planning a traveling gallery show of *Maus* drawings and other drawings. He divides his time between Santa Cruz and San Francisco and is soon to be back in New York, where he is consulting on an exhibit about the history of comics at Exit Art. He is constantly besieged by requests for interviews, but he rarely gives them. He suggested that the title of this article be "Art Spiegelman, Burnout."

Goffard: Your work is deeply personal—you write openly about your mother's suicide, your troubled relationship with your father and so forth. Does it take a conscious effort to drag these visceral things to the surface again and again?

Spiegelman: Well, not all my comics are autobiographical, at least in any overt and obvious way. It's only autobiographical in the sense that most art on one level or another can be traced back to the artist's history. But when I did "Prisoner on the Hell Planet" specifically, which is a comic about my mother's suicide, I wasn't even certain I was gonna let it get published. I was just doing it because I needed to do it. That's the way a lot of this work is developed for me. *Maus*, on the other hand, I was doing with the understanding that it would be seen in one way or another. But nevertheless it was something born out of trying to meet two needs at once. One, tell a story. It finally dawned on me after being a cartoonist for a good twenty years or more that what people wanted out of comics was a story, so I had to find a story worth telling, because the kind of comics I'd been working on up to the moment I started *Maus* were involved in kind of taking narratives apart and messing with them, rather than telling them. So it was fulfilling that need. On the other hand it also filled the more central need for me of trying to make sense of my own personal past and of history as I intersected with it.

Goffard: Does your work serve a therapeutic function?

Spiegelman: Look, *Maus*'s success sent me into a shrink's arms. It's just a process of trying to understand, trying to understand myself and trying to understand other things, and my medium for understanding is comics.

Goffard: In a *Progressive* interview you mention having one bad eye and being terrible at baseball as a kid. To what degree does an artist get into what he does as a means of proving his worthiness to himself and to the world? To compensate for his inadequacies elsewhere?

Spiegelman: Well, that's the Freudian interpretation. The Jungian interpretation is something else and the Marxist interpretation would be yet another thing. My sense of it is that, yes, to a degree it functions as a compensatory mechanism because you end up trying to find something you can do and get a feeling of mastery and accomplishment. I tended to feel rather isolated as a child. As I said in that interview, I spent a lot of time in libraries because I wasn't that good on the playground.

Goffard: You've had movie offers for *Maus* and you've resisted them.

Spiegelman: I don't think it would work. Basically movies are done by groups. Comics can be done by an individual. If there's one thing my father taught me, it's not to trust groups. I'm not interested in making a creation with a committee. I don't understand why everybody in this culture seems to believe it's not real until it's turned into a movie. I do understand all too well, actually. But to me *Maus* found its proper form and it took me thirteen years to give it that form. I'm not interested especially in seeing that diminished. I've had offers that I may pursue. People have come and said, "Alright, so you don't want to make *Maus* as a movie, what kind of movie do you want to make?" And that I may pursue, because that could be interesting to explore. But then I would be thinking it through from the ground up, as working in that idiom.

Goffard: Hemingway talks about success ruining a writer if it strikes too early in his career. Has success affected your work negatively?

Spiegelman: It's not as bad as what happened to Crumb, who got successful in his early twenties. I'm at least forty-three now, forty-four. But success is a bitch. So far it's mainly just made me have less time to concentrate. I'm sure that in the long run it will give me more time to concentrate because I'll get a bigger advance for my next book. But in the short-run it's just very distracting and a bit confusing. There are pleasures to it, but at the moment I feel like I'd be glad to forego those pleasures. My struggle was never for commercial success. I never believed that that had anything to do with me. It took me by surprise.

Goffard: Did the Pulitzer surprise you?

Spiegelman: Totally. I get to go to Columbia next month to pick it up.

Goffard: Does the popular acceptance matter to you?

Spiegelman: "Gooble, gobble, we accept you, we accept you, one of us." You ever saw *Freaks*? There's this great scene in the movie *Freaks* where the character, the beautiful Olga, is marrying a midget for his money, and she's having a wedding banquet, and a really twisted dwarf is standing with a wedding goblet atop of a table, and all the pinheads and Siamese twins and the Indian rubber men and the chicken-headed men are all drinking from this goblet, and it gets passed around, and as it's getting passed they chant, "Gooble, gobble, we accept you, we accept you, one of us" till she shrieks "Freaks!" and runs out of the room.

Goffard: Were there novelists or philosophers who influenced you especially?

Spiegelman: Yeah, sure. I'd say . . . I liked Kafka when I was growing up as a kid. I read Kafka. That was important to me. Faulkner. See, I can't tell how things influenced me. I can tell I read these things and they stayed with me. Vladimir Nabokov stayed with me, Gertrude Stein stayed with me. I'm trying to scan the shelves. Dashiell Hammett and Raymond Chandler and James M. Cain stayed with me. For philosophers—well, I read a lot of existentialism when I was in high school, that helped shape me. You see, it becomes a problem when you talk about influences because I think there's lots of stuff that I just picked up as stray strands, you know. It's hard to know. Probably some really shitty children's book that I don't remember made a permanent dent in my brain. Certainly *Mad* comics influenced me a lot.

Goffard: What's it like to be called the new Kafka?

Spiegelman: I hadn't heard that one, I'm glad.

Goffard: It's written in at least two different reviews.

Spiegelman: I missed both. (Laughs)

Goffard: You don't read the articles written about you?

Spiegelman: I scan them. There's so many of them now. I've seen lots of them but I can't say that I've read all of them. I'm glad *Maus* was a success, but I'm ambivalent about it. There are enough bad things that have come along with it for it not to be just like, "Oh, that's terrific." And it's a bit confusing, that's all. I'm grateful that after working for thirteen years on something it doesn't sink like a stone, that it floats out into the culture. But I expected when I was working on it that it would be more like a message in a bottle rather than like the big broadcast of 1992, you know. And it's not as clear-cut as like, "Ah, phui, I don't care about it." It has its upside, certainly. But it's also addictive, which I don't like. You end up saying things like, "Why aren't thirty people calling today?" This will tend to sort itself out, because the culture moves quickly so that somebody else will get it for ten minutes. It ends up leaving you kind of shorted-out. What was it that one friend of mine said? "You know, Spiegelman, it's not like you act different now that you're famous, you always fucking acted famous." I guess I've had a kind of conviction about my work, and I understood that it was worth something, even when it wasn't.

Goffard: Do you still do ten hours a day at the drawing board?
Spiegelman: I haven't been at the drawing table in any consistent way since August of last year. And I don't expect to be again until some time this coming July. It'll have been a whole year of dizziness as a result of *Maus* coming out.

Goffard: How long does it take you to do a page?
Spiegelman: I really have no idea. I never checked how long it took. I just kept working. So I don't know when a page started. There are pages in the last chapter of *Maus* that I started in 1979.

Goffard: Do you have ideas for your next project?
Spiegelman: Notions. "Ideas" would be giving them more glory that they deserve right now. But in order to pursue it and see these things through I'm gonna have to be able to have time again. The way success has really got a downside is that there all these distractions, like being interviewed a lot, and getting offers for all kinds of weird things that have nothing to do with my central interests.

Goffard: You've refused to refrain from smoking in class at UCSC.
Spiegelman: I'd warned them when I was invited to come out here. I said, "I've now lectured at enough different places and enough different times to know what makes me comfortable. I smoke when I lecture. If that's gonna be a problem, and I suspect it might be, then let's not do it." So it worked out, but then it blew up in the provost's face when a student complained. Not a student who wanted to take the class, mind you.

Goffard: One of the things people like about your work is that you resist moralizing when you portray the Holocaust. Mencken writes about

Wells developing a messiah complex which killed his writing, because suddenly every story had to instruct. Is there a pedagogic impulse in you?

Spiegelman: I'm sort of interested and glad, in a sense, that the book has a secondary life as a teaching tool. On the other hand it had nothing to do with me doing it. And I'm kind of shaky about it only in the sense that it's hardly the one-stop shopping mart to learn about what happened in the late '30s and early '40s in European and American history. It's not that it was born out of a pedagogic impulse. And so far as I have one it's completely satisfied by teaching the work of other comic book artists.

Goffard: Are there lessons to be learned from the Holocaust?

Spiegelman: I have no idea. See, I would find it a cheap shot to try to give any moral to it. It would be kind of diminishing what happened. My stories are a matter of presenting rather than projecting. Obviously it would be nice if people were nicer to each other. This is a moral? I doubt that it'll happen.

Goffard: You visited the concentration camps. What impression did the experience make?

Spiegelman: Dachau is thoroughly sanitized. It's shocking only in how benignly integrated into its landscape it is and how close it is to Munich, so it's really just the suburbs.

Goffard: Are the crematoriums still there?

Spiegelman: Not really. There are reconstructions of things there, but it's not like you're gonna see a lot except how clean and neat Germans can keep things. It's a museum of a sort. It was important for me to see it just to get a sense of scale and spaces for when I was drawing the Dachau sequences. The research was part of what took *Maus* so long.

Goffard: What's your perception of the state of America today?

Spiegelman: Pathetic. But I'm not interested in being a teacher, my friend. It's not like I feel I have any special right to give you a lesson on how America is going to the dogs. It's a bankrupt society in many ways. I feel very saddened by the death of communism. Because it's not like it means that America won, it means that America is dying slower. I think communism lost because it died first. Certain aspects of socialism are reintroduced into the American fabric. This is just going to become a more toxic place to live. Corrupt empires can last a very long time, but it'll become a more toxic place to live. It already has become more toxic, as I've watched it, more so over the past ten years. Living in New York you get to see it up close.

Goffard: Do the candidates impress you?
Spiegelman: That shit? That's just a silly circus. There are no genuine alternatives in American politics, so it's very hard to stay interested. I just consistently do the same thing. I do vote out of some kind of reflexive action, but without any conviction and always for someone who's slightly less toxic than the other candidate. I usually get to lose. I usually vote for one of the two monsters that's running. When you compare it to European politics, it's an incredibly uninteresting system. It just doesn't allow for representation of anything other than the most right-wing norms. We have a near-right and a far-right party.

Goffard: Can the artist serve a redemptive function—can he stave off the progress toward oblivion?
Spiegelman: Ai-yai-yai. Only from self. I think that artists aren't empowered in this culture in that sense. We were talking before about how things aren't real unless they become movies. Well, by the time they become movies they're pretty well funded so they're very much safely ensconced in the system that allowed them to get made.

Goffard: They're not dangerous any more.
Spiegelman: Can't be. It's just too involved with commerce, which is at the heart of the system. So anything that comes out can only come out through the cracks, or come out either by accident or as some kind of demonstration that the system works. Certain pockets are allowed to thrive because they seem to be not necessarily dangerous. Movies do have the power to shape and change things a bit within the culture, in a way that artists—if you leave it to include primarily painters and novelists and cartoonists, people working alone in their studios—have a much more silenced voice. I've got a best-selling book out. That means that maybe a hundred thousand people have bought it. Maybe by the time it's all over, more. That's what put it on the best-seller list, but that's not more people than you could get at some kind of local access cable show.

Art Spiegelman

NOAMI EPEL / 1993

As the son of Auschwitz survivors, Art Spiegelman set out to document his family history using the medium he knew best, adult comic books. The result was *Maus*, a two-volume memoir in pictures—*Maus I: A Survivor's Tale* and *Maus II: And Here My Troubles Began*. Spiegelman based the book on taped conversations with his father, Vladek. He drew the Jews as mice, the Nazis as cats, the Poles as pigs and the Americans as dogs. Spiegelman wove his father's memories of the Holocaust into a complex narrative exploring the painful relationship between father and son.

Born in Stockholm, Sweden, in 1948, and raised in New York, Art Spiegelman began drawing for the school newspaper at the age of thirteen. By fourteen, he was selling sports and political cartoons to the

Long Island Post. In the 1960s he became part of the underground comic movement, producing titles such as *Young Lust, Real Pulp, Bizarre Sex* and *Sleazy Scandals of the Silver Screen.*

In 1980, with his wife, Françoise Mouly, Spiegelman co-founded *RAW,* an annual magazine of avant-garde comics and graphics. In 1992 he was given a one-man show on "The Making of *Maus*" at New York's Museum of Modern Art. He was awarded a special Pulitzer Prize for *Maus* that same year.

I would say the thing that's uncanny to me is how rarely I remember my dreams unless I really go out of my way to do so. I went for a brief period, a few months, deciding to remember them and I'd write them down every day. Then it worked. But I have to make that kind of concerted effort. Otherwise, it's rare that I remember them.

On the other hand, I know that the dream lab is very active. Often I'll find that if I go to sleep laying the day's problem out to myself, and get a fairly clear fix on the various strands and bits of what I was working on right before going to sleep, letting those be my last conscious thoughts, I'll more or less consistently wake up with a solution.

With *Maus* this happened on an almost ongoing basis. There would just be the daily snag and the daily snag would have to wait overnight for me to come up with the answer. The kind of problems that I'm thinking about were narrative problems in construction.

One problem was where to enter things. Although there was a present and a past, I took liberties with when something in the present happened. Like a conversation with my father about his feelings about African Americans may not have happened at the exact moment that he was telling me about the liberation of Dachau, but it happened within that general time frame. There were ongoing problems of when to enter things and how to make them echo back into the rest of the text without being too blatant or obvious, turning them into just some kind of cheap symbolism.

There were also things I just couldn't visualize. I remember in the first book I had a lot of trouble visualizing this garbage pit that some friends of my father were hiding in. I had about ten different scenarios, none of which seemed to be very logical to me. They didn't look right in my head. That would be the kind of thing where I would go to sleep and wake up with a pretty fair image of what I had to draw.

While I was working on *Maus* I dreamt about the Holocaust a lot. Everytime I'd finish a section of *Maus* I would take some time off, do some other kinds of drawing, other kinds of writing and then I'd have to "reenter." Part of reentry was rereading the transcripts of my conversations with my father, listening to the tapes of our talks and reading Holocaust history more concertedly. Or reading survivors' testaments. And, until I would get inured again—which was actually a necessary part of working on *Maus*—I'd have a lot of really fitful and horrible dreams about being in the camps.

My father didn't tell me his nightmares per se, but it was clear from the fact that he would wake up in a sweat, screaming, that there were things that kept coming up.

In *Maus I* there is one dream that I incorporate, his prophetic dream. This was a dream in which my father's grandfather came to him and told him what day he would be released from the prisoner of war camp. It's a true story, a story he always remembered because that date became his magical date. It's the date on which he had been married, which was before he had gone to the prisoner of war camp and before he had that dream. Now I shouldn't say "date" as in January 3rd 19—whatever. It was a date that would change every year but it was the date on which a certain fragment of the Torah called Parshas Trumah would be read. I even looked it up and read it but, in and of itself, it didn't have much resonance. It was just some minor point of Talmudic Law. On your Bar Mitzvah you're supposed to read a piece of the Torah out loud as the confirmation that you've gone through this tribal ritual. And it turned out that mine was Parshas Trumah. Without anybody rigging anything. And so for him that became a magical date.

I recorded my dreams for a while because I was frustrated with not remembering them. I wanted to see if this was like a congenital problem or just prioritizing what my brain was going to be busy with during the day. It was kind of gratifying to know I could remember. I mean it was interesting to remember them, and occasionally I'd bring one to the shrink and we'd talk about it. A dream would trigger off conversation. There'd be an image that might send me down a path of unearthing buried dilemmas. But, on the other hand, looking long enough at a Dewar's scotch ad could do the same thing. For the most part, the dreams per se weren't that useful for analyzing myself.

Now, for me there's another kind of waking dreaming, which I call doodling. I mean, on occasion, I'll sit down and make a picture not knowing what I'm making and then I'll literally write around the image, covering every crevice around the square that has the picture. I find that often becomes a crystalization and a clarification of a lot of what's going on in my head. The process seems very much like what one would go through dreaming. A lot of random stuff sticks together, coalesces to make something that has its own logic.

I actually trust that kind of waking dream more, in terms of bringing me in touch with psychological issues, than the kind I do at night. Because I know that on some level or other that's what I'm doing. Once I've started ranging with the pen, I figure I'll start making images that have other connections.

Because they deal in essences, rather than nuanced description, comics move into the way, I believe, the brain works, which is in encoded, simplified images and concentrated verbal clusters. One not only thinks in words, but in images as well. Yet those images are very stripped down. We don't even think photographically, which is already a simplification of reality, but in terms of high-definition imagery. Not necessarily with the humorous notion that a caricature would bring up, but in kind of a set of caricatures. In other words, if you are thinking about a friend, you will remember their gait, let's say, or a pronounced brow or a specific kind of clothes they often wear, or a specific body gesture. These are very highlighted and exaggerated visuals that you conjure up. This is a description of how the brain recalls things and also a description of what comics are.

I had one dream about comics, incidentally. It took place a long time ago. This guy, who was very important in helping me get started as a cartoonist, had one of the world's greatest collections of paper ephemera and old comic strips in his basement. I would stay in his basement and occasionally just fall asleep there, drift off. I had a dream that consisted of drifting off in his basement looking at "Happy Hooligan," a turn-of-the-century comic strip about a kind of tramp character, who wore a tin can on his head. In the dream I have a tin can on my head. I'm trying to get the can off and it won't come off. It's permanently there. The dream has several episodes of me trying to get this can off by having people pull at it, by knocking it against something. Nothing works. Finally I sit under a tree and start sobbing. Then this other character kind of lopes in and says, "Don't worry, Buddy Boy, it's just the style you're drawn in."

This was a dream with a punch line!

The other interesting thing that happened in this dream was that there were these occasional and very rhythmic moments that were rather painful. These were the moments where I disappeared and reappeared again. And they would happen rhythmically. I realized those were the little white spaces between panels.

There's nothing like drawing a comic strip of your dream to help remember it twenty-five years later!

I remember when I was very, very young—I guess when I'd first been exposed to television—all of a sudden my dreams started having titles and credits. Even though I couldn't read! I was like five or six, so I couldn't really read the titles as they were going by, even on the cartoons, but my dreams would start with the same format that I had seen looking at TV.

Something that's referred to in *Maus* was actually a childhood dream image: all the kids in my class being separated out—Jewish kids, not-Jewish kids—and the Jewish kids being led away. That was something that happened in a dream. But it's not as though it was a recurring dream. It was just a strong image that stayed with me.

My wet dreams I remember. Like certain very strong erotic images that I first had when I was about twelve: a naked woman writhing in a net. Very erotic to me. Especially having her breasts and her vagina up against the netting. That was really hot for me. But explain why? I can't. I'll leave that to an analyst somewhere.

In the Sunday *New York Times* recently there was an article about how dreams move through your brain, positing not that what was charging through your head was random, but that it's a problem-solving machine. Kind of continuing the thoughts that weren't worked through during the day. In that sense it's not totally distant from the Freudian model. I can relate to this idea. It seems to me that part of what happens in your dream life is totally random. And some of the images are clearly your riddle for the week. You know, the things you're supposed to chew on.

I think some of what happens is just neurons firing, just random imagery. But there are bits of dreams that are also very specifically related to interpersonal problem solving.

I can think of various times where there were people who I consciously thought were just A-okay but my dream life told me they weren't. And that made me wary. Then I would discover all this other stuff that justified the wariness. That's happened to me several times actually. Though all it really means is that I'm an incredibly poor judge of character.

Dreams have helped me understand people who were troubling me. Like being unable to articulate consciously that a good friend was very jealous of what was happening to me. Having the fantasy episode in a dream was not just like an alarm bell going off, saying, Go away, but a way of empathizing and understanding what somebody else was seeing without having talked to him about it. Having that articulated to me in dream life helped me work things through to get our friendship into a new equilibrium.

One kind of dream I've had a number of times is seeing a work of art, usually a drawing or a comic strip, in my sleep. Like discovering a comic book that I'd never seen before. It would be just the best thing I'd ever seen. Ever. I'd be feeling incredibly jealous of this work. And then I'd wake up and not be able to remember anything except the feeling that I'd seen it. And then realizing, Hey, it's mine, I can do that. But by then the dream would've evaporated.

For a while I was actually doing work very specifically based on my dreams. I had three or four comic strips that were called "Real Dreams" and I was trying to make these rational narrative comic strips out of my irrational subconscious.

I pretended the dreams were totally narrative. Sometimes I had to add a few words to get them to be less disjointed, trying to turn them into one-page strips. The most interesting one for me was one where I ran an interpretation of the dream at the bottom of the strip. It was all done as a gag. I reinterpreted what was so blatantly and obviously a Freudian dream as having to do with Jews and Nazis.

One "Real Dream" starts with a quote from Macbeth saying: "Infected minds, to their deep pillows, discharge their secrets." Then there's me, describing the dream:

I was at a party. I don't know what we were celebrating. The hostess weaved through the room holding a large sausage to her groin. Every few minutes she would shake the sausage vigorously and vomit. The guests enjoyed the revolting display, applauding, except me. Ech! I figured I might feel better if I washed my face. But when I looked in the mirror, good God, my mustache washed off.

And below the strip, Dr. Shpiegelmann's dream interpretation:

The party is obviously the Nazi party. The hostess bears an uncanny resemblance to Odilo Globocnik, head of the Polish SS. The sausage, a Polish sausage, is roughly the same shape as the map of occupied Poland.

"Real Dream (A Hand Job)" (1975).

The "revolting" display symbolizes the tragic uprising of the Jews of the Warsaw Ghetto. And when the dreamer attempts to wipe away the horrors of World War II (his mustache) he is nevertheless left face to face with the naked truth of his own guilt.

I did about three or four "Real Dreams" and then I invited people to
send me their dreams. As they came in I realized I was much more interested in my own dreams than I was in other people's. I know exactly
how to dream up the imagery that will make my short hairs stand up
and get the various parts of me to light up and jangle. It's not as easy
with other people's imagery.

Occasionally I've drawn a dream and occasionally I just allow an
image to stay conscious, allowing it to come back so I can have it more
concretely present.

I only remember the dreams I've drawn. The other ones I can kind of
conjure up if I look back over my dream notebook. Let's see, here's one.
How's this?

> I'm taking care of [my daughter] Nadja. I pick her up by the head. She
> slips in my hands. I think she's okay at first. She's crying. I look again and
> see I've pulled part of her ear off by mistake. She's howling. Françoise and
> a friend of ours are aghast but put the ear back into position and it sticks.
> They've fixed her. The feeling of pulling the ear off is like pulling on an
> old kneaded eraser.

It took me a while to get used to having the idea of being a father
and having a kid, finding a way to do that that wasn't recapitulating my
father's and my relationship.

I tried to include a dream section in *Maus* that I ended up kicking out.
It would've been in the section in *Maus* where I'm with the therapist. I'm
talking to him about a dream that I'd had that had to do with the skit-
tishness about having a kid. So this is all from the same period:

> My downstairs neighbor, George, tells me he's going to the doctor or den-
> tist. Next time I see him he points out that his hands have been removed.
> His arms are shortened and narrowed in circumference. Somehow they're
> attached to wires in his mouth. He's quite casual about it, says it's tempo-
> rary. In the next few days I meet George at the mailbox and we enter into
> a mail competition: who gets more. I'm winning.

George, the person in the dream, had a child a month before I did. So
that's the topic of this dream. His hands being cut off by having a kid
seems to me like a real limitation of freedom. And then I dream of this
"male" competition with him about having kids.

That's what my dreams are like. You know, the usual muck. I find that
I can't work right after waking up, like some of my friends do. That's

because whatever is going on in the dream life has to clear out before I can start making the conscious dream.

The most comfortable time for me to work is in the afternoons and into the evenings. When life patterns allowed, it would be working through the night.

In the morning I usually do errands. You know, like telephone calls, letters. The early part of the day is just taking care of stuff where the genie doesn't have to come out of the bottle.

When I'm writing any sound just jangles, but when I'm drawing I start by listening to music. On occasion I use music consciously. In fact I have four tapes, ninety minutes each, of the complete works of the Comedian Harmonists, which was a German popular group in the twenties. I listen to a lot of twenties' and thirties' music in general—the kind of stuff that was used for the sound track in Betty Boop films. The history of the people in the Comedian Harmonists resonated so deeply into the stories of *Maus* that it was the best and most appropriate music I could find.

I would listen to these fourteen hours over and over and over again until Françoise was ready to drive me out of the house with my tape recorder, never to darken the door again. That music conjured up a lot for me. Yet, after a certain point, I wasn't hearing music. Or I would just be listening and not working. So I'd just get involved in talk radio.

I listen to whatever drivel talk radio I can find. Good talk radio, if I can find it. But even if it's just some kind of right-wing rant, I figure the left brain can kind of get occupied there and leave my right brain alone to draw. It has to be conversation, if it's music then it really starts seeping in to right brain activity.

I'll actually engage with the radio. Part of me will be going, "That son of a bitch, he can't say that! What about, you know, Nixon? What about, you know, whatever?" See, if I wasn't doing that, if I was working quietly, my mind would be moving around useless circles. Like thinking about somebody who had slighted me in some minor way. So my "That son of a bitch, he can't get away with that" takes all that and puts it somewhere in the air waves and leaves me alone so I can get my work done.

"Words and Pictures Together": An Interview with Art Spiegelman

SUSAN JACOBOWITZ / 1994

From *Writing on the Edge*, Fall 1994, pp. 49–58. Reprinted by permission of Writing on the Edge, University of California.

Born in Stockholm in 1948, Art Spiegelman came with his parents to the United States when he was three years old. He was raised in Queens, New York, and became a fixture in the underground comix scene. He and his wife, Françoise Mouly, founded and co-edited *RAW*, the critically acclaimed magazine of avant-garde comics. Spiegelman was catapulted into the mainstream of American culture (and international fame) with *Maus: A Survivor's Tale* (1986) and *Maus II: And Here My Troubles Began* (1991), his two-volume comic book re-creation of his parents' experiences in the Holocaust. For this achievement, Spiegelman was awarded a special Pulitzer Prize in 1992.

The *Maus* project took thirteen years to complete. Working from oral history taken from his father, Vladek, as well as from other sources, the first volume appeared after eight years in order to avoid any complications that might stem from the release of Steven Spielberg's animated feature, *An American Tail*, in which Jews were also depicted as mice. In *Maus*, Spiegelman moves back and forth between the present and the past, interweaving within a double narrative the story of his parents' trauma with some of his own frustrations and anguish as he tries to understand his place in history, exploring some classic Second Generation themes. *Maus* has currently been translated into sixteen languages and there are almost 400,000 copies in print.

Spiegelman is currently a contributing editor and artist for the *New Yorker*—one of his more striking covers featured a Chassidic Jew and a black woman entwined, kissing. His most recent project, through Pantheon Press, is an illustrated version of "The Wild Party," Joseph Moncure March's "lost" underground Jazz Age classic (1928), which garnered a cult following soon after its publication in a very limited first edition.

WOE: I've been reading back issues of *RAW*. Is *RAW* still coming out?
Spiegelman: *RAW* is in deep freeze at the moment. It's not dead and rancid, but it's not really in development. It was always a "mom and pop" shop, and Françoise and I are both so otherwise engaged at the moment. Françoise is now the Art Editor of the *New Yorker*. I'm working on a book of drawings to accompany a poem called "The Wild Party" and doing stuff for the *New Yorker* both as an editor and a cartoonist. So it was just too hard to keep the magazine afloat. It would only have stayed afloat if we had willed it afloat. It's just too hard to think about doing another issue right now.

Also, a lot of the artists we first published have gotten their wings and there are now lots of places they can appear. *RAW* isn't needed in the same way because there are other ways that work can now be seen.

WOE: What is the poem that you're illustrating—is it a poem you've written?
Spiegelman: No, "The Wild Party" was written in 1928. I found it in a used book store decades ago and was fond of it. I originally contracted to do twelve pictures, but that has grown to be about seventy and, as a result, I'm late on the book.

WOE: Your *New Yorker* cover, the one of the Chassidic Jew and the black woman embracing, was very intriguing, a wonderful piece. Will some of your work continue to have a Jewish theme?

Spiegelman: I'm not even quite sure what it is to be Jewish, but I know that whatever it is, I am. So if someone works out of a strong autobiographical position, it's inevitable that sometimes the more overtly Jewish component is going to come forward.

WOE: Are comics beginning to be more accepted in our society?
Spiegelman: From here it feels like there's the beginning of change, in terms of academic and highbrow museum interest at least. The landscape has shifted a lot in the last few years.

WOE: When I was a child, my father was always sneaking into my bedroom to throw away my comic books. Ironically, my 300 superhero comics are now my only financial asset.
Spiegelman: Superhero comics seem so much like boy power fantasies. It made more sense when, back in the fifties, girls could read love comics, not superhero comics. There were more genres around then. Crime comics, for instance.

WOE: There were a lot of female superheroes: Black Canary, Wonder Woman. Groups like the Justice League and the Avengers and the Fantastic Four all had women mixed in.
    Were there other early influences you could cite besides publications like *Mad* magazine?

Spiegelman: It's more a question of being seen in a certain light, in a certain company, than of accurately describing what may have influenced you. I believe that I was probably as influenced by some off-brand logo design—a weird cartoon character that I don't even remember seeing, for instance—as I might be by say, Winsor McCay or George Herriman. Or some bad kid books that don't even deserve to be remembered may have changed my life without me really knowing or remembering that. Out of the conscious influences that I have attended to and have learned from, Harvey Kurtzman is up there, and George Herriman's *Krazy Kat*, Winsor McCay's *Little Nemo* and *Dreams of a Rarebit Fiend* and Jack Cole's *Plastic Man*, a wonderfully drawn strip in the forties, and Milt Gross, one of America's great Jewish dialogue artists who actually was a screen writer for Charlie Chaplin. There are lots of cartoonists who influenced me. And I discovered Kafka as a pretty young kid. His work was important to me as an extension of the *Twilight Zone*.

WOE: Do you think of yourself as a writer?

Spiegelman: Sure, and as a drawer—actually as someone who probably fails equally well at both.

WOE: When you envision a project, do the pictures usually precede the narrative?

Spiegelman: It really has happened both ways. More often than not, I'm in service to an idea. First comes an abstract idea that usually has a verbal component before it has a visual component. This happens more often than not, although the opposite has happened as well. For instance, I would say that the Chassidic cover started out as a picture before it had any content. But usually, there's an idea and a surface to that idea. As a result, my drawings really shift in style a bit from picture to picture because I'm trying to find the appropriate visual container for the idea.

WOE: Have you considered working in prose, writing something without the use of pictures?

Spiegelman: I'm interested in all three. Pictures without words, words without pictures, and words and pictures together are all interesting to me.

WOE: At some point, especially when the problem arose with the animated Spielberg picture, you must have wondered if *Maus* would ever really get out and have an impact.

Spiegelman: Well, the Spielberg film propelled Part I of *Maus* into the world without Part II being complete, so I could beat the film to the cash-and-carry counter. I never really had expectations of *Maus* becoming a best seller or a cultural icon of any kind. I really thought of myself as kind of a cult artist: somebody who had a small respectful following and who would then get discovered after he died of lung cancer at the age of fifty. *Maus* really wasn't done with any eye towards major commercial success. On the other hand, it *was* a nod to external reality in that my comics prior to *Maus* had been getting more and more formal, structural (those words aren't really right). I was trying to understand the anatomy of comics, their language, rather than trying to tell a story per se. As a result, my work was very difficult for most people to understand. I realized that if I was going keep on doing comics—part of my definition of comics was a series of words and pictures intended for reproduction—pretty soon I'd be in a position where I wouldn't have to reproduce my work; I could just pass it around to the people who knew what I was talking about.

I realized that what most people really want is a narrative series of words and pictures with the emphasis on the narrative. That was a problem for me because I draw so slowly. To tell a joke or some kind of escapist fantasy story didn't seem to be worth the amount of effort involved. That's when it became clear that I should really expand this three-page strip I had done back in '72 because it was a narrative worth telling. To the degree that I thought, "Well, okay, comics are supposed to be narrative; by God, I can do that," I had an eye towards an audience. Not towards success, but at least towards an audience.

WOE: You also did "Prisoner on the Hell Planet." Was that the first time you tapped into your own experience and worked with something that autobiographical?

Spiegelman: I had already done that early three-page version of *Maus* a year before, but it was still a good six years before I ever even started thinking of *Maus* as a long book. A cartoonist named Justin Green was a very important factor in all of this because he really opened up confessional autobiography as a possible area for cartoonists to explore. It just didn't exist as a category before his work. He wrote something called "Binky Brown Meets the Holy Virgin Mary," which was about himself, Justin Green, and the guilt and repression and obsessive compulsive disorder that came from growing up Catholic.

WOE: "Prisoner on the Hell Planet" really struck me as very powerful, particularly because of the high rate of mental breakdown among children of Holocaust survivors. Do you relate your breakdown directly to the experience of being a child of Holocaust survivors?

Spiegelman: Well, it grew out of my experience. One set of kids I grew up with were kids of survivors, since that's what made up my parents' social set. Another set of friends had nothing to do with that. When I was growing up my parents' experience just didn't seem important to me one way or the other. Only after I moved away from home and went to college did I have any distance at all on what had happened to my parents, and I realized then that there was a stress in my household that wasn't everybody's experience growing up.

When working on *Maus* I thought it would be useful to go and visit some of the then-incipient Second Generation groups. I must say that I didn't have a strong feeling of commonality with the people I met there.

Which isn't to say anything one way or another, because there may have been a strong element of self-selection among the kind of people who would identify themselves as wanting to belong to a Second Generation group, and these people wouldn't necessarily be representative of all of those whose parents might have gone through one version or another of the Holocaust.

WOE: So being identified as a voice of the Second Generation—or something like that—doesn't appeal to you?

Spiegelman: I've been very reluctant to lend myself to that sort of identification because I don't really want to be a spokesperson. I'm glad to find that there's a commonality of experience that allows people to see something in *Maus* that's useful to them. For me it's just as interesting to meet Chinese and black kids who have had similar power struggles with their parents and are able to identify through that experience. So I'm just not able to peg my experience that simply. If I want to go to a support group of some kind, why should I go to a Second Generation group? I could go to a group of people whose mothers committed suicide, or a group for artists who are feeling blocked and frustrated in their work (at one point that would have been an appropriate group for me), or a group of former mental hospital inmates—I could locate myself in a number of different cross sections of fellow-sufferers.

This anecdote pegged it for me. I was invited as a guest to one of these Second Generation groups to respond to some film by a child of survivors, so I did. Afterwards, a woman got up to make an announcement, saying that the Second Generation singles party was going to be held at Temple Emmanuel six weeks later. I realized, "Wow, this is a problem," because I couldn't imagine the kinds of pick-up lines that would be involved—something like, "Which camps were your parents in?" I'm sure such groups are helpful to people and that I actually do have a lot in common with them, including my rather ironic distancing from the Holocaust. There's at least a certain type of commonality between children of survivors, but I'm really not interested in the blurring of uniqueness that's involved in finding commonality.

WOE: Do you think that the focus on the Holocaust, whether through Second Generation groups or Holocaust museums or special programs, is taking attention away from the atrocities that are currently being committed?

Spiegelman: Right now I'm waiting to hear from the Holocaust Museum in Washington, where I've proposed that they have a temporary exhibit called "Genocide Now." I thought that my proposal would just be rejected out of hand, but they're weighing it. I doubt that they'll do it. But I would be interested in dropping everything and curating such a thing because it would reshape the meaning of the Holocaust Museum, which now is more a monument to Jewish American political clout than to the actualities and dynamics of history and politics and race-hate.

I was very careful when doing *Maus* to stay close to things that were small and true so that it wouldn't become an easily inflatable float for a cause. Early on while I was doing *Maus*, the Holocaust TV series came on. It was appalling. For one thing, it moved towards eliciting emotional responses and, second, it recast the Holocaust as a "birth of Israel" story as if there was some use to the Holocaust, as if Israel was a worthy prize for that suffering. I've seen the Holocaust used and abused to various political ends: used by Palestinians, blacks, Zionists. In *Maus* I was really just trying to deal with actuality and not make it into a political tract so that there's an understanding of the universal dynamic that took very specific form in Hitler's Europe. But there's no agenda in that focus. I'm grateful that *Maus* remains in print, even as a kind of "Holocaust for Beginners" book, among other things. And yet I never intended it as a teaching tool of the Holocaust. I don't think it replaces the various histories that are around although it may well be many people's only close up exposure to this kind of material.

WOE: *Maus* is being taught in various survey courses at the university level around the country. What is your reaction to that?

Spiegelman: Well, gratitude because it keeps my book in print but also a kind of wariness because it turns *Maus* into a kind of official culture that may not allow it to live and breathe. Comics were never meant to he studied at school; they were meant to be read while the teacher thought you were doing something else. You could keep a comic book under your textbook. In terms of the way the Holocaust has entered into Jewish American consciousness, there's something sad and dangerous in that, along with the existence of Israel as being important to American Jews, the Holocaust is one of their defining aspects, more so than Tisha B'av or Sukkot or something (I'm lucky I'm able to conjure the right holiday names). It's like envisioning a future in which Christians walk around wearing crucifixes and Jews walk around wearing small gas chambers around their necks. It becomes this closed-off martyrology that doesn't necessarily open up into what it is to be a passive witness to ethnic cleansing.

WOE: That's a very disturbing phenomenon. The feeling of helplessness is particularly difficult to bear.
Spiegelman: Well, maybe *Maus* will create more sympathy for non-Jewish Poles. We've all become that. Up until a few years ago, I was saying, we're all Jews, even Yasir Arafat, Elie Weisel, whoever. But now, I'm beginning to think that many of us are Poles. The Poles were the victimized witnesses. They weren't the central dynamic. Some acted well, some acted badly.

WOE: But weren't they all complicit in some way?
Spiegelman: By definition, they were made complicit. And now we're all complicit. And we live our lives without the suffering going on somewhere to the side being the central event.

WOE: That's the really torturous thing about it. Growing up, I always imagined that, if it had been me, I would have done something. Now, as adults, we're confronted with the reality that sometimes there's very little that people can do. That's a very uncomfortable position to be in.
Spiegelman: Absolutely.

WOE: There's a photograph of your father towards the end of *Maus II*, the only real representation of him. He had a portrait taken of himself in a concentration camp uniform after the war. How was he able to put that clothing back on and sit for a portrait?
Spiegelman: It looks like he had a fine time having that portrait taken—he looks rather cheerful in an odd way. It's a troubling photo.

The thing that's interesting to me about what you just said is that that was the only "real" representation of him. Somebody is doing a paper on the use of photographs in *Maus*. It's an interesting subject for me and one which should be weighed very carefully because, in some ways, a photo is a wonderfully baffling bit of almost surreality in the book. One's image of a Holocaust survivor is not as a proud wearer of a uniform who (at least in that photo) looks relatively healthy, but as someone haggard, dressed in rags, which he was several months prior. But nevertheless, that photo is screwy evidence of God knows what. And the Vladek in that photo certainly isn't the Vladek that I knew as his son, fifteen, twenty, or thirty years later. I don't know what it's evidence of, except that it's this interesting photo that gives you another face to attach to the narrative that you've been in. Of course, I wanted something to pull you away from the Vladek screened through Art, and the photo offered that. One of the important components of the San Francisco show and a very important component of the one *Maus* "licensed" project that I'm working on (a CD/ROM disc) is my taped interviews with Vladek. His voice provides something in a way equivalent to that photograph. It's not filtered through his son; it's just there. Vladek was a good storyteller in his own right. The tapes have a strength for me.

WOE: What else will be part of the CD/ROM package?
Spiegelman: A number of rough sketches, photographic documentation that I used to make some of the drawings, preliminary drafts, notebook work, an interview that you can access on certain pages where it's appropriate.

WOE: So it's "The Making of *Maus*," something like that?
Spiegelman: The *Maus* books are available on screen, the two books together, and then there's a kind of menu on the side. From that you can access a transcript of the tapes and an audio of the tapes and family photographs where that's appropriate and a historical timeline where it's appropriate. I think there's some footage of my trip to Auschwitz that I used when I was working on the book. So there's the book and then other layers of historical, personal, and family information. The idea of being able to pull together a record of those things has always been interesting to me.

WOE: I understand what you're saying about not wanting to be identified as Second Generation for social reasons. But in other interviews, I've also read that being a child of Holocaust survivors was very important to you in shaping your voice and your consciousness as an artist, that it's a big part of your identity. I'm wondering about that in relation to your children. Do you think that some of the things that have been such big experiences in your own life will stop with you?
Spiegelman: If I had the choice, maybe. Since I don't, I haven't given it that much thought. If I did, I would probably choose to not let it affect my kids. On the other hand, I believe that it's inevitable. If nothing else, there's the existence of *Maus*. It's the family history. I did a strip with Maurice Sendak in the *New Yorker* where we were talking about that very point. I interviewed Maurice in this little comic strip—I drew me and

he drew him. Here are a few panels: I find out from him that he's working on illustrating Melville's novel *Pierre*. I say, "You're doing a book for grown-ups?" and he says, "Kid books, grown-up books, that's just marketing. Books are books." And I say, "I suppose, but when parents give *Maus*, my book about Auschwitz, to their little kids, I think it's child abuse." I want to protect my kids. When Nadja, my six-year-old daughter, was asked what I do for a living, she just said, "Daddy draws mice," and then went on to something else.

WOE: When you teach, how does that tie in with your work? Do you feel that it takes time away from your work?

Spiegelman: Well, at a certain point, it was taking time away from my work and I had to stop. When I was first beginning to teach, it was very useful to me to be able to articulate what it was in comics that was interesting to me, and by analyzing other people's work and what was important in that work for me, I was learning a lot. Only when I began to be a stand-up performer doing schtick, teaching the same class for the eighth or tenth or twelfth time, did I begin to realize that it was deadening rather than nourishing. That's when I pulled out. On the other hand, I'd like to coalesce my thoughts about this stuff by teaching; doing some teaching again will be useful, and I do want to do a book about the history and aesthetics of comics and maybe even some comics projects related to that subject.

WOE: Is cartooning something that can be taught?

Spiegelman: To a large degree, yes, although I think it's really like learning language, like learning to read and write. Creating comics is not exactly drawing—it's a kind of sign-making. Some people have good handwriting and some people have bad handwriting. But there's a thought process involved in organizing one's thoughts in comics that's certainly teachable. Nevertheless, if you want to be any good, it has to be more of a calling.

WOE: Are you teaching now?

Spiegelman: Lecturing, not teaching, although by next year I may have set something up. I want to teach the history-of-comics class at least one more time so I can organize my thoughts towards making a book on the history of comics. And so I'm talking about maybe teaching next year for a semester.

WOE: Do you have any regrets about becoming mainstream?

Spiegelman: I guess I'm deluded enough to still think of myself as not.

WOE: Well, let's see, I found twenty-three articles and five book references to *Maus* in the library.

Spiegelman: I guess that is mainstream. I figured as long as I didn't get it made into a movie, it wouldn't be mainstream. What can I say? It's a mixed blessing. I can't really complain about it—I'll start sounding like I have a Rolls Royce but the ashtrays are full.

The down side is that it's hard to escape from the false self created by others, and that's even true when alone at a drawing table. I have to shove it off and push it away and find out what's important to me outside of other people's expectations. At this point I'm carrying a 500-pound mouse on my back, which might even become my tombstone. Success and popularity are drugs, and it's difficult to arrange myself in a way to stay free of the desire for another fix. That's one of the more pernicious aspects of success. On a more minor level, my time is more fragmented because there are more demands made on me than when nobody gave a shit about what I was doing. So those are the problems.

There are too many up sides for me to focus on the down side of it. For one thing, the economic freedom to pursue ideas as they occur to me is really an exquisite luxury. And the ability to find somebody willing to take me seriously when I suggest an absolutely insane project that nobody would listen to except for the fact that I can say, "Well look, I have a Pulitzer Prize; you should be able to listen to this with a straight face." I can propose projects that would otherwise not be heard out.

At a certain point in my life, a lot of people asked me whether I was sorry or glad that I had taken LSD. It was a question that always left me stuttering because, since I had taken it, couldn't imagine what my brain would be like if I hadn't. And now it's equally true to say that whatever it is that's happened to me has so thoroughly happened that it's just a part of the equation. I can get nostalgic for moments when I was working for a world that didn't care and didn't understand and thereby be nostalgic for a more useful self, but that world is out of my experience now. Although I'm really grateful for the existence of *Maus*—it was wonderful to articulate something that profound for me, with such obvious resonance in the world—I'm left with redefining myself in a world that thinks of me as the *Maus* man. For instance, you asked me about other children of survivors. I think one of their common frustrations is what to do with this baggage. And at least on some level, *Maus* answers that for me.

Art Spiegelman

ANDREA JUNO / 1997

From *Dangerous Drawings* by Andrea
Juno, Juno Books, 1997, pp. 6–31.
Reprinted by permission of Andrea Juno.

Art Spiegelman was born in 1948 and lived in New York with his Polish
parents. He graduated from the High School for Art and Design in New
York and then attended classes at Harpur College (State University of
New York at Binghamton) until he was committed to a mental hospital in
1966. In 1971, he moved to San Francisco and began to publish in a
variety of underground comic publications. He co-edited an extraordinary book called *Whole Grains: A Book of Quotations* (1972)—a contemporary take on *Bartlett's Quotations*. In 1975, he and Bill Griffith
co-founded *Arcade*, an influential comix revue that published many of
the now legendary comix artists including R. Crumb, S. Clay Wilson,
and Justin Green. His early work was reprinted in an anthology called
Breakdowns published in 1977. It is a brilliant, urbane, and witty

collection in which he explores a variety of complex narrative and formal experiments that show the wide range of styles he is capable of rendering.

In 1980, Spiegelman and wife Françoise Mouly created their own "comix & graphix" magazine *RAW* which showcased emerging new aesthetics in comics and graphics and was highly influential in forwarding cartooning as an intellectual art form. *RAW* introduced European and Japanese cartoonists and artists and published for the first time many Americans such as Gary Panter, Chris Ware, Mark Beyer, and Charles Burns. He supplemented his income by making up *Wacky Packages* and *Garbage Pail Kids* for the Topps Gum Company, where he started working in 1966. *Maus, Volume I: A Survivor's Tale* (1986) and *Maus, Volume II* (1992) comprise the Pulitzer Prize–winning graphic novel which began in 1971. It's a masterful story of the Holocaust in comic book form as seen through the recollections of Spiegelman's father, Vladek. It is also the story of the tortured relationship between father and son as well as the son's tortured relationship to art. The powerful narrative is laced with textual and pictorial metaphors and irony. It has garnered more critical acclaim than any other comic work. Spiegelman is currently involved with a variety of projects. Among them are covers for the *New Yorker*, comic strip journalism, writing projects and lecturing. He lives in Manhattan with his wife, Françoise and his two children.

Andrea Juno: I read in an article that you wanted to "confound and implicate the reader." Because comics are a multi-layered form and you have to synthesize picture and text, I think it has the ability to confront the reader. Its seeming innocence can be a transmission for subversion. Do you think that's inherent in comics?

Art Spiegelman: It can be, but I don't know if it's implicit to the medium. In the early twentieth century, you have something that takes place in comics—they start to get associated with the lower classes. They're the part of the newspaper that's luring in people who are semi-literate—the new immigrants to America. Urban immigrants are flocking to the papers, and the kind of things they laugh at are looked down upon as vulgar by the more genteel classes. And that's where the early comics energy comes from. You have this strip called *The Yellow Kid* which takes place in a slum in New York City with kids being thrown out of windows, torturing animals, making fun of minorities. It's real popular, and pretty quickly social uplift groups are coming around trying to squash this stuff. A reaction happened even *within* comics, a reaction which keeps happening, and is interesting to watch between the vulgar and the genteel. Both the Pulitzer's *World* and Hearst's *Journal* were vying for *The Yellow Kid*. They both start to carry it, drawn by two different artists. The original creator did another comic strip called *Buster Brown*. Buster's this Edwardian-dressed kid who lives in the suburbs with his dog—his mischief is spilling ink, not spilling blood. There's also *Little Nemo in Slumberland* which again offers an upper middle-class suburban fairyland dream, as a response to the mayhem of the "vulgar" comics. I think this tug is still going on in comics. I'm not sure what side of the tug I'm on.

AJ: It's complicated when you win a Pulitzer.
AS: It is. Certainly, knew I was doing something for an audience that would read books. I wasn't necessarily trying to talk to the people who were reading *Batman*.

In the mid-'70s, Bill Griffith and I edited a magazine called *Arcade*. R. Crumb did most of the covers. Crumb and I had interesting arguments about the whole "genteel versus vulgar" tension of comics. After *Arcade*, he went off and edited *Weirdo* comics. I went off and did *RAW* magazine. *RAW* was doing a *Little Nemo* trip. It was definitely tugging things toward a more elegant presentation, selecting work by people who were conscious of themselves as artists. That's very different than *Weirdo*, a good magazine, but more interested in printing the jokes that were on toilet rolls as their fill-in material whereas *RAW* would print Gustave Doré. I must admit, it's more glamorous to be on the vulgar, *Weirdo* side of the argument. The tug probably has to do with the comic's association with subversion of social norms, with vulgarity, and a kind of immediateness and energy. What makes comics highly charged is the fact that they get to fly below the critical radar. People don't have any expectations when they approach a comic strip; thereby it's allowed to grapple with things very directly, it doesn't have to get past a lot of baggage.

AJ: People associate the form with something infantile and lowbrow—
AS: It looks cozy when you first come up against it.

AJ: And cuddly.
AS: Concerning the formal issues of comics it's worth noting that they recapitulate the way the brain works. It's primitive, not in the sense of cavemen, but like the early development of language. My kids could

recognize the "Have A Nice Day" smiling face way before they could talk. I think we're wired to understand simplified pictures. In other words, when you're remembering someone you don't conjure up a hologram of them, you conjure up a caricature. Comics are also an art of condensation. Even a text-heavy strip has fewer words than a short essay.

AJ: Then why do so many people have difficulty with comics? They find it demanding to simultaneously read text and look at pictures?
AS: I've heard that, and it probably reveals a cultural bias against the form. Philip Roth told me that. He said, "I really love your work but I can't look at it and read it at the same time." On the one hand it sounds really humble, like Gerald Ford's not being able to walk and chew gum at the same time. On the other hand, it's a little bit snooty, like saying, "I don't own a television set."

AJ: Didn't you start your work with trying to push the formal limitations of cartoons?
AS: In terms of my own development, in the early to mid-'70s, I became very interested in how narrative a comic strip had to be for it remain a comic strip. Could one create an undertow that dismantled the narrative while appearing to deliver one? How many obstacles could you put in somebody's path before the reader just caved in and couldn't handle it anymore? That was interesting to me for a few years. In comics, formal energies hadn't been tapped, although they had in all the other arts—literature, painting, sculpture, music. . . . Here was this young medium that, in a sense, was the last bastion of figurative drawing. As a result, nobody had become preoccupied with the issues that preoccupied modernist art elsewhere. This was a time [early '70s] when comics were spiraling into new territories by opening up sexual content and being much more overtly transgressive than they'd been before. They were exploring various kinds of content, and reviving certain earlier drawing styles from the 1920s to the '50s, but it seemed that the formal terrain just wasn't being plowed. I became interested in that, and found that everywhere I went, I was making discoveries, and that was fun. These discoveries weren't interesting to a wide audience. I was interested in the fact that comics were a mass medium. That's not something that I turn my nose up at. I think it's great. I think it's amazing that you have a mass medium which can be produced economically. After I put together a collection of strips which had some of those formal issues at their core, I wondered, "What can I do next?" Those questions gave me a good pocket of

energy to work from. I was also inspired by looking at underground or independent film. I don't mean low budget Miramax films, but—

AJ: Experimental non-narrative films like those by Stan Brakhage?
AS: Yes. I became very good friends with Ken Jacobs and Ernie Gehr when I was living in Binghamton, after my student years at SUNY. Although at first I found their work totally opaque, I eventually found my way in enough to understand what they were doing. It opened up a lot of possibilities for me. In comics, I was working out ideas that were inspired by their work. Since part of my definition of comics has to do with work for reproduction (by printing), I reached a point where I wouldn't need to reproduce my work because almost nobody knew what the hell it was about. So if I wanted to make work for print, I figured, "OK, I'm going to have to move around and deal with narrative more directly."

AJ: So your earlier work follows in the tradition of deconstructionist literature and film—explorations of how far one can take the narrative. What led you to do *Maus*?
AS: It just seemed to me that most stories had been told. Therefore, one could do another variation on the same story, or poke around elsewhere. Since I work slowly, it wasn't easy to say, "OK, I'll do a detective story." I mean, gee, it seemed like there were enough detective stories. In 1971, somewhere in the midst of all the other strips, I'd done a three-page strip called "Maus." I realized that *that* was a story worth telling. It had a lot of emotional charge and risk for me. There was an allure to trying to understand the story, and trying to figure out *how* to tell it. When I started to expand it, I didn't realize it would turn into a thirteen-year project. There wasn't a mountain of literature. I was able to do all my research in about three months. There just wasn't that much to read.

AJ: You mean about the Holocaust?
AS: Yes. At that time, especially, it seemed like a story worth telling. I felt I could devote whatever skills I could muster toward this story, and not feel like I was just doing some empty weaving.

AJ: *Maus* not only explores the Holocaust, but also your father's life in Poland.
AS: Yes, so much was connected to it, through my family. I also wanted to do a graphic novel which was a hazy notion being muttered about in certain circles. There were no examples of it. I liked the idea of reading a

comic book that you could put a bookmark into, a book which wasn't just a quick hit. I was also working on *A Life in Ink*, a story about the history of comics, but *Maus* had more difficulties, and I figured, "OK, take on something impossible. Otherwise, why bother?" It really was as basic as that. It had to do with turning thirty. With *Maus*, I found had to subsume many of my formal interests. I was still intrigued with what happens on a page, how pages are structured, how they fit together. But instead of trying to see how I could trip the reader up, the goal was to get people moving forward, to get my eye and thought organized enough so that one could relatively, seamlessly, be able to become absorbed in the narrative.

AJ: Didn't "Prisoner on the Hell Planet," the strip about your mental breakdown, precede *Maus*?

AS: The three-page version of *Maus* was done in 1971, and "Hell Planet" was done in 1972. "Hell Planet" was inspired by Justin Green's comic book, *Binky Brown Meets the Holy Virgin Mary*. Justin has the distinction of being the first real confessional autobiographical cartoonist in the history of comics. He did a comic strip about sexual Catholic guilt. I was living in San Francisco at the time, and actually moved into his apartment just as he was moving out. That's where I started working on "Hell Planet." It was basically my memories of the events surrounding my mother's suicide in 1968. I'd more or less forgotten about her suicide, and when I remembered, it all came back in a rush, and I started trying to note down what had happened and put it in the form of a strip. I wasn't even sure that I was going to publish it at the time. I was trying to find a graphic approach that was appropriate to the subject—a visual analog to the content. Every strip I did looked different from every other strip I did. "Hell Planet" was done in a woodcut German expressionist style—distorted and emotional drawing. It was about my getting out of a mental hospital, and my mother killing herself shortly thereafter. In the years since, I'd say that autobiography has become the primary mode of underground comics—like what superheroes are for the other branch of the comic family tree.

AJ: What do you think about this?

AS: In principle, it's fine. In actuality, it seems like everybody's telling the same story: "I was a lower middle-class guy who grew up in the suburbs and was nerdy and didn't have many friends and I picked my nose and masturbated." It's actually a better story than the superhuman being who comes down from the Planet of Argon, but it's ultimately as constricted a genre, unless somebody has extraordinary insights.

AJ: Well, what do you feel about your own confessional about your mother's suicide and your mental breakdown?
AS: I was dealing with extraordinary events in a life. I wasn't really—

AJ: This is not typical suburban teenage angst.
AS: Well, it was my suburban teenage angst. I'm a bit cynical about the genre of autobiographical comics, though there are good things being done within it. For me, *Maus* has an aspect of autobiography interwoven with other components. "Prisoner on the Hell Planet" was a misguided attempt at catharsis.

AJ: How?
AS: Catharsis doesn't happen. At that time in my life, it was useful for me to lay out particular events in my life, and try to understand them. But there wasn't that rush of liberation that I associate with the idea of catharsis.

AJ: Did you get that with *Maus*?
AS: No, of course not.

AJ: Of course not?
AS: I have a funny "anecdote" about this subject. When *Maus* came out, I suddenly found myself in a very sharp spotlight. I was about to run away, and then *Good Morning America* (I think that was the show) called. I'm going, "Oh, don't know . . . what the hell! This is *ridiculous*. I'll do it!" The day before I went on the show, I talked to a fairly intelligent interviewer for hours. He interviewed me about my whole life. A few hours later, he calls back, and says, "Here are the five questions that Kathie's going to ask you, and here are your answers." (I think it was a woman named Kathie Lee, I was on a couple of those shows.) The whole interview was scripted; I was told what pictures would be shown while I answered. I had to wake up really early for the show, but I went in there pretty prepared. I meet Kathie Lee, and she's trying to make small talk with me before the show. She's obviously never read my book, but she had seen an article on me in *People* magazine. When the interview starts, she asks me question number one. Duck Soup—I'm with her. She asks me question number two, I'm with her. I mean she didn't have a hard job. Somebody else did all the planning. All she had to do was

read off a fucking teleprompter. But somehow, she missed question three. She asks me question number four, and I know that the pictures that are about to come up are related to question number three. I do my best to answer in such a way that I can make use of the illustrations. She asks me question five and flashes pictures from question four. It's getting harder! I sort of admired the fact that we'd gotten through it. We'd fucked up, but nobody would know. She realizes she's fucked up because she has ninety seconds of interview time left, and nothing to ask. At this point, she turns to me and says, "So how do you feel?" Now I was prepared for why the Holocaust, why mice, why comics, but not *how do you feel*. She really threw me there. [laughs] I didn't know how to answer. I said I felt all right, but it was a little early in the morning. I realized that wouldn't get us through, so I pretended that she had asked me whether art was cathartic or not. I answered that question. I don't think she even realized she had been on the edge of an abyss. She's lively. She went on.

AJ: Can I bring up a quote?
AS: Yeah.

AJ: In an interview I read in the book *The New Comics* [Berkley Books], in response to why the subtitle of *RAW #1* was called *The Graphix Magazine of Postponed Suicides*, you answered with a quote from Nietzsche: "The thought of suicide is a great consolation: with the help of it one has got through many a bad night." You continued, "To think about suicide isn't necessarily to commit suicide. It's to acknowledge the possibility and to acknowledge the precariousness of being alive and to affirm it." This sort of goes back to the catharsis issue—as an alternative to conceiving that somehow art is a process where suddenly the big light shines and everything is resolved.
AS: It's just something to do. Thereby you have to postpone this other thing, which might be suicide. The work has its own problems to solve, problems which the artist gets involved in. I'm not sure that it's the same as catharsis. I associate "catharsis" with coming or blowing your nose. It's a clearing out. I don't think I've ever had that sensation from doing comics. It's just too labor intensive and slow. Instead, there's a useful accretion of thought, but it's not the same as having a good cry. Because it's a synthetic medium—you have to draw and write and put those two forms together in a fairly organized way—it doesn't provide the rush of energy that abstract expressionist painters like Jackson Pollock might

experience. With comics, you're cobbling together little things and carefully placing them. It would be like the catharsis of making a 100-faceted wooden jewel box. It's highly crafted work. The mere fact that you've got to draw the same figure thirty times, walking through a door, lying in bed, jumping out a window, . . .

AJ: How long does it take you to draw a page?
AS: I've done one in a couple of days, but it's not unusual for me to spend a couple of months on a page. With *Maus*, once I figured out the basic premise, I was able to do a page in about eight work days. Over a week; less than two weeks was typical.

AJ: So let me ask you the Oprah question.
AS: "How do you feel?"

AJ: [laughs] I don't believe in catharsis, but you have taken your own life as material, your father, your family, etc., and I wonder what the consequences of that are? Was there a growth?
AS: A growth? I think of it as a large wart. [laughs] Well, there's change, but you know, if you don't change after thirteen years, you've got to be made of stone.

AJ: But I would argue that many people in our very unhealthy culture don't grow. Creative expression is not encouraged and most people become more encrusted as they get older.
AS: I can't figure out exactly what happened because my father died in the course of my making the book. That alone is such a major shift. I can never know what his death would have been like if I wasn't making a book about him at the time. Certainly thinking about him for the years after he died was a way of internalizing him differently than if I hadn't been making that book, and that was useful to me in rudimentary pop-psych ways. But the book has had its own life now which has caught me up in its undertow. I have relationships to it other than the pure one that existed while I was making it with very little expectation. I wanted to work on a mass medium, but I thought a mass medium was 7,000 copies. I would say that the response to *Maus* has left me kind of dizzy.

AJ: How many copies has it sold?
AS: I'm not sure. I think, in English, each volume is up in the 400,000 copy zone. I don't keep good track. But without any major pushing, it

still sells about 20-plus thousand each year. It's still selling enough so that I know it's out there in the world. Part of the sales come from the fact that the book is used in colleges, in courses on everything from the Holocaust to post-modern literature to the dysfunctional family.

AJ: What's your take on that?

AS: Well, good—it stays in print. But because *Maus* has actually entered into the world in a certain way that became grafted onto the book, I can't separate those things anymore. It's a complex problem for me. It's not the problem of genocide, or the problem of becoming one's father, but the problems just have to do with the all-American story of success, and it's *weird*. The ramifications have really slowed me down as a cartoonist, not because I've got to go out and be interviewed, but because I feel timid about making comics now. I'm more comfortable doing other kinds of work. Even though I would like to be reabsorbed into a long comic project, I again find that I get in my own way. That has more to do with expectation—it's much easier to work with no expectations. When I did *Maus*, I'd set up an ecosystem that worked. I was getting my money from one place, and creating something else.

AJ: You had—

AS: Bubble gum.

AJ: Topps.

AS: Yeah, I was in the bubble gum industry. For many years I worked for Topps, and I put in a couple of days a week making up Wacky Packages and Garbage Pail Kids. It brought me a five-day week for myself. So that was pretty clean. Now, I don't have to work with the bubble gum company. I could go ahead and do another comics project without having to earn a living elsewhere because I'd have a contract just waiting for me to dive in. But I've tried several things and haven't been comfortable working on them. Part of it is just knowing that the way I work is like contracting for an almost fatal disease—signing on the dotted line means I'm in for anywhere from seven to twelve years. It makes me wary of saying yes. I've been doing a lot of shorter things, as holding actions and exploratory probes. The *New Yorker* was a useful job to come along for me; it allows me to do cartoon graphics for their covers. Part of the pressure goes away for me when I don't have to work on comics. It allows thought to develop more freely because I don't have that 2,000-pound *Maus* chasing me.

AJ: All those eyes looking at you.

AS: I keep brushing them off my shoulder: "What comic is *he* going to do next?" It's unpleasant to have to think of myself in the third person.

AJ: Your situation brings up the twentieth-century dilemma—should an artist be a star? Were they better off when they were considered as low as whores and pimps?

AS: The situation of fame is certainly not something I want to sit here and whine about. Economically, it makes things a lot easier than they were. Now, if I get some nutty notion in my head, there's usually a way to implement it. Before, I'd just be looked at cross-eyed. The down side has to do with the objectification of myself, an objectification that just isn't useful to me. Some cartoonists handle it very well. Matt Groening doesn't seem to have any problem with this stuff at all. Lynda Barry told me, "You don't understand—when you were in high school, you were the class creep, and when Matt was in high school he was the class president."

AJ: So he knows how to be politic.

AS: He knows how to deal with people and he's just not—he doesn't have these conflicts. Crumb thoroughly freaked out over what happened to him in the '60s. His way of dealing with it was to head for the hills. Run. That's probably a very intelligent response.

AJ: He went to France.

AS: Eventually. But even before that, there was an insane flurry of activity over *Fritz the Cat*. He rejected it all. My response has been more complicated. I haven't rejected it and I haven't been able to live with it. My problem is microscopic compared to what some people go through, but it's enough to already have thrown me. It didn't take much. [laughs] I'm lucky I haven't dealt with film or TV; that's where the fame machine kicks in. Crumb's had to face it again, because of the movie made about him. Without TV or film exposure, cartoonists stay in subcultures. There are many wonderful cartoonists who are known to hundreds of people. In some ways, I find their situation very enviable.

AJ: Your books have spawned a growth of their own that has nothing to do with the original intent.

AS: God, there was a stupid article in the *LA Times* "Lifestyle" section about "Generation J"— the new Jews interested in their roots and heritage. They profiled a woman with a shaved head and concentration camp imagery tattooed all over her body. And she's citing *me* as an inspiration. I can't be responsible. I don't have the money for a shrink who could get me out of that one. So yes, work has unforeseen consequences when it goes out in the world.

AJ: You said that when you started *Maus*, it took three months to learn about the Holocaust. What do you think about the present deluge of literature?

AS: I think what you might be asking me about is a subject that is a cause of concern—the fact that *Maus* shows are frequently requested by Jewish museums. I don't want *Maus* to be shown in Jewish museums. It's not out of anti-Semitism. It's out of malaise and unease with the idea that the single binding mechanism for Jews should be the Holocaust. I have no strong interest in any religion, Judaism included. I'm very interested in the cultural condition of the diaspora Jew.

AJ: Could you explain that?

AS: Stalin pejoratively referred to the "rootless cosmopolitan." I actually like the idea of not being at home anywhere. "Rootless cosmopolitan" is an accurate description of life at the tail end of this century. It's an appropriate adaptation to a world where nationalism is crumbling. I don't really associate it with Jews anymore; it's just like we live on the subway that goes from Tokyo to Paris to Bali to New York, and you can get your McDonald's food at every stop. I take pleasure in that kind of borderless culture, and Jews have practice at it. They've got their own lingo that they take from country to country. The self-deprecatory Jewish humor seems like a good survival technique. But I'm not comfortable with the idea of people finding their Jewishness by identifying with mass victimization of other Jews just because they were Jews.

There's something a little bit wacky about the Holocaust becoming a weird badge of honor for Jews, and I don't want to lend my work to it. It caused my breakup with my gallery. I spent a year and a half getting out of my contract, so I could have more control over where the work is shown. I've begged Jewish Museums to do community outreach programs. I want the work to be presented to as broad a community as possible. I prefer that the work be shown in other kinds of museums, other kinds of gallery situations, at universities. A few years ago, when I had conversations about having a *Maus* show at the Holocaust Museum in Washington, D.C., I indicated I didn't like this idea. The Holocaust Museum didn't need *Maus*, and *Maus* didn't need the authority of the

Holocaust Museum to make itself understood. On the other hand, I'd
be game to curate a show about Bosnia. I actually acted as a catalyst to
get a show about Bosnia, a show which, to me, was a justification of
that museum's existence. Unfortunately, I got kicked out as curator
fairly early on.

AJ: Why?

AS: I wanted to call the show "Genocide Now" and that's where we ran
into trouble: "Does it have to be called Genocide Now? Got a better
one? Can't we just talk about atrocities in former Yugoslavia?" Well, if
the situation in Bosnia looks and smells like a genocide, it probably is.
They were still against the title, and the best alternative I could come up
with was: "Never Again and Again and Again." They didn't like that title
either, and that was about the time I checked out. But they pursued it,
and I'm glad that a museum could put on a show that didn't have connections to the current identity politics which have consumed America.

AJ: I know it's thorny territory.

AS: It is, and I feel like I'm speaking out of both sides of my Maus—my
mouth—because Maus has been a beneficiary of identity politics. Maus
is still alive and well in college courses partially because you've got to
read one Chinese author, OK, Amy Tan; you've got to read one black
author, well, let's see, Alice Walker; you've got to read a Jew, Philip
Roth—uh, maybe a comic book would be more fun for the kids. Maus is
on these kind of lists, and it's symptomatic of things gone terribly, terribly askew.

AJ: There's a frightening identity politics of the victim.

AS: I ran into some interesting versions of this with the New Yorker covers. I've learned to stay under cover more because there were too many
crazy problems between me and the magazine, and the magazine and
the rest of the world. But, at first, it was so much fun to do these
provocative images—like the Valentine's Day cover of a black woman
and a Hasid kissing. Some people were upset, but it worked out fine. I
was naïve; I didn't understand why. Because I'm Jewish, and still of the
tribe, I was allowed to make the comment. On the other hand, when I
did an Easter cover depicting an Easter Bunny taxpayer crucified on a tax
form, there was no end of negative comment. The New Yorker lost
advertising. That cover really got me in trouble. The real offense of it
was that I was a Jew commenting on Christians. Nail him to the cross

one more time. I got much more hate mail for that than for anything else I ever did—pencil-scrawled "we'll get you" letters.

AJ: Did you get hate mail like that after *Maus*?

AS: Relatively little, most of the hate mail was from jealous cartoonists. There was nothing like the letters I got from anonymous crazy men about the *New Yorker* cover. I didn't feel well backed up by the *New Yorker* because they were willing to apologize as soon as somebody took offense. I found the response amusing, and thought it should be treated as amusing. I was lecturing in Germany when the cover came out, and I had to fly back to respond to the flak. I went on a TV news show with this Reverend. He's the head of some Christian Anti-Defamation League. He talked about "Christian bashing." The idea of Christian or Catholic bashing was funny to me because they're the majority culture. WASP bashing.

AJ: Which is really in vogue now.

AS: Yeah, and I *really* feel sorry for the poor beleaguered upper-income executives who have to suffer that. [laughs] This Christian organization managed to create a flurry of attention around itself by protesting the movie *Priest*. When the *New Yorker* cover came out, they were on a roll and were not about to give up. The TV reporter asked me, "How would you respond to Reverend so-and-so who says that this illustration is very offensive to all Christians?" And my response was to stretch my arms out and say, "*Mea culpa.*" I thought that was pretty good. But I was told by the publicity department of the *New Yorker* that I shouldn't make anybody mad. So I felt like I was being undercut.

AJ: Were you *that* surprised with the *New Yorker's* response? It's not like they're a bastion of radicalism.

AS: I was more surprised by the intensity of response, but I was also very pleased by it, because it showed that an image can still have power. In a world of photographic images, the fact that a drawing can still provoke a response is encouraging. There were people who liked it—I met them; I received letters. But over all, the negative response was so overwhelming. It makes me feel like I'm not on the same planet. It's like when somebody told me the enormous amount of records Whitney Houston has sold. I started asking around, and not one person that I know owns a Whitney Houston record. Nobody. That means everybody I don't know has two Whitney Houston records, and all of them found me by the mailbox after the *New Yorker* cover came out.

AJ: You said earlier that your interest in *Maus* stemmed from a belief that most stories have been told, and *Maus* was one of the few—
AS: I certainly found a story that I had an interior compulsion to deal with, and I haven't really found anything else as compelling, although I do go to movies and sometimes read novels. They're fun, it's just that I wouldn't want to have done them. There are people who are able to make wonderful things with the notion that a story's just a coat hanger, an armature on which you can drape a lot of ideas. And that works swell, I just haven't been able to figure out where to drape yet. And I'm not even sure to what degree I'm interested in making up a story rather than working on a found object, working on something that happened. I know that I'm more prone to read nonfiction than fiction.

AJ: What do you read?
AS: Well, it depends what I'm researching. There's books there and books here; various different piles. In this pile, there's *Among the Thugs* by Bill Buford, *The Arrow of Time*, a book on eugenics, a book on chaos theory, one on narrative theory, a biography of Philip K. Dick.

AJ: Are you a fan of his work?
AS: Yes. There was a time when Philip K. Dick was the only writer I wanted to meet. We actually corresponded for a while, and I eventually met him. When I was in college, he was the only person describing accurately the same border problems I was having—not being able to figure out where I ended off and everybody else began—not being able to figure out what I was causing and what was being caused onto me. And so, of course I took a leap into infinity and figured out that I was God . . . and four days later I figured out that I was God in a straitjacket, you know. Going into the nut house had to do with getting the bends—coming up for air too quickly from a very claustrophobic home environment by going away to college. Over the years, nothing's changed except I've managed to keep it under control better. I have a stronger sense of what other people's sense of reality is. It's like that TV show, *Family Feud.* Two teams play against each other, and they're not trying to figure out the *right* answer, but the *common* answer. For instance, the host will ask, "What items are in a refrigerator?" Now, in my fridge, you'll find Kodak film and some obscure brand of yogurt. But that's not the right answer. The right answer is milk, butter, or eggs—whatever their demographic testing has told them is the most common item. If you get those answers, you win. That's the game. You're rewarded for knowing what

everyone knows. Well, it's not just on *Family Feud* where you're rewarded for knowing what people know. In life, you have to know what people expect you to know. Otherwise, you end up in the nut house. Now, it's easy, because I've had practice at it. But, when I was twenty, I'd had no practice whatsoever. I wasn't aware of the conventions, and that was a problem. I think that's often described as schizophrenia—that's what I was diagnosed as. My inner landscape is not that different than it was when I was being dragged away, it's just gotten more nuanced. These are issues that Philip K. Dick describes even though he's one of those great examples of a great novelist who's a terrible writer. Or great writer who's a terrible novelist.

AJ: So you actually met him?
AS: Yes, In 1966 or '67, I found a book of his called *Zap Gun* on a drugstore shelf. The blurb said, "A world gone mad and only a cartoonist can save them." It was one of those messages—I thought, "I was meant to buy this book." The second book of his I read, *The Three Stigmata of Palmer Eldritch*, really freaked me out. Halfway into the book, I barricaded my door, wouldn't let my roommate in, and spent the next two days foraging for crackers and not wanting to deal with the outside world because it was way too scary to have it in a book. I wrote him some letters, didn't get an answer, and left it at that. But when I moved to San Francisco, someone in the community of underground cartoonists had met him at a science fiction convention, and said he knew who I was, that my name came up in conversation. At this point I had gotten his address and when I was in Los Angeles, I thought I'd look him up—I figured, what the heck, I'll drive out to his house. His phone had been disconnected, but he was there. I went in, we started talking, I stayed for three days without sleeping very much. It was very electric.

AJ: Did you have an immediate rapport with him?
AS: I think so. Although I've since learned that Phil had immediate rapport with lots of people; he was good at having rapport. He was a very charming, entertaining person. We talked about a range of stuff that I've been talking to you about the edges of: what it was to go nuts, talking about his work, how he did it, what it was. I just wanted to know what his thing was. Then it wasn't as clear to me as it is now, how his work is a very thinly transposed autobiography, even though it appears as science fiction. It's amazing just how prescient a lot of it was. Technological and social possibilities that he couldn't have possibly known in the

mid-'60s. . . . I saw him again, just before he died. We talked all day again, and then the next day, he totally clammed up. His wife Tess told me, "Don't take it personally; Phil's been in the middle of a six-month depression. Yesterday, was the first time he's spoken to anybody."

AJ: Schizophrenia is obviously a pretty meaningless term and our society has no ability to differentiate "altered states of consciousness." Chester Brown has a wonderfully eloquent comic strip essay that addresses the complexities of the misunderstandings and willful political control that surround that medical term "schizophrenia." He also mentions some of my favorite theorists such as R. D. Laing, Thomas Szasz, and Stanislav Grof who I think are very valuable. There's a paucity in our language to describe these states which makes someone like Philip K. Dick very useful. It seems to me that unlike Dick, you obviously have other apparatuses in your personality that allow you to be functional. I've observed that one can lose boundaries but it depends on what other parts of your personality can at least—

AS: Make up for it. The compensating mechanisms. Well, for one thing, I don't have to function in real time very often. When you have a deadline you have to keep yourself pretty much reeled in and then between them it's OK to sprawl, to go into a fugue state. As a result it's possible to accommodate. But it's also possible to get lost, so it's dangerous. I've tried to set this up so I have something like a bunker. Earlier we were talking about the problems with the aftermath of *Maus*. A lot of demands were being made on me fairly continually and I wasn't good at continual. It's OK if you have time to fall apart and then regroup. I don't understand it, I just know that some of the time I can't answer the phone, not because I'm too busy but I just can't figure out what on earth it is. This thing rings. I want to answer it as soon as I can figure out how it works. So—let it take care of itself.

AJ: Then again, it can be a poetically healthy reaction to the intrusiveness of telephones.

AS: I don't know. I think what happens is after a while you just get the rhythm of the ways in which you don't function well—you get used to them. You just bear with it, get veered off into another dimension, but you know you'll be back and you can cope again. It's why I couldn't do a daily comic strip and Bill Griffith can. He's got a tighter mechanism. His breakdowns only come once every fifteen years, not every fifteen minutes. Right now, I'm actually just coming out of a miserable two or three months where I really was in an almost permanent fugue state. During the day, I'd rally for half an hour so I could do something like bring a child home from school.

AJ: What do you think then of the pharmacological use of—
AS: I haven't taken any drugs besides caffeine and nicotine and a little bit of alcohol for a long time now. But I don't rule it out. It's just that it's hard enough to stay focused.

AJ: Actually, I was thinking about the medical establishment's use of drugs from Prozac to—
AS: I don't do that. No, I'm much more interested in the other drugs. I don't medicate myself much in either direction except for the caffeine and nicotine stimulants which are socially acceptable. Drugs like Prozac just seem to be maskings. I'm not interested in masking it, I'm interested in riding it. Actually, I have a predisposition to think well of psychedelic drugs which unmask things. On the other hand, since my main issues have to do with reeling enough of myself back in to get something done, I'm not interested in figuring out how I can reel myself out past that point. But I miss it. I mean, do you do this sort of thing or—?

AJ: Not since the mid-'70s. Like you, I also want to produce creative work and, at present, don't have the leisure time it would take to regain my grounding. But back then I was studying the work of Stanislav Grof and had some very profound experiences with LSD and peyote. Grof was using LSD as a kind of microscope/telescope into the human (un)conscious, inward as well as outer expansion.
AS: One of my oldest friends, a cartoonist named Jay Lynch [*Young Lust*] had a very good one-liner. At some point when I was still having a lot of trouble with these boundaries, he said to me, "Of course we're all one, but don't spread it around." I thought it was a pretty reasonable attitude.

In the days when I was doing drugs of any kind, there was a brief period when I'd try anything. Just to know what it did. As I said, I was most interested in psychedelic drugs. What I *wasn't* interested in were the middle zone psychedelics like marijuana and hash because I wouldn't feel any pleasure. I'd mainly just get either thoroughly confused or crazy-paranoid-unhappy with my surroundings and myself. I wasn't able to see what the fun was. I never had that pleasant buzz that my friends had. But when I was totally blowing my brains out by taking mescaline or LSD, it was genuinely interesting. I wouldn't put it in the category of fun, but fun isn't a meaningful distinction. When it was a bad time, it was such an intensely bad time that it wasn't even a bad time anymore. I have vague desires to just do more of this, even though for the most part, it's well flushed out of my system; we're talking about twenty years ago. But I suspect that it would just make it that much harder to get through a day. On the other hand, it's tempting.

AJ: Getting back to comics, what other forms interest you?
AS: Comic strip journalism is one thing. I did an obituary for Harvey Kurtzman, the creator of *Mad* magazine, in the *New Yorker* using the comic as an essay-like construction. When *Maus* came out, I went to Germany and my publisher took me to Rostock to a housing project where the "foreigners get out" types had burned down the homes of gypsy guest workers. I interviewed the people around there, and did a comic strip about that for the *New Yorker.* I also did a story on the picture collection of the New York Public Library, and interviewed the one guy who seemed to understand the sorting system of this crazy collection. It's the kind of story that, ten years ago, would have been a prose piece in the *New Yorker.* It was reportorial, and involved distilling the best parts of a lengthy interview down to a four-page comic strip. There are some cartoonists who are doing it very well like Joe Sacco.

AJ: Yes, I like his comic book *Palestine*—
AS: Now he's doing something about his stay in Bosnia. But he's running into the same problem I run into, which is in an age of the camera, it's difficult to use illustration as your form of documentation. By the time you've figured out the material and drawn it, news is old because comics are very labor intensive. Still, I've been trying my best to get the *New Yorker* to pursue this type of reportage.

They've sent Bill Griffith to Cuba, Sue Coe to Liverpool to cover the trial of two children who had murdered another child, and Gary Panter to Waco. A few of those stories did appear, and it's an exciting way for a magazine to approach current events. When it comes to news, magazines have the same problem illustrators have. They can't be as current as CNN. Therefore, their best tactic is to be reflective about events that have taken place, to try and understand them. One of the ways events can be well understood is by combining short bursts of words and pictures. Sue Coe did a journalistic piece on garment workers for the *New Yorker* fashion issue, and it was a great piece, the best thing in the issue. It's great when powerful work like that can happen.

AJ: This brings up another issue—your role as an editor, namely of *RAW*, which was so influential and ahead of its time. How did that start?

AS: It goes back to my admiration of Harvey Kurtzman. He was a cartoonist, a cartoon writer, and an editor—he was functioning in all those different areas. One of the things that Kurtzman was able to do very, very well, was ferret out talent. That was a model for me. And *RAW*, which I did with Françoise [Mouly, Spiegelman's wife]—

AJ: Both of you started it together?

AS: Um-hmm. After Bill Griffith and I both got ulcers from *Arcade*, I was smoking four packs of cigarettes a day. "Never again" is the only attitude to have to putting out a magazine. But somehow I got together with Françoise and that's what she wanted and there we were, doing it again. So in 1980, we started *RAW*.

It filled certain needs for us. Françoise wanted to get involved in publishing and originally wanted to publish books. The problem—Françoise's way—was that she went about it by deciding that she should learn how to run a printing press as the first aspect of being a publisher. So before I knew it, we had a printing press in our loft and she was learning to print. And after that—see, I'm unteachable, I know a few things and I've learned those things so I can function with them, but Françoise is more of a polymath type and likes learning curves that she can jump onto. She learned distribution, production, editing, and all of the other facets—which makes her wonderfully overqualified for most normal publishing jobs. Then it became obvious that it would be easier to distribute a magazine. With a book, you have to build up a new constituency each time, whereas with a magazine you can gather an audience with common interests.

Around that time, I was getting hired by magazines such as *Playboy* and *High Times* as a consultant to help them with what they should do with comics in their magazines, but they would never take my consultation. It was very frustrating. I'd always be told, "No, no, we want comics about dope or sex." In *Playboy* they had writers that they were giving a great degree of latitude. Why can't they give the cartoonists the same latitude? So we did the first issue of *RAW* as a one-shot just to show what comics could and should be. We felt there was a *screaming* need—there was a vacuum that needed to get filled. The energy of underground comics had run dry. So *RAW* was done without any intention of ever having a second issue. But it was useful for the cartoonists and it sold out its print run—

RAW was able to present work by people who didn't have a home and weren't doing mainstream cartooning. Charles Burns was a case in point. Even though his work was very fully realized, he couldn't get published in the undergrounds since it wasn't about dope and it didn't look like R. Crumb—it just didn't fit in. Underground comics had gotten fossilized.

We also thought there was a lot of energy in Europe that had been ignited by what had happened in America ten years earlier but nobody here was seeing any of that stuff.

AJ: Who were some of the people you published?
AS: Let's see. Mark Beyer, Winsor McCay, Kaz, Gary Panter, Bill Griffith. Very peculiar cartoonists like Ben Katchor, who had no place to publish. Mariscal, who since has become very well known for, among other things, inventing the symbol for the Barcelona Olympics. Jacques Tardi who's seminal in adult comics in France. The Bazooka group in Paris: Bruno Richard, an artist who called himself Kiki Picasso and another one named Lulu Picasso. They were doing very sophisticated graphics that were comics-inspired. Françoise did one comic strip page about never doing comics. . . . At the time, it was very fresh and exciting finding people that were odd bedfellows—the idea that Sue Coe and Drew Friedman should be in the same magazine is not obvious.

AJ: It also had its dark edges.
AS: I guess, but only slightly more so than *Arcade.* I think the main difference was that it was published by Françoise and I as "ruthless cosmopolitans." It didn't feel as all-American as some of the underground comics felt. We staked out this territory somewhere in the middle of the Atlantic that allowed a cross-fertilization to happen. I guess I'm really proud, looking back on the *RAW* magazines, of how many artists were first seen there. For example, choosing certain European artists that are now central pillars of their country's graphic culture but in 1980 they weren't.

One of the problems we ran into is that comics aren't that easy to edit. And cartoonists aren't that easy to work with. It's much harder to take a comic strip and dismantle it than it is to edit a manuscript. It was a lot easier picking work from Europe that had already been published, so we could know what to choose. And also, on occasion, one could "help" things along in the translation, let's say, that could otherwise be seen as an absolutely unforgivable tampering with people's language. But with the American work, it led to a lot of tensions because cartoonists are an especially impossible bunch to work with, in that there's no money in this. Therefore, all there is is egomania. It's the currency of the avant garde. If you published the work, you were exploiting the people you were publishing; if you didn't publish them, you were denying them something. There was no winning. I just didn't have nerves of steel. The social tensions of *RAW* became impossible. It was inevitable. I couldn't be an editor *and* a peer. Ultimately, I wasn't that interested in being editor. I think now that *RAW* isn't happening, a lot of cartoonists are very wistful for it because it was useful.

AJ: There was something magical and exciting about *RAW*. It juxtaposed both high and low culture, using graphic art and comics.
AS: The genteel and vulgar smashing up against itself. It had a harder-to-define sense of what was interesting than just publishing comics. It had words and pictures and used pictures to communicate. But it also appeared so fully realized. It gave the impression that there was really a generation of people all working in tandem. That's hardly the way Françoise and I experienced it from the inside.

AJ: Then you *are* a good editor.
AS: I think a good magazine is greater than the sum of its parts but it should be made up of great parts. It wasn't a disposable magazine. RAW was trying to be more like a museum than a gallery—something that could be built to last. It took a lot of energy to do. Once we managed to do it twice a year. Once we did it in two years. So it was a biannual in both directions. Bill Griffith, when I was working with him on *Arcade*, was always prolific and is now producing a daily comic strip *[Zippy the Pinhead]*, whereas, I was built to work on something for thirteen years. I admire the other approach, it's just not what I can do. And I think *RAW* is a reflection of that particular impulse, of wanting to get it right no matter what it took, as opposed to wanting to get it out and build on your former achievement in the next strip and hopefully, over time, leave a trail of other pieces of work that got you there. I'm more interested in figuring out how you get to an entire continent and then burn all traces of the road that allowed that new continent to get discovered. *RAW* had some of those qualities of being fully realized territories. The advantage to it was that it got picked up on by people way outside the obvious constituency that would never look at comics. I think it changed the way the New York gallery and museum world viewed this kind of picture

making. And it created a violent reaction against it on the part of other cartoonists who were very interested in keeping the cheesiness of comics alive and well. There were cartoonists who were really upset by the idea of comics aspiring to any kind of condition where it brushed shoulders with the other arts. All of which made it a useful catalyzing agent. After a while we ran out of energy.

AJ: What current work is exciting to you?

AS: I'm not as in touch with it as I was, but I would say that Chris Ware is one of the best cartoonists around. I'm glad that we got to publish him pretty early on. I like Dan Clowes, Julie Doucet, Chester Brown. In France, the work of Pierre Le Police is very good. I'm not as fully engaged as I was; I don't seek out the xeroxed self-published magazines to the same degree.

AJ: Why not?

AS: There's been a general withdrawal, withdrawal from the consequences of *Maus*, withdrawal from the consequences of *RAW*.

AJ: When *Maus* came out, there was a media frenzy about "adult" comics, and even in the book publishing world, there was a sense that comic novels would be a new genre.

AS: *Maus* was exempted from being a "comic" and the "graphic novel" category was created—*graphics* being respectable, *novels* being respectable. Booksellers probably decided that a double whammy of respectability would help make the stunted hunchback dwarf look better by dressing it up in evening clothes. The problem was that *Maus* took thirteen years to do, and there wasn't another book that somebody had been working on for thirteen years to put on the shelf next to it, and there certainly weren't another dozen to put out next to it. However, in the last ten years, there have been several well realized, long comic books: Howard Cruse's *Stuck Rubber Baby*; Seth's *It's a Good Life, If You Don't Weaken*; Ben Katchor's *Julius Knipl: Real Estate Photographer*. People have to accept that the category will establish itself slowly. It won't be an instant publishing phenomenon. It's similar to the way that when we were doing *RAW*, it was inconceivable to me that magazines like the *New Yorker*, *New York Times Sunday Magazine*, or *Time* would run comics. But they all do now.

AJ: Do you think comics, in general, are still stigmatized?

AS: Younger editors carry less prejudices toward the medium. It's like there are these moles in various organizations: magazine editors who are predisposed to use cartoonists as illustrators, and, whenever possible, allow them to function as cartoonists. A publishing house hasn't opened its doors and said, "Let's do as much of this as we can." But, over a period of time, I think work accumulates, and as a result of that, there'll be a larger constituency. I must be in one of my upbeat days. Depending on where the hormones are on a given day, my other answer is, "No, print is dead. This is the last generation." I feel like the last blacksmith.

As technology and computers advance, I don't know in what part of the mix comics will be in a hundred years. I suspect it will be like a serious artist of today who's interested in the stereopticon or lithography. I think that as the march continues through time, these things get discarded and they're just left as toys for artists.

Presumably there'll be some people who are interested in what the specific properties of comics are but it's a rarefied activity. One of the arguments of why I felt it was worth making the *RAW* gambit was to move toward "respectable culture" which exists with a support system of museums and universities and, to a degree, publishing houses.

AJ: You mean intellectual—

AS: As opposed to the joy of Bazooka Joe comics. I think that move toward the cultural apparatus is actually useful in allowing a medium to survive. If it's not going to exist in that game sanctuary, it'll still exist. Most novelists and poets I know who aren't trying to write best-sellers are dependent on a university and grant system. Comics can be done without that and they *are* being done without that, but to the degree that it's available, it's useful. It's a tricky one, because it has a big down side. It can fossilize and damage the work and lead to an academicized form. But it was at least worth trying. And if it leads to pendulum swings, all the better. It's not like the *New Yorker*'s the answer to anything; it's a mess and it doesn't use the best of what's going on. It uses some of the best by accident every once in a while. It's kind of this happy accident, and the more happy accidents, the better.

AJ: Like your controversial covers or Charles Burns doing a sideshow carnival cover—viruses entering into the system.

AS: I'm actually about to do something that's dangerous. I'm not sure I'm doing the right thing, but—some people came over from the Museum of Modern Art and wanted to buy my *Maus* sketches. It seemed reasonable since they'd shown some of the *Maus* drawings there. Fine. Then the conversation turned to my other comics. I said,

"I could show it to you but I'd rather you didn't buy it." When we were putting the *Maus* show together I spent a lot of time in the basement of MOMA and saw all this great stuff that never gets out of there. Anything they would have taken from me would be the equivalent of burying it in a vault. I asked, "What other comic art do you have in your museum?" And the woman actually came back to me with this entertainingly crazy list. It was like, "Oh, we have a comic strip by Otto Soglow and four or five other very obscure works." It wasn't because they were the best obscure works—they don't have George Herriman's *Krazy Kat* in their collection. But it was what happened to get stuck to the back of a canvas when it was being donated to the museum. So I said, "There was a time when you didn't show Howard Hawks's movies or any movies at MOMA. I think there was a time when you didn't have a photo collection. Maybe you should consider comic strip art worthy of inclusion. But you'd have to understand it differently than just looking at it as if it was just a drawing that happens to look nice as a drawing. It's just an accident when it makes a nice drawing, it's not essential to it being a good comic strip." And the conversation expanded from there and turned into me giving a lecture to curators from various New York City museums in my studio next month. Comics 101, a slide lecture.

AJ: Why is it dangerous?

AS: For one thing, if I'm successful, it means I won't be able to buy the original art that I like and covet by other cartoonists of the past—I'd price myself out. And it's also dangerous for the aforementioned reasons that there's something great about the fact that comics manage not to have to deal with that world, and maybe they're better off for it.

AJ: It's also dangerous to privatize information.

AS: It's an inevitable meeting and I feel all I'm really doing is acting as an accelerator again.

The Very Briefest Taste of a Part of the Early History of Comics

Andrea Juno: Adam Gopnik wrote an article in the *New Republic* (June 22, 1987) about the misconception people have about comics. They think comics have a primitive history and that they are some relic of the infancy of art. He basically opposes these notions, saying that, "Cartoons are not a primordial form. They are the relatively novel off-spring of an extremely sophisticated visual culture." He goes on to talk about the development of the caricature among artists in Italy in the

1600s, like Carracci, and then to the late 18th century English use of the cartoon as a form of popular political and social satire. He writes, "Our mistaken beliefs about cartooning testify to the cartoon's near magical ability, whatever its real history, to persuade us of its innocence. Even though cartoons are in fact recent and cosmopolitan, we respond to them as if they were primordial. . . . That educated people don't know very much about cartooning just shows that we don't usually think it worthwhile to educate people about it."

Art Spiegelman: The nice thing about comics is that they have a relatively short history, so you can know their history in a way that you can't know world history, or even art history. If you're a painter, you're stuck with thousands of years or more of baggage. The Gopnik article is among the best I've read about *Maus*. But when he talks about the history of caricature and cartoon, he conveniently passes over the stuff that he considers lowbrow, which is comics. The cartoon has a related but different history.

AJ: Could you clarify the difference between cartoons and comics?

AS: A cartoon comes from the notion of the original sketch for a mural. The word actually comes from "carton," from board, drawing on a board. The cartoon is a schematic simplified drawing, usually involving exaggeration or distortion. Comics are clusters of cartoons strung together to indicate time. And that's what especially interests me.

I think comics arose out of the invention of the printing press. It's possible to trace the genealogy back to certain kinds of picture writing and medieval art, but I think it's the invention of printing that is related to comics. You're widely disseminating a picture to a semi-literate or illiterate audience, teaching catechisms and eventually spreading political and social propaganda and commemorating events and crimes in multiple images. I looked up the word "comics" in the dictionary and found out that it was a narrative series of pictures. Looking up "narrative" led to "story" which came from medieval Latin "*historia*," which specifically refers to the stained glass storytelling windows in churches. So the roots of "story" are related to the roots of "comic strip." I feel comfortable with this architectural notion of what a comics page is—a bunch of picture windows stacked together in a building to form a narrative.

So I kind of have a schematic family tree in my head. Comics come from these 13th century medieval woodblock prints of multiple images to tell a story. The first real stopping-off point is William Hogarth who was telling stories in sequential scenes: "Scene of the Rake as a Young Man," "Scene of the Rake in His Dissipations," "Middle-Aged Man" or whatever. His highly impacted drawings would take pages to describe. They unfold like a play in seven scenes with various clues in each picture that refer back and forth to each other. As a structure, it's as tightly woven as a staged play.

But the first direct progenitor of the comic strip is Rodolphe Töpffer who worked around the 1830s. He was a writer who could also be considered the granddaddy of semiotics as well as comics. He wrote an essay called "On Physiognomy," which was a study of the classification of people through their facial structures—stupid people have small, low foreheads while smart people have high foreheads. He said physiognomy didn't make much sense as a science, but it did make sense as a sign system. He experimented with simple lines. The interrupted line still makes a recognizable image. He worked out very interesting notation systems.

He was a school teacher who really wanted to be a painter like Hogarth, but he couldn't draw very well so in his spare time, he'd do these comic stories. They were sequences which were very sophisticated for 1830. He used his theories of sign recognition in a way that he could draw something once so that the next time he didn't have to draw it as completely. He made basic discoveries: changing sizes and shapes of panels, clustering things on a page so that they have interesting design, accelerating and slowing down the reader's attention as he scans the page, having words and pictures communicate with each other while not repeating the same information so they complement each other.

He was influenced by Laurence Sterne, the novelist who wrote *Tristram Shandy*, which had this loopy structure. Both Töpffer and Sterne shared a kind of whimsical interest in structure that reads like James Joyce but for different reasons than Joyce. Joyce was at the tail end of the novel whereas these guys were at the very beginning of their mediums. They were exploring what the medium might be for its own sake.

Töpffer printed his comics with a primitive kind of lithography which allowed him to make about 15 to 20 copies before the plate ran out. No one would have ever seen it except that one of the copies got to Goethe who said, "New medium, great thing, everybody should know about this." As a result, they have stayed in print ever since. This was my inspiration when we were doing *RAW*. It didn't matter how many you made, you just had to get them into the right hands.

Töpffer was amazing. In some sequences he anticipated cinematic crosscutting before there was anything like a movie camera. He was able to capture multiple moments of time. I would really like to know whether the drawing of multiple motions at once in comic strips precedes the invention of narrative photographs of multiple developments on a plate—like the work of Muybridge or Marey doing multiple exposures on one plate, like a horse running or a bird flying. I'm curious to know which happened first because it would tell me whether this was a cartoonist's invention or a result of a technological leap through the invention of movie—of cameras.

AJ: That's a fascinating question. I always had this intuition that artistic and technological leaps seem to appear at the same time, feeding off each other.
AS: As far as I can figure, this precedes any camera work.

AJ: Whether comics precede photography or not, this marriage of motion images brings up many issues of the development of our visual language and how we cognate, how we see—
AS: I'm pretty sure that comics come first. From the middle of the 19th century on, there's this impulse toward wanting things to move. The motion picture camera offered more satisfaction so its history got to travel farther and faster leaving comics on a stunted limb of the family tree.

The 5,000 Pound Maus: On the Anniversary of Kristallnacht, Art Spiegelman Revisits His Legacy

ELLA TAYLOR / 1998

From *LA Weekly*, 13–19 November 1998. Reprinted by permission.

Art Spiegelman's *Maus*, the best-selling comic book in which the co-founder of *RAW* comics, now known for his out-there *New Yorker* covers, explored his tortured relationship to his father, Vladek, and to the Holocaust, tells the story of Vladek's survival in Auschwitz. Spiegelman is in Los Angeles this week to give two talks: "Comics 101" ("the history and aesthetics of comics distilled down to something that can be said while someone stands on one leg") and "Representations of the Shoah in *Maus*," a speech to Second Generation, a group of children of Jewish Holocaust survivors. In a telephone conversation from New York, Spiegelman made it clear that, like most artists, he's more comfortable talking about his craft than about the meaning of what he's crafted. But his presentation to Second Generation coincides with the sixtieth anniversary of Kristallnacht (November 9, 1938), when anti-Jewish violence erupted throughout the

German Reich, setting the stage for the genocide that was to follow. Millions of Americans know little or nothing about that event or its ramifications. For that reason, and because Spiegelman is the only artist working in a popular medium who has addressed the Holocaust without trying to extract hope or inspiration from it, I tried to pin him down on the significance of his work and other popular representations of the Shoah.

L.A. Weekly: Popular culture can have an important role to play in raising awareness of the Holocaust. On the other hand, much of the pop language on the subject is reductive and tries to fold the catastrophe into received genres or narratives that lean toward uplift.

Spiegelman: I agree. I would say that one thing specific to my work has been that I wasn't interested in teaching anybody a damn thing and don't think the world can be made better. Talk to some Bosnians. I never did *Maus* as Auschwitz 101. It's useful to me that it has had this secondary life as a didactic tool, because it keeps my book in print. I don't mind being a good citizen, if it happens while I'm just busy living my life.

L.A. Weekly: To me, *Maus* is one of the few successful attempts to confront the Holocaust from within popular culture, precisely because it doesn't seek to sentimentalize it.

Spiegelman: I never thought of it as popular culture. It's just culture. I was interested in understanding my origins. It didn't occur to me that

First tier of "Mein Kampf" (1996).

there was anything unusual or odd about doing it as a comic book. That's the idiom that I talk. It's what I understand.

L.A. Weekly: Did you know you'd get flak for depicting the Jews as mice, the Nazis as cats, and the Poles as pigs?
Spiegelman: By the time *Maus* was published, I'd been warned by my publishers that it would be a good idea to lay low somewhere without a telephone.

L.A. Weekly: But as you were drawing it, that didn't occur to you?
Spiegelman: I'm stupid. What do I know? And it turned out that the flak was rather mild. However, in the last decade there's been mostly a very understanding and supportive response, certainly within the community of the directly affected and afflicted. And a cry—a squeal, let's say—of outrage from the Polish community. That's where it's still a problematic book.

L.A. Weekly: Speaking of problematic, I wonder what you thought of Roberto Benigni's film *Life Is Beautiful*?
Spiegelman: I think I would like Benigni a lot as a dinner companion. I have the reputation for being—at least since the *New Yorker* covers started coming out—a member of the shock troops. And yet I must say that I was shocked by the movie. I think Benigni overreached. I understand the movie has been very well received, and it makes me very confused about the planet. It's a bizarre film, done, obviously, with good intentions, which usually are paving stones for getting one place or another, sometimes to an Oscar.

You know, Benigni said something fairly interesting in some interview I just read, that it was important to banalize the Holocaust. That was kind of a shocking statement. I would bet that people who hear about *Maus* from the outside assume that it's more of the same. If I heard about the idea of this—"You know, somebody did this comic book. It's about the Holocaust. It uses animals. Oh, it's really amazing. I laughed, I cried"—I would shudder.

L.A. Weekly: Did Benigni elaborate on why we should banalize the Holocaust?
Spiegelman: So we could get on with our lives. I don't think this was sinister. I think this was actually part of those aforementioned paving stones of good intentions.

L.A. Weekly: Now that *Schindler's List* has lifted the lid off the Holocaust . . .

Spiegelman: [Laughs] That's one way of putting it. I vowed to stay silent about these things, and then every once in a while somebody just pushes the wrong button and I end up saying something. I got a lot of flak for my responses to *Schindler's List*. I got roped into a panel discussion, published in the *Village Voice*, in which I said that the only thing the film conjured up for me was six million emaciated Oscar statuettes.

Many people have approached me about turning *Maus* into a film, and I've always resisted. I was offered one thing where I would have final cut, and I said, "I don't want final cut. I don't want to make a movie." And they said, "But if you did want to make a movie, how would you do it?" I said, "All right, I'd use real mice."

It took thirteen years for the book to find its proper shape, and all I saw were almost insurmountable obstacles to making it work as a film. There's a kind of smoothing out of textures in trying to accommodate different aesthetics, psyches and personalities and needs that comes very naturally to the pyramid-building project of making a movie, compared to the papyrus-scrawling project of making a comic, where one can remain in God-like charge.

Out of all the critics writing about *Maus*, Lawrence Weschler wrote one really wonderful phrase that I've held on to—that *Maus* achieves "crystalline ambiguity." To not simplify that which cannot be simplified, and yet make things as lucidly complex as they are. And using the idiom of comics tends one toward that, because one works with a language that requires efficiency, both visual and verbal. It's an art of essentials.

L.A. Weekly: And yet it's not reductive. There's so much going on.

Spiegelman: Well, if you ask about what makes it appeal to people, I can now talk to you as a fellow critic, rather than as the person who made *Maus*, and say that many of the people reading *Maus* did not have parents who went through the Holocaust, but they all had parents. People would come rushing up to me, saying, "My father threw out my coat, too!" I think the fact that comics tend to fly below the critical radar allowed it to get through.

One of the reasons *Maus* is so powerful has to do with comic-book language. Comic books work on you the way you work inside yourself, much more so than almost any other medium. When you meet somebody and remember them, you tend not to remember them in the form of a hologram. You remember them in the form of a caricature—not necessarily a humorous caricature, but a fictionalized image. And that's exactly how you visualize in your head. It's a kind of streamlined iconography. When I think of what I'm going to say before I say it, I think of it as about seven words, and yet by the time I finish talking, you've got like a $10 phone call.

It has to do with the fact that we think in language, but we don't think in syntactical grammar. We think in essentialized verbal clusters. And by the time that unfurls, it's a lot more language. And this is wonderful for a novelist and not the way one can function as a cartoonist. Because even a densely loaded word balloon can only hold a burst of about thirty-five or forty words. So one moves through these sets of signs that are actually articulations of something that echoes very deeply inside our head. And I think that's why it was found in various experiments—before comics began to be seen so negatively in the '50s—that comics were incredibly useful teaching tools. *Superman* DC Comics in the late '40s did a bunch of phonics workbooks. And the only problem the teachers had was getting the students not to do the entire phonics workbook in one day. That's awesome.

L.A. Weekly: You mentioned that *Maus* is taught not only in history courses, but in courses on the dysfunctional family. How, as the therapists say, does that make you feel?

Spiegelman: I believe that universities and museum cultures are necessary repositories that allow the work to become something other than a passing parade. So I'm very grateful for the various lenses which people bring to bear on it. I was told it was used in a course on the American Indian. Well, this is what moved some professor, and he found through that lens he was able to get at other things he wanted to teach. It's cool. It was used in autobiography courses, courses on postmodern literature. I can only be grateful. I must say that the thing that made me agree to come out to Los Angeles was a lecture called "Comics 101." And as long as I was out here, I figured I'd also try out this thing in talking to my fellow sufferers [at Second Generation]—something I rarely do because it feels like talking to the choir. On the other hand, the image I have in one strip I made a few years ago—it appeared in the *New York Times Magazine*—has me being chased by a 5,000-pound mouse. I can't live under this large mouse and keep moving forward with my life.

Interview with Art Spiegelman

BRIAN TUCKER / 1999

From *X-Tra*, Spring 2000, pp. 3–19.
Copyright © 1999 Brian Tucker.
Reprinted by permission.

Art Spiegelman emerged at the beginning of the 1970s as an underground cartoonist bent on testing the formal limits of comics.
Spiegelman also distinguished himself as an editor and publisher of influential books and magazines devoted to comics. He co-edited (with Bill
Griffith, creator of *Zippy the Pinhead*) the underground comics magazine
Arcade in the mid-'70s. He worked for years at Topps, Inc., where he
authored or supervised parodies of consumer culture aimed at children,
including Wacky Packages and Garbage Pail Kids. Spiegelman has also
worked as an historian and educator about comics, teaching courses on
comics at venues including the San Francisco Art Institute and, from
1979–87, the School of Visual Arts in New York. Beginning in 1980,
Spiegelman collaborated with Françoise Mouly (his wife, now art director

of the *New Yorker*) to publish and edit the graphically lavish international comics anthology *RAW*. He has also published, designed, edited, written, or illustrated a variety of other projects, including a children's book (*Open Me . . . I'm a Dog!*) and many cover designs for the *New Yorker*. As J. Hoberman put it, "The tension between the marginal avant-gardist and the mass-market audience informs the entire Spiegelman enterprise."

Maus, his book-length comic, has probably generated more critical attention than any other work in the history of the medium. Using the cartoon convention of anthropomorphic "funny animals," *Maus* dovetails the harrowing, painstakingly researched details of Spiegelman's parents' lives as Polish Jews who survived Auschwitz with the story of Spiegelman's own strained relations with his father, and with his acutely self-conscious account of the thirteen-year process of assembling the book.

What follows is the edited transcript of a telephone conversation held December 10, 1999, a few days before Charles Schulz announced his retirement. The editor is grateful for the kindness of Michael Silverblatt, who was instrumental in arranging this interview.

Brian Tucker: When we set up this interview, I explained that many of the readers of *X-Tra* are artists and art students, people who have a formal art education which basically ignores the history of comics. And you, with a jocular tone, replied, "Well, now that they've canonized Norman Rockwell, that will all change." I'm curious why you made that connection. Do you see Rockwell as having something in common with comics that has separated them both from academic respectability?
Art Spiegelman: Yes, sure. Rockwell was in my mind just because I'd been reading about him.

BT: Because of the Rockwell show at the Guggenheim.
AS: Yes. Let's see, there are two or three reasons why the Rockwell show is re-entering art history. One of them just has to do with money, because the art world always has to do with money. But the second reason has to do with the result of battles within the academy about what should be canonized and what shouldn't. Stuff that I don't fully understand, but I guess is called "post modernism," that ultimately leave things on a more level playing field than they were before, so that it's not as obvious as it was fifteen or twenty years ago that there's a "high" and a "low": there's an understanding that these values have an

arbitrary quality. That's one thing that allowed, say, Norman Rockwell through a portal that lets him be considered as a capital "A" artist rather than a capital "I" illustrator. The third reason has to do with attitudes about irony and sincerity that are only tangentially related to the high-low comics issue.

BT: I wonder about the things that enforce that division, and whether what separates comics from legitimacy has to do with the taint of illustration, or whether it has to do with narrative demands, or with class affiliation.

AS: That's easy. It's all of the above. There's no conflict between any of those. On one hand, the narrative demands are among the things that make both comics and illustration more attractive to the art world now. Because the art world's found a way to deal narrative back into the game that it should never have left. There was a period, when I was growing up, where anything that smacked of narrative content was beneath contempt.

BT: That was the Clement Greenberg idea: anything literary was to be despised.

AS: Right. And then, things changed. Partially, by re-entering figuration into the world of art via the strategy of pop: the most formal approach possible to representation, but, thereby, a way back toward representation. And by the so-called "photo-realism" that flourished for awhile. That also was a way, through formal means, to re-enter narrative content into pictures.

BT: I think feminism had something to do with legitimizing narrative in the art world, too: the idea that personal stories are legitimate subject matter.

AS: Yeah. The culture of victimization in general.

BT: The culture of victimization promotes narrative art?

AS: Narrative content, yes. When you say "personal stories," I'm broadening it from being feminism to being feminists, gays, Jews, blacks, all of these things. All of which, again, is part of the breaking down of the canon, and it all may be somehow connected to the notion of "outsider art," which is another means of trying to accommodate the, um—

BT: Diverse?

AS: Yes, the diverse possibilities of art making that were under the hegemony of a very specific ideology. You know, there was a specific notion of what could make it Art. Inside of all of this, I'm not trying to condemn abstract art. It's not like, "Oh, and this thereby is canceling out all of the heroic '50s experiments."

BT: Your own work in the '70s seems to have been deeply influenced by that kind of modernist investigation of the conventions of the medium.

AS: Yes. So I'm embracing it all, including the culture of victimization, even though that phrase sounds very pejorative. So, let's see, threading our way back to Norman Rockwell—yeah, the fact that there's a class thing at work: people liked it, therefore it can't be very good. Second, there's the sentimentality of it which, at the moment, is becoming a very attractive feature of the work, because we're drenched in irony, and the ultimate of any concept is its opposite. And a third thing is that Rockwell is interesting in that he's not, exactly, an illustrator. Even though that's the category for him. He tells stories, he doesn't embellish stories. That's the real job of an illustrator.

BT: To embellish an existing story?
AS: Yes.

BT: So you're crediting Rockwell with more authorship than most illustrators?
AS: Yes. With the same authorship that exists in the painting that became a marriage license. You know, those art history lessons—

BT: Oh, the Arnolfini Wedding?
AS: I think that's the one. It has a little mirror set in the background.

BT: Right.
AS: There are all these embedded narratives. That was an arbitrary example, but up to a certain point it was always the task of a painting to tell a story. That's certainly the task of medieval painters, but well beyond. In that sense, there's a blur between illustrating and painting when the narrative is either self-contained, or refers to a story that one can intuit from the cultural references without an actual text. Maybe it's not illustration anymore. And at that point, I would say illustration and comics have something in common. But there's a self-contained authorship that makes comics interesting as art. Whether as narrative art or visual art is another issue, one that we were kind of inching up on.

BT: Whether comics are more closely allied with literature or visual art?

AS: Yes. Because they really do sit somewhere between a lot of things. Even though we started out by talking about illustration, the closer comics are to illustration, I would argue, the less they are like comics.

BT: What is an example of a comic that is fairly extreme in coming close to illustration?

AS: Oh, a lot of what happens in what's left of superhero comics. There's a comic book artist named Alex Ross who does very realistically painted comic book panels. Almost photographic. In the history of comics, I would say the beginnings of that tendency—and the beginning of the end of what I'm interested in—are people like Hal Foster and Alex Raymond, the guy who did Prince Valiant and the guy who did Flash Gordon. Because those really are bringing the illustrator's craft to comics. And comics are at their strongest, to my understanding, when they move toward a certain kind of abstraction. Because it gets closer to what comics do.

BT: Okay, that hangs a question out there. So what is the thing that comics do?

AS: Comics are an invented language. They are a synthesis of verbal and visual language, because all of the visual elements are in place as part of a narrative construct. They make use of things that look like written language and, indeed, are written language, but often with inflection and embellishment that doesn't usually exist in typography. Typography is impoverished: it has italics and bold face to help you inflect. Comics have a lot of subtler ways—they're closer to handwriting. The visual aspect of the text actually has a lot more possibility for expressiveness than all but the most avant-garde typography.

BT: Because everything can be customized.

AS: You can whisper. You can shout. You can turn some things, as Walt Kelly did, into Old English Gothic text to indicate something about the nature of what's being said. So the visual element of what's written becomes very important. So, on the one hand, there's all that. On the other hand, there's a kind of visual sign system that's in place for comic story telling, so that when it moves towards illustration it's misguided. Illustration is often a project that has to do with rendering things so that they create false windows. (There are other kinds of illustration, obviously.) Where illustrators and painters really overlap, that Rockwell spot, has to do with the satisfaction that people get from going, "Looks just like a cow." And no matter what you do in a comic book, it's always going to look like a very small cow. And, therefore, you're better off just getting its cowness across.

BT: That makes me think of Scott McCloud's book [*Understanding Comics*]. But before we leave Rockwell, it seems to me there are some important distinctions between what Norman Rockwell was doing and the kind of comic art that you do, and that you've supported—that appeared in *Arcade*, and *RAW*, and so forth—which tends to be, at least, very idiosyncratic, and in some cases downright oppositional or counter-cultural in relation to the monologues of the big institutions of society.
AS: Now we're into the Mutt 'n Jeff of form and content. Those guys come coupled. There are two conversations there: one has to do with the formal aspects of comics, one has to do with the content of certain kinds of comics.

BT: Do you think you can divorce them?
AS: Oh, you can't. They're Mutt 'n Jeff. The apostrophe "n" connects those two characters. Abbott 'n Costello, Mutt 'n Jeff, Laurel 'n Hardy. Form 'n content. But, when you're talking about the underground comics and the kind of comics that appear in *RAW*, part of it has to do with formal concerns and part of it has to do with the content of it. What I was just hearing you talk about had more to do with content. That's not to say that we shouldn't talk about the content.

BT: Well, I guess it is content, but there's a question of the basic position of the artist in relationship to the culture at large.
AS: Yes, but there's a vast continuum here. This week, what I've been thinking about most is a cartoonist who I haven't ever thought about seriously before, and that's Charles Schulz. Schulz is as Norman Rockwell as it gets, and yet he also gets very close to the bone, to the essences of what happens in comics. That being, just to spell it all out, pulling together this kind of comic writing to make a very, very personal world. It's amazing that it actually exists as everything from Hallmark cards to hookers for life insurance. Peddling, you know. But at the heart of it all is an operation where there's one person with a single vision, an author, making something very specific and very sophisticated. Not sophisticated meaning, "Oh, that's a sophisticated greeting card." But genuinely complex.

BT: Would you say the same is true for Rockwell?

AS: Less so. That's why I'm saying that if Rockwell can walk through the heavenly Guggenheim gates, it should be easy for comics. There's much more to chew on.

BT: Well, you've done more than anybody I'm aware of to promote the consideration of comics as a serious medium among the intelligentsia.

AS: I'm sorry.

BT: (Laughing.) I'm wondering what you see as being at stake. What happens when comics become respectable?

AS: Oh, it's a dangerous dance with the devil, which is why I was apologizing. In part, this comes from my being more interested in what comics might do than what they have done in many instances. It's been a lifelong concern, at least since adolescence. Because a lot of what's done is relatively boring. But that's true in every field, isn't it? Nevertheless, there's something exciting at its core. There's something very basic that I think is an interesting mystery at the core of comics, which isn't best displayed by things like *Garfield* or the *X-Men*. So a lot of it has to do with potential. As I outgrew certain kid's comics and still remained interested in comics, it was like taking this whole way of thinking along with me. It ends up putting me in this odd position of being the evangelist for serious comics. Which is a really dangerous place to be, because part of what makes comics very interesting is their populism, their ability to float through culture without getting zapped by the anti-aircraft missiles of cultural attention.

BT: Right. And so that's what's at risk.

AS: That's the risk. And the reason for taking those risks probably has to do with something tawdry, mainly survival. At this point, I see that comics were this great twentieth-century medium. As we sit here a few days before the twenty-first.

BT: So comics are totally in the past tense?

AS: Well, it's dangerous. Sometimes I feel like I'm sitting here touting stereopticon cards as a really interesting medium.

BT: It sounds as if part of the reason for including comics in the art discussions is simply because the discussions are more interesting.

AS: The discussions are more interesting, and comics require cultural attention to flourish at this point. Their populism will just be part of it, insofar as comics are interesting in connection to, say, graffiti. That is transmuting comics into something else, where certain similar issues will be taken up in different media. For example, I'm sure there will be a place, for a while, for the graffiti aspect of comics on the internet. But in terms of comics qua comics, that's something else again. And that's something that I just happen to have fallen in love with, and therefore would like to see live. For that to happen, a degree of institutionalized attention is probably necessary. In other words, the apparatus that comes with universities, with museum attention, with academic focus. The same kind of life support system that actually does function to keep everything from painting to literary novels to poetry part of a world where everything else is at the mercy of sheer commerce.

BT: Do you see that happening?
AS: Yes. Comics certainly aren't as central in the culture as they were mid-century. There was a moment when comics were so popular, the Senate had to investigate comic books and try to squelch them because they were seen as the most dangerous thing in our culture. That was the 1950s—

BT: And this resulted in the comics code.
AS: Yes. All because comics were such a mass medium. Really, they were. The number of people reading comics was staggering. The numbers were large enough to make it loom as a genuine threat in the culture: this could actually taint our society if it wasn't kept under control, because it was so widespread. They were read, not just by children. And the numbers of children that read them were awesome. Around the same time, comics were also a very important part of the newspapers. Newspapers themselves are less important in the culture now, and they devote less space to comics. So, by this point in the century, comics are already specialized, but they're specialized in a kind of Yahooland—not the internet Yahoo, but the Jonathan Swift Yahoo—of comic book shops.

BT: Do you see the idea that you're promoting, where there would be legitimacy for people who are working seriously with comics—a subsidy, through university teaching positions, or whatever—is that happening?
AS: Yes. I remember years ago applying for grants to help me get some of the comics I was making made, and being turned away almost automatically. But at this point, I'm not the only one who's received a Guggenheim for making comics.

BT: Who else?

AS: Ben Katchor has. I imagine it happening again. I would say even that special Pulitzer that was awarded to me is a sign of the times. I know that comics are being taught in lots of universities. My work has found its way into lots of post-modern lit courses, as well as core curricula, humanities courses, and . . . blah de blah. I know that Scott McCloud's book stays alive as a university inclusion. There have been a number of comic shows of one kind or another, dating back to the '60s, probably, that will keep happening more and more often as comics move into an orbit where its concerns and so-called "fine art" concerns are more or less a blur. And in Europe—where it's not like the promised land or any-thing—but in Europe, there are museum shows. And there is a university devoted to comics study in France.

BT: Where is that?

AS: Angoulême. It's this town that has an annual comics festival, but it's not exactly like the kind here that focuses on things like *Star Trek* and weird costumed babes. But it's a comics festival, and a town in France that is overrun by this event for a week. It includes lots of museum-quality shows of comics works, including in the town's museum. It has an ongoing project all year 'round of "Comics Studies," some of it seeming very academic, and some being very solid historical research. The week culminates in some awards for various comics. But they're about as attended to as, say, the "Tonys." They're announced on the evening news.

BT: Wow.

AS: So, to that degree, France has allowed comics into their canon of activity that's not necessarily to be ignored, frowned upon, or dismissed.

BT: Well, maybe that's what it takes here. So often, some sort of European validation is necessary before Americans are comfortable—

AS: Yeah. The French have been doing this for a generation. Umberto Eco, as a young man, was part of a European cluster of intellectuals, that also includes Alain Resnais, who started a kind of intellectual fan interest in comics moving. That changed the landscape for comics in Europe. And then Japan is a whole other planet, one that I don't fully under-stand. But from way over here, it looks like it's a done deal. Comics can exist in every pore of their culture.

BT: There doesn't seem to be a class identification with comics in Japan, from what I gather.

AS: Or an age thing even, it's just up and down, across the board, stupid, smart—all of the above are just as easily integrated into their culture as cathode ray images are in ours.

BT: Before we leave the talk of marching up the museum steps with comics, can you clarify your role with regard to the big museum show about comics that may or may not happen here in Los Angeles?

AS: If it does happen, I was the catalyst.

BT: So you did instigate that show.

AS: Well, that show was a result of an event that happened about three years ago. I had a show in '92 of my *Maus* work at the Museum of Modern Art. A few years later somebody called me who represented a group called "Friends of Drawing" of the Museum of Modern Art. She was one of the curators in the drawing department. "We realize we don't have any work by you in our permanent collection, except for a couple of your lithographs in the prints department, and we'd like to buy some of your drawings." I said, "What do you have in mind?" She said, "For starters, some of the *Maus* work." I pointed out that I wasn't breaking up the final art, but I had been pressured into selling some of the preliminary sketches through the gallery I was connected with up to around the time that she had called. I said, "I suppose I could let you look through some of those sketches if you want." And they came over, a few curators, and "friends" who donate the money to buy these things. Then they looked at my other comics and said, "Oh, we'd like to get some of that stuff too." And I said, "That's ridiculous, I'd never sell any of that to you." "What! Why?" "Well, when I was putting together the *Maus* show, I was in the basement of your museum looking at all this great stuff you had that never gets up for air, and I was thinking: this was a fate worse than death, just to be in this vault below the museum. And I suspect that unless you have a body of work or an approach to this stuff, most of my comics would end up stored away next to Pavel Tchelitchew's *Hide and Seek* painting, never allowed to be seen." And it took them aback. I said, basically, that they don't know enough about this stuff. And that led to me agreeing to tell them more. So I was going to give them a lecture. Comix 101. And as long as I was doing this I figured I'd invite other curators. So I had curators from the Guggenheim, the Whitney, the Library of Congress, the MOMA, the

Met, the Brooklyn Museum, and a few influential galleries, all gathered in my studio to get a slide talk on comics. With the goal being a long, long, long overdue comics show. Not a high-low show, but a low-low show. Where you don't have to pit comics one-on-one against paintings to give them validity. You'll get a sense of what they're like at the Museum of Modern Art from the fact that they weren't miffed at my bringing in all of these curators from other museums, but the "Friends of Drawing" were very upset that the "Friends of Prints" from the MOMA might be there.

BT: (Laughing.) That's very nice.

AS: Ultimately, this worked to ferment a lot of interest. The MOMA was quite serious about this, but it finally exploded. I don't know which curators exploded it—it's a very Byzantine structure. It exploded so much that one of the curators quit the museum.

BT: On what grounds?

AS: I don't know the exact reasons. It had to do with debating whether or not the show could happen, and strong resistance on the part of some curators. I think—I'm speculating a little bit—it may have had to do with the problem of granting comics the status of being prints.

BT: The actual comic books?

AS: Yes. Because there's no reason why a show like the one I would be interested in seeing happen wouldn't include printed Sunday comics on newsprint, for instance. As opposed to just the actual board that the artist worked on. One could argue, even, that to show only the board would be like showing the piece of wood that Dürer inscribed, rather than the print made from it. Considering something produced in millions of copies on rotogravure offset as a print creates real dilemmas for people who have spent their lives trying to keep the distinction in place between printed work and art print.

BT: Limited edition fine prints.

AS: Fine prints, yes. One of the debates that would have to have taken place is, "What? What do you mean, giving center stage to these off-register things printed on pulp paper without any attention to the quality of it as an object per se?"

BT: How did talk of this show migrate to Los Angeles?

AS: Well, the MOMA was one front. Another front was the Whitney, where I wasn't as keen on seeing this happen because the Whitney's been doing a lot of shows that flirt with non-art territory, but without acting to actually consecrate something as fully worthy of attention.

BT: What's an example of that?
AS: Oh, I don't know . . . Keith Haring's show. Over the past decade, there's kind of a desperate trendiness on the Whitney's part that this comics show could have fit right into. Nevertheless, that whole bunch of curators exploded out of the museum over unrelated issues within a few months. The whole museum changed: directorship, staff, and everything. But one of the people who was involved with this lecture experience that I set up, and who had been involved in some comics show projects in the past, was a curator in a place in my neighborhood called The Drawing Center. A non-profit gallery that specialized in drawing. A couple of years after this lecture, that curator, Ann Philbin [now Director of the UCLA Hammer Museum], calls me up excitedly to say, "Guess what? I'm in charge of this whole museum. We're going to be able to do our show." And from that it began growing. But as I began to see what it was growing into, I realized that I would need to clone myself to be involved fully.

BT: So you instigated it, and supplied them with the—
AS: With the notion of what such a show should and could be. And I would be glad to help them to prepare a map that they could use to explore with, and even find people to go on the spelunking expedition with, as long as it's not me in charge.

BT: For the record, could you describe the basic premise of the show?
AS: A show of comics from the get-go to tomorrow. A very large survey, with focuses on specific artists, that would be large enough to contain rooms devoted to some of the key players: [Winsor] McCay and [George] Herriman, and whoever.

BT: What would you call "the get-go?"
AS: One place that is very comfortable for me to start is with this guy Rodolphe Töpffer in the 1830s. To start there, you have to parenthetically include something prior to him, which would probably be Hogarth. And, arguably, back from there to some medieval prints. In fact, there's a person connected to UCLA who's done a wonderful set of books—

BT: David Kunzle. [*The History of the Comic Strip*, two volumes, University of California Press.]

AS: Yes. They were an intelligent opening up of what a real definition of comics might include. It seems to me one would go specifically to works designed for print. I don't think it would be real important to have a stained glass window, even though the roots of comics definitely travel through those church windows. So much so that, as far as I can figure out, the word for "story" comes from—is connected to—church windows. You know, like the stories of a building.

BT: Right. I recognize that idea from an early piece of yours. I think it's right at the beginning of the *Breakdowns* anthology, where you're ruminating on the nature of comics.

AS: Yes. So once you connect it to stained glass windows, it's clear that these are kinds of picture stories, using little windows next to each other to tell a story, often connected, often with written language as part of the picture. Either telling an explicit story or referring to stories that are known so well that you just have to conjure them up. But part of the definition of comics probably includes works for print. And when you move toward secular work, you travel through some political propaganda art, and art that's specifically in place as social propaganda—to propagate certain "proper" view points. That includes Hogarth, with his "Rake's Progress" and "Harlot's Progress," and from there to something that's much more middle-class bourgeois, which is stories for sheer amusement. That's Töpffer. Just for the frolic of it all. That's really the beginning of something else. So we'll start with Töpffer, and then we'll go through to Chris Ware, and beyond.

BT: Would you envision including a reading experience? Like a table with comic books on it? Actually get people handling them?

AS: Probably. That's happened in a number of the shows that have been done in small venues already. And, ultimately, it's the reason why in the shows that have a high and low connotation—where they show paintings and comics—usually, the paintings win the wall and the comics win the catalogue.

BT: Makes sense.

AS: So any show would have to be accompanied by print. Either an amazing catalogue or lots of books available to read in a library situation and/or to buy. The way that one could go up to a certain point in giving demonstrations about film as art, but there is a moment at which you just have to have a theater available to show these things.

BT: Are there particular artists or critical volumes that you commended to the attention of those curators in the Comix 101 lecture?
AS: Artists for sure. Critical volumes is much harder. This isn't a territory that has encouraged a lot of good thought; certainly not that's been gathered together in one place. So it's easier to point people toward histories than toward critical work. Even the histories tend to be pretty often mucked up. So one of my longer term projects is a "Comix 101" book. It's something I've been supposed to do for years. Even the Scott McCloud book in some ways is connected to this—I mean, Scott McCloud was sitting in on the lectures I was giving on comics in the early '80s.

BT: At the School of Visual Arts?
AS: Yes.

BT: How do you assess that Scott McCloud book?
AS: Scott's a very smart boy and a lot of it is well codified, and some of it is one step too codified to be comfortable for me.

BT: Can you give me an example?
AS: Well, what's sticking out in my mind that I really like, for instance, are the zany charts that are in his book—drawings from abstraction to realism, and a kind of pyramid.

BT: That pyramid, yes. [A diagram placing various approaches to comic imagery within a triangular field, with the three corners labeled "picture-plane"-"meaning"-"reality."]
AS: But that's typical of a lot of other charts that remind me of, like, Jack Chick's religious pamphlets. Insofar as they're tongue in cheek, I enjoy them. But if they get in the hands of very earnest academics, they can be dynamite. In the bad sense of that.

BT: I was just looking at that pyramid diagram. I noticed how he drew a little line to connect your Vladek Spiegelman [from *Maus*] with Mr. O'Malley, from *Barnaby* [a strip by Crockett Johnson, published in the 1940s].
AS: I'll take the compliment, wherever it comes from. To some degree these things are interesting. I think even Scott McCloud would say, "let's take this with a grain of salt." If he didn't say it in so many words.

BT: I think he almost does say it in so many words. I think he really wanted to get the conversation going.

AS: As a part of that conversation, it's very good. As something that can set too many things in place and become a straight jacket, that's what I mean by being dangerous in the wrong hands. An earnest academic can turn this into Lacan in no time. That's part of the danger that we were—

BT: Part of the danger, but maybe it needs to happen.

AS: In the right hands, it's fine. There's a guy in France named Thierry Groensteen, who is curator of the museum at Angoulême. He's really a smart guy. And he does very well at dealing with the stuff without too much jargon, and yet putting a pretty fine point on things.

BT: Has he written? Has he published anything that's translated?

AS: Yes, a group of essays, but nothing translated as far as I know.

BT: We've gone on for a while and haven't talked about any of your current projects, and I'd like to do that.

AS: Alright. Right this minute, I'm working on something relating to a project called Little Lit which Françoise, my wife, and I are doing together with HarperCollins, which is basically a *RAW* magazine for kids in children's book form. That's the first of a series of annual books that will be coming out next Christmas.

BT: Are these original stories or retellings of traditional fairytales?

AS: The first one is retellings of traditional fairytales. There are some original stories in this one and depending on the theme of the given issue, there'll be more of that.

BT: What artists are involved?

AS: Some of the *RAW* gang, which would include Charles Burns, and Chris Ware, who did a very elaborate endpaper/game with diecut pieces. Then, a strip by me that's a retelling of an old Hassidic fable. Dan Clowes, the guy who does "Eightball." David Mazzucchelli, doing a Japanese-style thing. Lorenzo Mattotti from Milan. Joost Swarte, in his clear line Tintin-style, telling a Dutch fairy tale. A reprint of a Walt Kelly story from his pre-Pogo days. Kaz. And some children's book artists as well. A woman named Barbara McClintock, who has been doing a number of kid's books and has been winning prizes as a children's book artist, deservedly so, with a retelling of "The Princess and Pea" that looks like Grandville might have had a hand in drawing it. David Macauley, the guy who did *Cathedral* and *The Way Things Work*, doing his first comic book story. J. Otto Siebold. Harry Bliss, who is a cover artist for the *New Yorker* that Françoise discovered as part of her gig as art director at the *New Yorker*. And William Joyce, who did *The Leaf Men*, *Dinosaur Bob*, *Santa Calls*—he's a well known children's book artist. So it's children's book artists and avant cartoonists doing comics. In full color and large, very large size.

BT: This seems to be a thread throughout your career: work that's directed at children.
AS: Sure. On the one hand directly for children, in the form of Garbage Pail Kids and Wacky Packages, and here, specifically for children's parents, to let them have something that they would actually like. This all has to do with my stupid evangelical hat (a dunce cap?)—trying to keep comics alive. And understanding that unless kids learn how to read comics and enjoy them as kids, then it's less likely that adults will be reading comics in twenty years. Françoise and I have observed our own kids: both learned to read from all the comics that were around the house. It made them like reading.

BT: Was that the case with you as well?
AS: Yes. And for Françoise too, actually. It feels so natural for me, and seems intrinsic to the whole nature of comics that it would, of course, get people to like reading. Even more so than most children's picture books. There's more story, and more moment-to-moment drawings. Just prior to that 1950s moment we were talking about—the "comics cause juvenile delinquency, let's put a comics code on them and stomp them out" moment—there were some very successful experiments with using comics in schools to teach phonics and grammar. It was all squelched because the whole comics project became tainted. And yet, they were very successful. The only problems, for instance, that some schools were having using a Superman comics grammar exercise workbook was to keep the kids from doing it all in one night. That's amazing. So the idea that comics would very naturally fit into a more global literacy project is a no-brainer. It's just so obvious that it belongs in that mix. And so, without dumbing it down, Little Lit is part of that endeavor. So that's one major thing that I'm involved with, aside from my ongoing work at the *New Yorker*, which includes writing more essays about comics, doing comics, and doing covers.

BT: I heard tell, awhile back, about an opera.

AS: Yes. That's becoming more and more time consuming.

BT: The story of comics censorship in the '50s, is that—

AS: That's at the heart of the story, yes. Opera is the wrong word—let's say it's a music theater piece. Although it's "A Three Panel Opera." *Drawn to Death: A Three Panel Opera.* It's about the rise and fall of the American comic book, told through the destinies of various comic book artists.

BT: I heard that you were collaborating with [composer and arranger] Van Dyke Parks on this, and then I was told that was no longer the case.

AS: Yeah, it seems to no longer be the case. We spent a year plus thinking we were working together, but not making that much progress, and finding that there seemed to be some kind of impasse between my words and his music sitting together. I'm not a good enough lyricist for the occasion. And yet, what I needed to do was write a libretto that could have music. So, for the moment, that's not how it's proceeding. I'm working with a jazz composer named Philip Johnston. It seems to be working well. He's doing just what I always envisioned would happen with this.

BT: That's great. What is the timetable for this?

AS: On May 18 and 19 we're supposed to have a concert performance version of this up at St. Anne's in New York. That will be before the very elaborate visual end of this gets plugged in. But it will be a first public airing of a large chunk of it. The person producing it is talking to some people at CalArts, as well as people at the American Repertory Theatre in Cambridge and some other places including BAM, all of whom are sort of interested in helping abet this thing. It looks like the NEA is helping it happen also.

BT: Have you been making drawings or comics in conjunction with *Drawn to Death*?

AS: Yes. It will be very visual. There will be a book of that material in some form as well.

BT: Is there an anthology of your work coming out?

AS: At the moment, there is a kind of phantom book out in the world. Somebody has put together a retrospective of my work that's been going to different farm team museums in different parts of the world, so there's a catalogue that I did that accompanies the show. [*Comix, Essays, Graphics and Scraps,* Sellerio Editore-La Centrale dell'Arte, Rome, 1999.] It's fairly elaborate for a catalogue, but it's one step well short of a book. It includes some of my essays on comics, and some of my work that's out of print, and some preliminary drawings for *Maus,* and some work I've done for the *New Yorker* and elsewhere that otherwise hasn't been gathered together. So, for the moment, it's as close as I have come to an anthology, although it's not quite a book and it's not quite out in the world since its main use is as something that accompanies the show and isn't available through distribution. I've asked for some copies to be distributed here, at least through comic shops and comic distributors, and—it's a complicated problem that has to do with a crazy printer in Palermo who's been doing this—it's been about two years, with one misprint after another, ordering copies and getting half the number of copies I wanted. The long and short of which is there will be about two or three thousand copies floating around outside of the sight of the traveling exhibition. But only that many. So it's a sort of anthology that sort of exists.

BT: I read an interview you did with Andrea Juno a few years ago that's in her book, *Dangerous Drawings.* You talked about how, in the wake of the incredible success of *Maus,* you were feeling timid about your next move making comics. You just mentioned a comic that you made that's going to be part of the Little Lit series—are you still feeling that way about making comics?

AS: To a degree. It's easier for me to think about making short strips than engaging in a book length comics project, so I just keep putting that off. I'll make pokes in that direction and then just back away, going "Oh, my God." If you can avoid doing it, why would you contract to have a ten-year bout of the Asian flu?

BT: But you're expecting at some point to take to the sick bed?

AS: It could happen. Part of what I've been saying all along has to do with the fact that, even though the popular perception is that comics are kind of dopey—and a lot of what people do is indeed dopey—it's actually, as far as I can see, maybe the pinnacle of artistic possibility. It's a bit like the abstract form of opera. It allows all of these other arts to engage. As a result, it's harder than almost anything else I can think of doing. Harder than writing, harder than drawing, is this drawing-writing in comics. So, yes, I'd like to tackle it again. But it requires, at least the way I do it, a minimum of half a decade to make a book.

BT: Do you feel that the long form is the main event?
AS: Not necessarily, but wouldn't mind it again, if I found a long form work that was so compelling for me that I had to do it. Otherwise, I'm lazy like everybody else. Everything you do is to avoid something harder. And right now, that's just too hard.

BT: You seem to do an incredible amount while you're procrastinating.
AS: I try to keep myself out of trouble—like right now I'm screwing around with this other muse that I know nothing about. This music theater thing doesn't come out of any long-lived secret desire to be Cole Porter or Bob Fosse. Or Verdi. It's just something that grew and seems interesting to try.

BT: In that Andrea Juno interview, you also talk about the problems of fame that you encountered with *Maus*, and you said that you were lucky that you hadn't had to deal with the worst of it, since you weren't involved in television or movies. Do I understand that you are developing a television project now?
AS: Well, there's talk about me being the Sister Wendy of a comics history thing for television.

BT: Would this be PBS?
AS: It's too soon to say that. But it's possible that it's PBS. If that happens, so be it. I think all of this stuff still ends up flying within the lower realm of cultural radar. I think that what Dan Clowes said about fame is about right: it was something like, "there's no such thing as a famous cartoonist, it's like being a famous badminton player."

BT: Yeah, but if your mug is on TV—Sister Wendy has a kind of fame.
AS: A kind of fame, although I've used that quip several times without anybody knowing what I'm talking about. Maybe it's just the circle of people I'm traveling with.

BT: Maybe you should use Leonard Bernstein. You know, he did those explanatory Young People's Concerts.
AS: That's true. I learned everything I know about classical music from Leonard Bernstein. I was grateful for that. Was he famous?

BT: Yes, I think he was. I think that there was an aspect of the culture in the '50s—there was a middle class striving for cultural cultivation. The "middlebrow" thing was really evident. I think he was part of that. But it still goes on to some extent; have you seen those PBS shows that Wynton Marsalis did?
AS: I haven't.

BT: They're directed at kids, but absolutely adult friendly. Of course, they have the advantage of actually having live performances of music. They're excellent.
AS: Sounds great. Yeah, so it's a good middlebrow project—it's not about becoming famous. If anything, that's a good argument against it.

BT: That's why I brought it up in the context of what you were saying in that other interview. It almost sounded as if going on television would be revealing a masochistic streak.
AS: Well, it's just an acknowledgment that if you're involved in. . . . Someplace early in the interview you talked about me as a "promoter."

BT: Did I use that word?
AS: Yes. The word sat. And, I guess so. I'm not trying to hustle anything for a specific economic end. But to the degree that Wynton Marsalis or Leonard Bernstein were promoting their mediums, I am [a promoter]. It's one part of what I am and do, that is central to me. I acknowledge and accept the fact that I'm a comics promoter. Without even liking most comics. It's a very odd dilemma to be in. And as things seem plausible, to move forward in one place or another, I've taken those things on, for better or for worse. So, on one hand, *RAW*, I think, was that. It seems like Little Lit is another version of it. *Maus*, even, was a demonstration of it. I mean, *Maus* grew at least as much out of my interest in making a long comic book that could have a bookmark as out of any other goal. I was very interested in *Maus* happening in bookstores; I'm very interested now in seeing Little Lit happen in the children's book part of a bookstore. And I've been involved, for better or for worse, with *Details* magazine, trying to get them to use comics artists as journalists.

BT: Do you see yourself getting back into publishing comics anthologies like *RAW*?
AS: I don't know. I'm not predicting it now because it seems like there's less urgency for it. When we started *RAW*, Françoise and I, there was no

place to publish anything, and no place to demonstrate what could happen. *RAW* was partially responsible for changing that.

BT: What do you see as the successor to *RAW*?
AS: It's not any one successor. It's just that all of the cartoonists that we would have ordinarily been responsible for pulling on to our raft, our little life boat, have one way or another that they can get into the world. Like Chris Ware: his work is published by Fantagraphics, and a book collection of his work is coming out through the people who published *Maus*, Pantheon. Dan Clowes' work also comes out through Fantagraphics. A woman named Debbie Drechsler, whose work I like, is being published by something called Drawn & Quarterly. There is a book called *Blab!* that, at least, takes on some of the graphic energy. There is a very small outfit called Top Shelf that seems to be poking around for talented people that wouldn't be commercial.

BT: What do they publish?
AS: There's a book called *Top Shelf* which is an anthology, and then—

BT: It's good? I should look for that?
AS: As a way of seeing some of the more interesting experimental stuff which isn't, for the most part, fully developed. I think they've published Eddie Campbell, who might be better known than some of the other people that they've had. It's something that comes to mind as one of the places, ranging from small scale to larger scale—larger scale being Pantheon putting out *The Jew of New York* by Ben Katchor, small scale being Top Shelf, and then next up in line being Drawn and Quarterly— that are doing the work of continuing some of this material. *RAW* was created because it was a vacuum at that point. We kind of went in kicking and screaming.

BT: What's your perception of the audience for serious comics? Is it growing?
AS: I think so.

BT: Do sales figures bear that out as far as you know?
AS: Which ones?

BT: What does, say, Dan Clowes, sell? [*Eightball*, one of the most prominent independent comics titles.]
AS: Dan Clowes must be around ten or fifteen thousand copies. A movie is being made [based on Clowes' *Ghost World*] that will reflect back into

his book sales eventually. And he's got two books coming out from Pantheon, so I'm sure that will help amplify it. Talking about serious comics and market is a little bit like talking about the poetry market. Yes, there might be one. (Laughter.) I don't think that is what impels it, but there's a demonstrable audience as long as people aren't involved in making money.

BT: There's a curious thing about the serious comics market. The best comics shop in LA is a store called Meltdown. It's an excellent store: you walk in and instead of seeing the *X-Men*, it's Mark Beyer and Basil Wolverton, and original art by Seth and Dan Clowes and such on the walls. They have an adjacent store which is called Baby Melt, where they sell toys and they commission comics artists—I think Clowes and Chris Ware both have done designs for T-shirts for little children.
AS: Sounds good.

BT: Standing at the counter, I noticed a sign about why they don't accept checks. It listed the names of people who had bounced checks, and all the names were male. I asked the guy behind the counter what proportion of their customers are male. And he told me, very proudly, that unlike most comic book stores where it's 98% male, their audience was about 90% male. Is this consistent with your experience?
AS: It's consistent with most of the comics that are published here. In Japan and Europe, those numbers would be very different. There are actually fairly large numbers of attractive women around Angoulême: it makes me very interested in the invitations I receive from that festival. And it looks to me that in Japan it's probably an even split between X and Y chromosomes. Here, most of the comic books are about pre-adolescent male fantasy, so there's a predisposition to more of the same.

BT: Sure, But even in a store like this, which is clearly positioning itself away from that—
AS: But [they're limited by] the small number of things that are available. You were mentioning Dan and Chris' work: there are more guys than girls.

BT: Yes, by a wide margin.
AS: And doing it, more or less, for guys rather than girls. Because it has to exist in the margins of these shops that were created more for guys than for girls. As it moves out into another realm—I'll bet you the people buying *Peanuts* anthologies are skewed in a whole different gender

graph than what we were just taking about. But then, is *Peanuts* not serious comics? Because it advertised MetLife? I don't know, I'm thinking about the answer to that myself. But if *Peanuts* is serious comics in some way, then that gender thing just falls apart.

BT: I'd like to ask the obligatory question about what artists working in comics—or, for that matter, artists who aren't working in comics—you find interesting.

AS: The most recent artist I find interesting is Spike Jonze. I really like that movie, *Being John Malkovich*. I don't run around to galleries a lot anymore, and as they have been fleeing out of my neighborhood to make way for high-end fashion stores, I see less and less fine art except as it's reproduced in magazines. Let's see. . . . On [Michael Silverblatt's] recommendation, I'm reading *Brief Interviews with Hideous Men* by David Foster Wallace. It looks pretty good to me. There are people that I was interested in and remain interested in, like some of the so-called underground filmmakers of the '60s—

BT: Stan Brakhage?

AS: Yes, and Ken Jacobs, very much so, because we're close friends. I follow what he's up to, so far as I can. Then among cartoonists, some of the suspects that have already come up in one way or another. The people that I itemized as being from the *RAW* crowd are still working. Kim Deitch is still working and is really great. Mark Beyer should be doing more, he's really great. Gary Panter. David Mazzucchelli. Some of the old underground cartoonists: Spain Rodriguez is still interesting to me. Robert Crumb. Debbie Drechsler. The people who would be up front in that store you were just describing are among the people whose work I'd probably be prone to want to look at. I spent a lot of last year trying to find and look at Jack Cole's work, in preparation for that essay [about Cole's *Plastic Man*, for the *New Yorker*], and he's now a figure in the *Drawn to Death* piece. I've been looking a lot at Rodolphe Töpffer lately, because I want to write about him. And very recently, I've been looking, as I've said, at Charles Schulz.

BT: You said you don't see much of what goes on in galleries and museums. Are you aware of people like Jim Shaw and Mike Kelley, [gallery artists who have done work that is engaged with comics]?

AS: Jim Shaw's work I know. We were thinking about using it in *RAW* back a ways ago when he was being shown in a gallery around the corner. I always made a point of going to see his work. But Mike Kelley, I just know him by reputation. And then, there's a California graffiti artist who is highly considered at the moment. [Barry McGee.] Does sort of a Basil Wolverton-like head—it's this highly cross-hatched and rendered graffiti. I remember walking past an opening, seeing more skateboards than I'd seen in my neighborhood in decades. Well, anyway, I follow that to a degree. I'm more interested in the stuff that grows out from comics than the stuff that sinks its roots back in. But I'm open-minded.

Asked about [the reference to Pavel Tchelitchew] after the interview, Spiegelman replied: When I was a kid, *Hide and Seek* was one of the biggest crowd-pleasers on permanent display at the MOMA. It showed a woman hiding her eyes, counting against a tree that's made up of neuronal paths with hidden fetuses and embryonic baby heads. Almost fluorescent psychedelic colors. One day some curator realized it was kitsch and banished it to storage.

Art Spiegelman: Walking Gingerly, Remaining Close to Our Caves

NATASHA SCHMIDT / 2000

From *Index on Censorship* 6, 2000,
pp. 126–33. Reprinted by permission of
Index on Censorship.

People tell Art Spiegelman he makes them laugh. He says he doesn't really understand humor and is only trying to tell his particular set of truths in the hope that there's "some resonance beyond the laughs." He describes his most serious work, *Maus*, which has appeared in twenty-one countries, as both a "diaspora novel" and part of the "comix" genre.

By working with comix, I can ratiocinate. They get to fly below critical radar, and thereby go into your head. Comix echo the way we think, in the sense that thought takes place in bursts of language and in icons that exist in one's head. Comix are about the only medium I can think of that accurately does that. Talking strictly as an outside observer, after the initial, much more intuitive genuine impulses that moved me through all this, I would say that since comix are a way of showing time spatially, they have advantages in terms of trying to palimpsest the past and present into the same narrative.

A lot of humor comes from taboo. Maybe all humor ultimately comes from some version of taboo and then one has to gauge how funny is it and how efficacious at doing something other than just making you laugh. There's a lot of laughter that comes from the nervousness of "oh, jeez! You're not supposed to say that and you said it."

I was watching a show called *Politically Incorrect* after the political debates, and one of the panelists asked, "Why is our military budget so high? We don't have any enemies any more." And another more conservative member of the panel says, "What about China?" and then Gore Vidal says, "A great laundry people." It's funny, but in a way you wouldn't have dared do if the enemy was Israel and you were to say, "They're great pawnbrokers," or an African nation and you said, "All great singers and dancers." The Chinese and Japanese don't have as good a lobby [as the Jews] for sensitizing people to these things. The more sensitized the community, the more difficult it is to make the jokes. The joke here is about conjuring up stereotypes.

Ultimately, cartooning is a conservative business, even when you have so-called liberal and radical cartoonists. Almost by definition, cartooning tends to use stereotypes, you're dealing with a recognizable iconic picture. It ends up saying, "Yep, those Chinese really are good at laundry, ha." But it doesn't tell you how to get past that. Much harder to take that stereotype and do some kind of judo with it that actually undoes it. And when you do, then you're in dangerous territory.

I had a cover that was first accepted and then rejected with horror by the *New Yorker* at the tail-end of the OJ Simpson trial. I drew something that portrayed "the race card," since this was exploited repeatedly throughout the trial by OJ's lawyers. It ended up in the *Nation* instead—but minus the caption. The idea of showing OJ with a minstrel face was not about reaffirming "all blacks are watermelon-eating coons," but a way of showing that he was playing himself up as a black victim. It's a paint job, as much a mask as the Klan mask on the Los Angeles Police Department. One thing that makes it so complicated is that I'm not black, therefore I don't have the same right to say certain things; though, in the same issue of the *New Yorker* that this was destined for, Maya Angelou describes the OJ trial as a minstrel show.

I certainly wouldn't subscribe to the notion that the only person with the authority to speak is the most directly affected. That would be to say,

"It's a hermetically closed subject, don't pay attention, don't listen, it's strictly among us insiders." It can't be that way. It's a matter of how sensitive and intelligent the commentator is. *Life Is Beautiful* made me bristle, not because he wasn't Jewish, but because, ultimately, it's kind of stupid. And *Schindler's List* made me bristle because Spielberg was kind of stupid—it's equal opportunity stupidity. One Jew, one not.

Everybody moves through this territory attempting to bend it, evoking the Holocaust for different reasons. That's why I tried to stay very, very blinkered while working: all I was trying to do was understand what my father was telling me and keep that the focus. I wouldn't make any other grand claims for what *Maus* was. I certainly never expected it to be "Holocaust for beginners": I never meant either to trivialize or aggrandize the survivor: it was just a matter of me dealing with my own family crucible, which isn't to say it's the only way one can move through this terrain, but it certainly was what was given to me to do.

Because there's so much blood and pain, it seems reasonable to walk gingerly. I used metaphor to try to understand the genocide, but I didn't turn the genocide into a metaphor. The thing about *Maus* is that it's a diaspora novel, not a Zionist novel. It's about a destiny that exists in which Israel hardly figures, as opposed to most popular American culture about the Holocaust that posits Israel as some kind of happy ending, like *Schindler's List*, where the survivors get to end their story in Israel: the payback for the Holocaust is getting a homeland. To me, this is some kind of a booby prize. When you've proved that nationalism is an absolutely virulent disease, the solution isn't to give the people who got clobbered a nation, it's something else.

We went through this thing in the last century that knocked the underpinnings out of our civilization. We live as if the Enlightenment still held, and yet there's this demonstrable, gaping hole in the center that says, "actually we're far closer to the caves than the moon," and clearly, we're capable of getting there again. Maybe Bosnian Muslims this time instead of Jews. It was such a large-scale failure of civilization that it can't help but stay a traumatized arena.

I'm not a humorist. I read all these books on the psychoanalytic theory of humor to try to understand. Nevertheless, I find I make people laugh, and I don't understand why. If you keep saying something that you perceive to be true, occasionally people laugh because you're saying something you're not supposed to say. I'm more interested in irony than in humor. For me it has to do with measuring the distance between what's said and what's meant.

Art Spiegelman and Françoise Mouly: The Literature of Comics

CALVIN REID / 2000

From *Publisher's Weekly*, 17 October 2000, pp. 44–45. Reprinted by permission of Publisher's Weekly.

It's not quite 9:30 AM, as *PW*'s interviewer walks through the still quite deserted streets of SoHo toward the modest office of *RAW*, the pioneering magazine and publisher of alternative comics and cuffing-edge graphics art cofounded by Art Spiegelman, author of *Maus*, the Pulitzer Prize-winning Holocaust memoir-in-comics, and his wife, Françoise Mouly, who is art director of the *New Yorker*.

Spiegelman answers the buzzer and he's trim, energetic, and immediately full of brainy chitchat about comics and publishing. Wearing a pale blue oxford shirt, suit vest, and green slacks, he quickly steers *PW* toward a coffee bar ("first I need caffeine"), and as we walk and talk on this warm September morning, he lights the first of a steady succession of cigarettes. Jumbo coffees in hand, we return to the amiable clutter of their office where Mouly joins us, striking and stylish in a black dress. Like Spiegelman, she is full of cheerful and lucid conversation delivered in French-accented English.

This month, HarperCollins is publishing Spiegelman and Mouly's *Little Lit: Folklore and Fairy Tale Funnies*, a large-format collection featuring stories by comics artists and children's illustrators who provide an underground comics spin to the children's picture book genre. *Little Lit* is the latest in an ongoing publishing series by these two comics and graphic design veterans; it is distinguished by its quirky story telling and extraordinary graphics, and, like any edition of *RAW*, is replete with surprises, such as Chris Ware's delightfully illustrated board game.

Together, Mouly and Spiegelman are the first family of edgy, cosmopolitan comics. Spiegelman, born in Stockholm, Sweden and raised in New York City, is a veteran of the underground comics movement of New York and San Francisco during the 1960s and early 1970s. A prominent figure during the tumultuous period of America's counterculture, social protest, sexual revolution, and psychedelia, he was joined by such legendary underground comics artists as Robert Crumb, Bill Griffith, S. Clay Wilson, Justin Green, and Gilbert Shelton, just a few of the iconoclastic West Coast artists whose works helped to usher in the current American renaissance of alternative comics—idiosyncratic, introspective graphic works self-consciously intended to be received as art, liberating a medium that had been aesthetically suppressed by the anti-comics hysteria of the 1950s and the subsequent commercial domination of mainstream superhero comics.

Beginning in 1974, Spiegelman, along with *Zippy the Pinhead* creator Bill Griffith, edited *Arcade*, a legendary comics anthology from San Francisco. "One of the most edited comics anthologies to come out of an anarchistic scene that was more totally focused on sex and drugs," Spiegelman tells *PW*. "There were a lot of different subcultures of artists interacting and bickering with each other—all of which made it a vital scene. For the first time, the comics were being done for one's peers and not for money."

Exhausted by the effort required to exhort an unruly herd of cartoonists toward deadlines, Spiegelman returned to New York City in 1975, where he met Mouly, a French architecture student who was working as a bilingual secretary, electrician, house painter, and cigarette girl to pay the rent on her SoHo loft. Of course, comics would bring them together. Very much interested in the sophisticated comics of French artists (many

of whom were also influenced by the American undergrounds) and looking to improve her English, Mouly thought she "could learn English by
reading comics. The *New York Times* was too hard for me, one issue
would last me three months." Turns out that the comics on the newsstands were very different from those she knew in France. Tiring of her
complaints about local comics, mutual friends introduced her both to
Arcade and to Spiegelman. "*Arcade* had some really interesting
comics," she says. "That was my point of entry into work that I could
understand."

By 1977, Spiegelman was consulting and producing illustrations for
the *New York Times*, comics for *Playboy* and, appropriately enough,
High Times, but none of these publications was interested in expanding
beyond the conventional work they published. "Various people would
hire me as a comics consultant and then not follow my advice," says
Spiegelman. At the same time, underground comics seemed to have
gone into hibernation. Mouly was becoming interested in publishing.
She set up a small printing press in her loft and began publishing postcards and booklets, learning about design and distribution. That year, the
two of them cofounded Raw Books and Graphics in hopes of publishing
the kind of work they were seeing from younger comics artists here and
abroad. "I fell in love with publishing graphics arts," says Mouly.
"Architects get to dream up projects, but seldom get to build them.
Here, I got the little press, and you could dream up a project, print it out,
and make it happen." *RAW*, says Spiegelman, was to become a demonstration of "just how luxurious and intelligent comics could be."

It wasn't long before they expanded well beyond Mouly's little letter-
press. The first issue of *RAW* magazine came out in July 1980: oversize
format, lavishly produced, and full of unusual, very urban and very personal graphics work. It also became known for its wry tone and sly, ever
changing subtitles: *The Graphix Magazine of Postponed Suicides* in issue 1
became The *Graphix Magazine of Abstract Depressionism* by issue 5.
RAW featured artists who had taken courses from Spiegelman at the
School of Visual Arts in Manhattan, like Kaz, Drew Friedman, and Mark
Newgarden, and Europeans who were influenced by American undergrounds, like the Frenchman Jacques Tardi and the Flemish cartoonist
Joost Swarte. It also featured the first installment of *Maus*, the autobiographical comics story by Spiegelman about his father's torments in Nazi
concentration camps that won a Pulitzer Prize in 1992 and set a standard
for literary accomplishment for American cartoonists.

To their surprise ("we expected that we were doing a one-shot," Spiegelman says), *RAW* was an immediate success, introducing a succession of artists and unpredictable graphics styles and an ironic, literate interest in trashy fringe culture that influenced an entire generation of American comics artists. "It sold out quickly and people seemed to want more," he recalls. "The artists wanted to do it again. So we got dragooned into making another one." Over the next ten years, *RAW* evolved into a smaller format trade paperback magazine and a series of one shots, copublished and distributed by Penguin, offering up the best young cartoonists.

RAW the magazine no longer publishes, but RAW the graphics arts publishing experiment continues. Now with two teenage children, Spiegelman and Mouly both emphasize that they have put the RAW aesthetic to work in *Little Lit* ("Comics aren't just for grownups anymore," quips Spiegelman), essentially creating alternative comics aimed at kids that adults can read as well. "I learned to read from comics," says Spiegelman, "and our kids learned to read from comics. By now, RAW has fulfilled its mission; it has helped to launch a generation of different comics for adults. What's needed now is to make something for kids." Besides, says Spiegelman the cartoonist, self-interest is at work: "Unless you have kids reading comics, in a generation you won't have grownups reading comics."

But traditional American comics, he says, "have an odd aroma that goes back to the 1950s," the era of anti-comics hysteria; he emphasizes that *Little Lit* was an effort to replicate the more "fully functional comics culture of Europe." Since joining the *New Yorker* as art director in 1993, Mouly says, she misses the "thrill of self-publishing," and she began to push to start a new series of kids' comics. "I think educators are wary of comics because kids gravitate to them, and they don't have to be forced," Mouly tells *PW*. "Comics are enticing in a way that a page of text isn't."

"There is all this buzz and discussion about e-books, what a comic is, on the Internet," says Spiegelman. "All those things have a place, but there's something really wonderful about a book as a book, just a nice thing to touch and hold. A book that you could enter into, learn to love and think about as you get older." But remember, reminds Mouly, "this is a man who's done a few controversial *New Yorker* covers"—and Spiegelman tells *PW* he's got a pet peeve about children's books. "Some kids' books are just so drippy with condescension. There is some idea of

Front cover of *Little Lit: Folklore & Fairy Tale Funnies*, edited by Art Spiegelman and Françoise Mouly (2000).

what a kid is that is somewhere between a chimpanzee and a pinhead. *Little Lit* is not based on underestimating kids."

And despite his own reputation as a supreme ironist, Spiegelman proclaims that *Little Lit* is also intended as a challenge to a cultural marketplace long overwhelmed by irony. "When I was a kid, Mad magazine was salvation," he says. "Everybody's lying to you—that was their message. It was so well heard that an entire generation has become so ironic that it's almost catatonic," he tells PW, while also cheerfully acknowledging that many of the RAW and Little Lit contributors, "like Dan Clowes and Chris Ware, are definitely at the highest development of what an ironic stance can be." Laughing, Mouly quickly interjects, "It's ironic to hear you say this." Sincere or not (it's hard to tell), Spiegelman impishly points to a fast-approaching age of "neo-sincerity, which is sincerity built on a thorough grounding in irony, but that allows one to actually make a statement about what one believes in."

Little Lit's fractured fables have been created by an unusual collection of American and European comics artists—those who use words and pictures in sequential panels—and noncomics illustrators. Why these particular stories? "Fairy tales have been market-tested, focus-grouped for centuries. They're resonant stories," says Mouly. In the book, Spiegelman combines a little irony and a bit of sincerity as he deconstructs a royal identity crisis in the story "Prince Rooster," an oddball father/son conflict about a very neurotic emperor, without clothes in this instance, because he also believes he's a rooster. In "Humpty Trouble," children's artist William Joyce (Dinosaur Bob) shows that you can put Humpty back together again. There's a classic Gingerbread Man comics strip from 1943 from the late creator of Pogo, Walt Kelly; Italian fabulist Lorenzo Mattotti submits a strange, intensely colorful story called "The Two Hunchbacks." Most of the artists are RAW contributors, and many have also worked on New Yorker covers for Mouly—"a band of people that could make this rather arcane storytelling process work," Spiegelman says. "So those were the artists we went back to." Others, such as David Macaulay, the popular explains-it-all-for-you illustrator and author of The Way Things Work, contributes an update on Jack and the Beanstalk—his first comic strip. "He was really excited," says Spiegelman. "Comics can be hard to learn, but they are a self-teaching machine. That's why kids can learn from them. They're willing to slow down and look."

Little Lit the series is a copublishing venture between Spiegelman and Mouly's editor, Joanna Cotler, and her children's books imprint Joanna Cotler Books at Harper-Collins, and the RAW brain trust. RAW does the production and oversees printing, and "Joanna gets to talk to marketing folks and all the people who sit around large tables," says Mouly.

We had the opportunity to do our book exactly as we conceived it."
Cotler also published Spiegelman's first children's book, *Open Me . . .
I'm a Dog!* (1997). "She's been a dream to work with," Spiegelman says.
"She got me, she gets it." And there will be more Little Lit books to
come. "Our goal is to have a Little Lit shelf," Mouly says.

They live together, work together, and share an agent (Deborah Karl).
Laughing about their communal approach—"We have collaborated on
everything from the children to the *New Yorker*"—it was only natural
that they would start a series like Little Lit. They clearly take a serious but
bemused pride in their ongoing project to make the world a better place
through comics.

Pig Perplex

LAWRENCE WESCHLER / 2001

From *Lingua Franca*, July–August 2001,
pp. 6–8. Reprinted by permission of
Lawrence Weschler.

Maus, Art Spiegelman's Pulitzer Prize-winning comic-book memoir of the Holocaust, has proved a literary sensation in country after country since the first volume was published fifteen years ago. (There have been more than twenty translations.) Until recently, however, one country had been persistently and conspicuously unwilling to embrace the book: Poland, the homeland of Spiegelman's parents and the setting for much of the book's action.

For years, efforts to publish a Polish edition were stymied by the visceral reaction of Polish editors and commentators to what they took as the central scandal of Spiegelman's entire project. Depicting Jews as mice and Nazis as cats was entirely unobjectionable, they felt, but Poles portrayed as *pigs*? Impossible! One publisher after another hesitated at the quite real prospect of reader boycotts and protests. Finally, this year, a small Kraków outfit has released a Polish edition of the book. At the behest of Adam Michnik's *Gazeta Wyborcza*, the country's most widely circulated newspaper, I undertook the interview with Spiegelman that follows.

"There were a few countries whose translations really mattered to me," Spiegelman explained in his SoHo studio, taking a drag on his ever present cigarette. "France, for example, in part because my wife is French and in part because of the long and highly sophisticated tradition of literary comic books over there. And Germany, of course, where the book proved a considerable best-seller and even gets assigned in classes.

"But a Polish publication of the book has all along been particularly important to me because—how should I say this?—well, the kind of ambivalence the Poles feel toward certain aspects of their past is mutual with me and goes back to my earliest memories. As I was being raised in Rego Park, my parents regularly expressed negative feelings about the Poles; but those feelings were regularly being expressed *in Polish*, so that Polish is really my mother tongue and the comforting lullaby music of my infant life."

But, I asked, what about the issue of having portrayed Poles as pigs? Countless Polish publishers have told me that if the Poles in *Maus hadn't* been portrayed as pigs, there'd never have been the slightest problem about publishing the book.

Three panels from the Polish translation of *Maus*.

"To begin with," Spiegelman said, stiffening slightly, "let's be honest about this: On this particular subject, if there weren't any problem, *that* would be a problem. Look," he continued, taking another long drag on his cigarette. "For the hundredth time . . . "He paused, redeploying his thoughts. "I'll tell you a story. Shortly after the first volume of *Maus* was

published here in the United States, I felt the need to visit Poland—
Sosnowiec, Auschwitz, and so forth—for research purposes, to help
me visualize the places my father was going to be talking about in the
next volume of the book. When he said that he and my mother were
stumbling through the streets of Sosnowiec late at night, frantic for
shelter. . . . In my mind a street at night is West Broadway in my SoHo
neighborhood, and I needed to see what streets in Sosnowiec actually
looked like.

"So I applied for a visa—this would have been in 1987—and I got a
call from the Polish embassy in Washington, asking me to drop by the
New York consulate; they were going to be sending someone up from
Washington to interview me. The day came, I went up to talk with the
guy—entirely cordial. He indicated that they would be granting the visa,
but he, too, wanted to know, very concerned: Why Poles as pigs?

"My initial reply, I suppose, was a bit facetious: 'At first,' I told him,
'I tried to render Poles as noble stags, but I eventually found it just too
hard inking in all those antlers.' But then I went on, trying to explain
how in the American cartoon tradition, pigs simply don't carry any particular negative connotation: Porky Pig, for instance, is every bit as cuddly and beloved a figure as Mickey Mouse. Although it wasn't lost on
me that as far as my mother and father were concerned, the main thing
about pigs is that they weren't kosher. Beyond that, in terms of the narrative conventions of the text, the main thing to be noted about pigs is
that they are not part of the book's overriding metaphorical food chain.
Pigs don't eat mice—cats do. Pigs are relatively innocuous as far as mice
are concerned.

"The embassy guy nodded politely, but clearly he wasn't buying my
explanations. 'Mr. Spiegelman,' he said gravely, at length, 'the thing you
don't seem to understand is that in Poland calling someone a swine is a
much, much greater insult than seems to be the case here in America.
Swine, you see, is what the Nazis called the Poles.'

"Exactly!" I replied. 'And they called us vermin. That's the whole
point.' You see, I didn't make up these metaphors, the Nazis did. I was
just trying to explore them, to take them seriously, to unravel and
deconstruct them. I must say, I keep waiting for some Pole to take
umbrage at the fact that I portray Jews as rodents—I mean, I'm not
holding my breath or anything, though it would be nice.

"But actually, it's interesting when you look at those metaphors in the
context of the sort of suffering competition that so seems to define

Jewish-Polish relations nowadays. Because if you think about the Thousand-Year Reich as a sort of animal farm, to borrow a metaphor, Jews as rodents or vermin were pests to be destroyed and exterminated first thing, indiscriminately, as a matter of course. Whereas Poles as pigs, like all the Slavic races in the entire Nazi conception, while not to be coddled, weren't to be indiscriminately destroyed: they were to be put to use and worked for their meat. Neither status was enviable, but it's a distinction worth noting nevertheless.

"Beyond that, though," Spiegelman went on, "the main thing to ask is that people try to see past those initial metaphors. In terms of the narrative itself, in terms of what actually happened to my mother and father, it's all very complicated: There were pigs who behaved well and pigs who behaved shabbily, just as there were mice who did likewise. I mean, look"—he reached for a volume of the American edition, leafing through for a particular page (page 136, as it happened, in the final chapter of part 1)—"on this single page, for instance, you've got the entire range of responses: My mother and father are desperately roaming the streets of Sosnowiec, seeking shelter, wearing pig masks, and first they knock on the door of the pig-woman who used to work for them as my brother's nanny, and she slams the door in their face; then they make their way to the home of the pig-man who used to work as the janitor in my mother's father's house, and he offers them shelter in his stable, at great personal risk. Both have pig faces, and yet one behaves with great generosity, while the other, if one wants to be generous about it, behaves out of sheer self-interest. And that's what things were really like."

Pausing, he took another deep drag on his cigarette. "That literal-minded way of thinking can get ridiculous. If *Maus* is about anything," he concluded, "it's a critique of the limitations—the sometimes *fatal* limitations—of the caricaturizing impulse. I did my damnedest *not* to caricature anybody in this book—and anyone who caricatures my efforts in any other light, I'm sorry, that's *their* problem, not mine."

"The Paranoids Were Right"

Alana Newhouse / 2002

From the *Forward*, 6 September 2002, pp. 1 + 14. Reprinted by permission of Alana Newhouse.

"I grew up being told by my [Holocaust] survivor parents that the world is an incredibly dangerous place and I should always be prepared to flee," Art Spiegelman told the *Forward* during a recent interview. On September 11, 2001, their predictions came true. Their son—best known as the author of *Maus*, a graphic novel about his parents' persecution and escape from the Nazis that was called a "masterpiece of comic literature" by *Publishers Weekly* and went on to win the Pulitzer Prize in 1992—found himself running from a world suddenly filled with danger. "In that sense, the paranoids were right," he said.

Spiegelman, fifty-four, lives only blocks from where the World Trade Center stood. He and his wife, New Yorker art editor Françoise Mouly, were walking on the street when the planes struck and turned around just in time to see a hole open up in the north tower. By Spiegelman's account, he was traumatized by the event for months afterward.

"I found that I actually was more or less trapped in September 11," he said, so he embarked on a mammoth effort to make sense, or as much sense as could be made, out of what had happened in his backyard.

"One way I've dug myself out of traps before is to dig myself into another one," he said. This second trap turned out to be a project he has titled "In the Shadow of No Towers," an autobiographical comic strip that will be serialized monthly beginning this week by the *Forward*, the only newspaper in America to do so.

Perhaps the most immediately striking element of Spiegelman's latest creation is its size: The comic "strips" will be on full pages, as comics were in the early part of the last century, a decision that the author relates directly to the targets of the disaster. "The buildings were so big," he said, "I needed a lot of space." But the full pages offer something emotional as well, what he called a "sense of scale and beckoning presence that one would spend a lot of time with." One needs that time, because the events behind the story are neither simple nor easy to digest.

Still, Spiegelman said that comics offer one of the most effective ways to express emotion, especially emotions related to a complicated and painful disaster. He has done this before, with *Maus*, whose second volume was also serialized in these pages, and whose protagonist turns up again in "In the Shadow of No Towers" as a stand-in for Spiegelman. "This was a means of representing myself at a time when I couldn't even see myself in the mirror clearly," said Spiegelman. Instead, he relied on an image of himself with which he was already comfortable.

Spiegelman characterized the pages as "mosaics," montages of strips angled right to left as well as up to down, broken up by circles and squares overlaid diagonally—expressions of the author looking at September 11 from a number of different angles. They are not easy to produce, Spiegelman conceded, and the density is intentional. "They have an immediacy, but they unpack for a while in your head," he said.

The process has been very different from, say, the now-famous *New Yorker* cover of black-silhouetted Twin Towers that he created immediately after the attacks, which he has said was "channeled," rather than drawn. This comic strip, on the other hand, "was a chipping-away to get at the squeamish animal inside."

In addition to the *Forward*, the project will also be serialized in the German newspaper *Die Zeit*, a twinning that amuses Spiegelman, who

Cover of *In the Shadow of No Towers* (2004).

thinks of the two as a "German-Jewish coalition that's allowing me to do this."

"September 11 forced me to take inventory of everything left in my brain," he said. "Over the past few years I had stopped doing comics because they were too hard." Spiegelman said he finds drawing illustrations, like those used for *New Yorker* covers, easier than the multiple drawings that a comic strip comprises, but he said he was using only half his brain to do them. In the aftermath of the terrorist attacks, Spiegelman said, he realized that it was cowardly not to use his brain to its fullest potential. "I made a vow as we all huddled safely that day, in the shadow of no towers, that I would draw comics again."

A Conversation with Art Spiegelman

GENE KANNENBERG, JR. / 2002

Previously unpublished interview.
Transcribed and edited from the original
audiotape by Joseph Witek and printed
by permission of Gene Kannenberg, Jr.
This public interview/slide presentation
was conducted as a joint presentation of
the International Comic Art Festival and
the Small Press Expo on 6 September
2002, in Bethesda, Maryland.

GK: You've often remarked that one of the good things about comics is
that it's a form which flies under critical radar. One of our guests at ICAF
this year, Roger Sabin, co-authored a book on the underground comix
and alternative comix and 'zines which actually uses that as its title,
Below Critical Radar. But you've reached the position in your career
now where everything you do is certainly far *above* critical radar; your
work immediately draws lots of attention.

AS: I know, that's a problem.

GK: I was wondering if you could talk about two issues related to this: first, how it affects your work to know that your work immediately draws this attention—if it actually does affect it at all—and, second, your work as a scholar of comics, your work in bringing other comics above the critical radar themselves.

AS: It's a Faustian bargain. Doing comics became very difficult after *Maus*, and for a long time I was doing less and less and less. In the wake of September 11, I began to think, "OK, you've survived this particular event, and you're frittering away your time doing covers for this cake-eaters' magazine, and so—you should do comics." The problem is that comics take so long, you have to assume you're going to live forever—at least the way I do them they used to take forever. You have to assume a long life to work on this comics stuff, and that was hard to assume after September 11. So I thought I should go back and do more it more full-time. After *Maus*, I just felt that there were eyeballs mounted on my shoulder at all times, and that made it paralyzing.

Nevertheless, the Faustian deal was that a lot of the energy for comics, and a lot of what got a lot of the people downstairs, the SPX cartoonists, interested in this was that comics didn't have that art-school baggage. You just made them. On the other hand, it seemed to me that at a certain point comics have shifted away from having a real function except as a feeder system for Hollywood; they don't have any economic function in our culture anymore. But they grew up as something to peddle newspapers at the turn of the last century, or as a way of peddling fantasies to kids in large numbers at a time when it was really a mass, mass medium. And as that drifted away from being the core operation, what ended up happening instead was, like Marshall McLuhan said, that after something stops being a mass medium it either becomes art or it withers away and dies. So after they invented the camera, people who had invested in buying lots of pigment had to find another reason to use it, because the way you made portraits was no longer this painstaking craft that you had to learn. So painters had to redefine what painting might be. And in a sense the same thing has happened to comics, at least in America (I don't know enough about Mars, and Japan), but ultimately here, for comics to have a future requires a different frame to happen. And I figure that that frame has to include the same protective devices that perhaps are surrounding the other arts. There should be a system that allows for granting, a system that allows for study. And as a result, yeah, comics are now beginning to make that move, so it's possible to see comics in these new [museum] shows; that's happening more and more, grants are being given to cartoonists, like Joe Sacco got a Guggenheim this year, Ben Katchor got a MacArthur. All of these things make it more possible to pursue something that's not as much a career as a calling, because there's not a good place for most people to do this and make even a bad living. So it requires that apparatus. What makes it a Faustian deal is, a lot of cartoonists want to be able to sneer at the academy, but you need to have the academy there so there's somebody to sneer at.

GK: It's not *all* sneering.

AS: No, it's not. It's a boho dance, as Tom Wolfe put it in his book on art. So that structure is a useful one. And for me, I wish I had hobbies, but I really don't—except for smoking I don't have any extracurricular activities. As a result, I'm interested in comics. Sometimes I'm interested in making them, sometimes I'm interested in looking at them, sometimes I'm interested in thinking about and writing what it is that I'm understanding about them. I like researching. I like looking into old comics and finding out information about the people who did them. And if anything, I've got to confess that over the last few years I actually like the meta-literature about comics more than I like reading comics. If I can find some old essay about a cartoonist, that's actually more interesting to me somehow than reading a new comic, sometimes. It's definitely a mixed blessing to have that as an ongoing love affair with this medium.

GK: In an article a couple years ago in a magazine called *X-Tra* you mentioned Thierry Groensteen, from France, as one of the writers about comics who you thought was doing the right sort of things. I was wondering if you could talk a little bit about what you think makes good writing about comics.

AS: The stuff I really like the best is the stuff that does for me what your friend said that writing about fiction did for him, so it's not so much critical writing—me and Gary Groth just had a nasty exchange of e-mails about the review of *Little Lit* that appeared in the *Comics Journal*—and that certainly doesn't make me want to look at anything, except being in the dark somewhere. On the other hand, I really like Donald Phelps's stuff. He wrote a book called *Reading The Funnies*. He goes into these delirious drunken prose descriptions of the comics that he really loves, the older ones. And he does it in such a way that I get convinced on the people I've never thought twice about, like J. R. Williams, who did *Out Our Way*. He makes a very convincing case for it. And he writes about it in a way where you can barely follow—I'm one of the few people who could follow this stuff—but he's talking about very specific pictures by Harrison Cady that have never been reprinted, and somehow the enthusiasm, the rush, the erudition that comes with it make his stuff to me the best comic criticism, because he only writes about what he loves.

GK: So there's got to be some kind of obvious engagement between the critic and the material.

AS: I'm not that interested in seeing somebody putting somebody else down very effectively. What passes for criticism is usually the consumer's guide stuff, like this movie's worth seeing, this one isn't worth seeing, this one's worth a ten-dollar ticket. On the other hand, when somebody really is able to put into words what it is that you're trying to understand about somebody's work, and shoves you toward that work, that's great criticism. And then the other thing I like to read is just historical information about people. Bob Beerbohm's here, and he's been digging into Rodolphe Töpffer and other very, very, very early ur-comics. Man, that's fascinating, because there's no way to find this stuff out unless you've got a full-time life as a researcher. And so right in that area that I guess is sort of vaguely under the umbrella of criticism, is historical writing about comics. And that's what I appreciate in Thierry Groensteen's work as well.

GK: We've got a couple of examples of your own comic strips about art about comics about art—by Art. [Slide of "High Art Lowdown"]

AS: Violating my own rule immediately—there's only negative statements, negative comments in the form of criticism of the High/Low show about comics that the MoMA did back in the early '90s. I did it as a project for *ArtForum* criticizing the show, and ultimately it was a useful catalyst in terms of forging this Faustian bargain that I think should be formed, in that I was then approached by the Museum of Modern Art because they wanted to buy some of my originals. I met these people when I was doing a show of *Maus* work in '92 at the Museum of Modern Art. I said, "Well, I don't want to sell you any originals; they'll stay in your basement forever." When I was putting together that show of *Maus* stuff, I got to see all this great stuff that they have in the basement that never comes up for air. They said, "What do you mean?" And I said, "Well, you don't understand comics. I don't even know what comics you might have in your collection, so why would you want my stuff? You'll have to always put it in some kind of peculiar context to look at it." They said, "We have comics in our collection!" I said, "What?" And they came back, and they own one Frank Giacoia *Batman* daily, a *Little King*, not the best, but a *Little King* by Otto Soglow, and one really great thing, which was a Lyonel Feininger, but mostly it was just a few things that had gotten stuck to the back of things that had been donated in the twentieth century that they didn't really know what to do with. So they said they wanted to know more.

It turned into this lecture that I gave, that I have variations of, Comix 101 for the ineducable, which are museum curators. [laughter] I invited about forty curators from different museums to my studio, all huddled together getting a lecture on comics. What I was proposing was a Low/Low show to make up for this High/Low show, saying that when you put a comic on the wall next to a painting, the painting always looks better; it was made for a wall. On the other hand, when they print the catalogue, the comics always look better, because they were made for publication. And, I said, on the other hand, if you just show comics on the wall there's nothing to compare it to, so if you put it on the wall, people will look, it's there. And somebody should just do a show of comics. And it took years for this to engage, but now it's actually under-way. One of the curators who was there is now the head of the Hammer Museum at UCLA in California, and the first thing she did was call and say, "Art, we're going to do the show!" She hooked up with, I think it's L.A. MOCA, and so it's going to be in two museums. I don't want to be one of the curators; people already hate me enough for passing judg-ment on them as an editor. The last thing I want to be is a curator, figur-ing out which art should be on a museum wall. So it will be curated by a guy who had done a show at the downtown Whitney years ago. And it will be a historical overview, with a deep focus on about fifteen artists, and they'll give them each rooms. A long overdue event.

GK: So they'll each get their own artistic context, plus you'll get to see each one in terms of each other, not next to, say, a Vermeer.

AS: If you don't know anything about comics and you see one page by some obscure cartoonist who happens to be really good and then a page of Winsor McCay that happens to be really good, there's no way to really find out that, "well, yeah, but then there's also this whole . . ." It's like the tip of an iceberg sometimes. So it seems like a very reasonable structure.

GK: Did they say when this will take place?

AS: I think it's in 2005 or 2006.

GK: OK, so just around the corner!

I think we have one more example, one of my favorite examples of comics about comics, your essay on *Peanuts*, on the work of Charles Schulz, from the *New Yorker*.

Page 2 of "Abstract Thought Is A Warm Puppy" (2000).

AS: That started out as a written essay similar to those on Jack Cole. When I started thinking about doing this was before he announced his retirement and right before he died. And right after he announced his retirement there were essays beginning to appear on Schulz everywhere.

GK: Suddenly people remembered that he was important.

AS: He was there every day and had been taken for granted forever, so I decided to try to see if it was possible to do all the things I was beginning to write in prose and condense them down to a comic. Much harder to do in comics than in prose. It turned into a three-page strip for the *New Yorker*. It all grew out of—it sounds like I'm bragging—I got a fan letter from this guy who said he was Charles Schulz and invited me to 1 Snoopy Place for the weekend. I couldn't resist! So I showed up there. I had taken Schulz for granted, I must say. I liked him when I was very young, and then at a certain point it became like wallpaper. It would never have occurred to me to list him as an influence; it would be like saying Rice Krispies was an influence—it might have been, but that's not what comes to mind. But then meeting him I was really impressed with his genuine dedication, including drawing despite the tremor in his hand; every day he drew the strip himself and didn't use ghosts. He was very impressive, so I came back having really fallen in love with this guy in a way. And it led to this; this slide is page two of it. It ended with something that made him give me a call actually the day that he died to say that it was one of his favorite things that had happened about him now, because of, I think, that last panel. The penultimate panel says, "Unfortunately, his deceptively simple approach has been widely emulated by lesser talents who have brought about a distressing erosion of cartoon craft," above a panel of Cathy and South Park and Dilbert. And then the last panel is Schulz against a tree saying, "It's not my fault!" I think he liked that.

GK: One thing that I really like about this strip is the fact that you weren't just writing an essay about *Peanuts* in comics form, but that you used the *Peanuts* form as well; you used the daily four-panel format, the Sunday format, some of the four panels went across, some were formed in a box, you've got the picture of your mouse-surrogate stand-in reading an original. It was a great commentary visually on the *Peanuts* mode as well. Could you get your own thoughts to somehow match the flow of Schulz's own dialogue?

AS: Well, it was really hard to do, because I felt obligated to have punch lines, and then I had all these thoughts I wanted to get in. One of the things in general that makes me so slow as a cartoonist is that I think of it as a medium of great condensation. When I was teaching at the School of Visual Arts, the students who couldn't think their way out of a paper bag were always drawn into the cartooning department. Oh, he could barely draw, his portfolio was the back of a science notebook, but they wanted to take his tuition fee, so they bring him to us and say, "You have a promising future as a cartoonist." So that's cartooning as kind of the dopey end of the arts, which is the opposite of the way I found it, because it's so much harder to keep everything that condensed. Although my father was never interested in me becoming a cartoonist, and I can't say that I learned much at his knee that was useful for becoming a cartoonist, but one thing that was useful is, because of his own paranoias, he taught me how to pack. It was very important at a young age to see how much you could fit into the small volume of a suitcase. I always thought of it as a useful kind of early training.

GK: I'm no artist, but I've tried to make some comics on my own, and the whole process of distillation, of taking a story idea and then trying to break it down and figure out, OK, what is the most efficient way of communicating an idea, made me just appreciate people who can actually do this all the more.
AS: It's hard.

GK: We had promised that there was going to be only one *Maus*-related question, and you almost started to cover that question, but I just want to throw it out for a little more discussion. I think that it's possible that, second maybe to only Hergé's Tintin books, *Maus* probably has more critical material written about it than perhaps than any other comic ever.
AS: A three-hundred-page book, and thirty thousand pages of essays . . .

GK: I was wondering if you could talk a little more about how a critical reaction like that affects your work. How did it affect your work, and does it continue to affect your work now, or is that sort of in the past?
AS: It took me a long time to get over it. It was really a problem to have—it's much easier to think of yourself as a genius if nobody's looking. If somebody says, "You're a genius! What are you working on now?" [adopts whining voice] "I want to go to a bookstore—I don't want to work." And so, it really took a while to get past it. But I don't

read most of the academic writing that has been done on *Maus*. I know it's out there; people send it to me. And half of it I just don't understand. A few pieces that I've read have actually been very intelligent. A lot of it's written in a kind of jargon that I can't follow. I found in general that one of the ways I used to make people nervous, even before *Maus*, was that since I did articulate about my own work, academics were happier with idiot-savant cartoonists. And only now that this jargon has been perfected, is it possible for everybody who's not in the club to be an idiot-savant, because they're never going to understand what the framing device which the criticism is. So I really can't follow half of what's been written about me.

GK: We'll try harder. Second question, just to sneak up on the lie of only one question. You've created these books that people read and that people have enjoyed for a long time; how does it feel to know that your parents kind of live on in the memories of all these people who never met them? When I've taught the book, students care passionately about the people in *Maus*.

AS: A lot of people who only bought volume one say, "How's your dad doing?" [laughter] I think it's like Woody Allen once said, "I'm only interested in immortality if I can be there to enjoy it." On the one hand, when I finished it I realized that I had made like a thirteen-year-long Yahrzeit candle, a memorial candle of some kind. On the other hand, it somehow is out there as a separate entity. And what I'm finding now is, *Maus* stays in print because it's taught in a lot of schools, and younger and younger kids are studying it. So at a certain point, even though I didn't care if my kids read it or not, I had to make sure that Nadja, my daughter, at least knew about it so it wouldn't take her by surprise. Even when she was like nine years old, or eight years old, she said Joanna, one of her friends, had just read *Maus* and she asked, "Do you think I should read it?" Her friend's nine years old, what's she doing reading *Maus*? Nadja said, "Well, what is it?" I said, "Well, it's a comic book." She then asked, "Is it a true story?" And I said, "Yeah." She said, "Is it sad?" I said, "Yeah." And she just went off like Snoopy: "Nyah, later for that!" I would have thought like thirty would be a good age. And ultimately though, within a few years, she still insisted that she hadn't quite read it, but I know that she knows every panel in that thing. And my son still thinks that the only book I've done is *Little Lit* and *Open Me, I'm a Dog*, but *Maus* is looming; it's something he'll have to know about because his peers will start reading it in classes.

GK: This slide of "A Jew in Rostock" is still about the influence of *Maus* on your life. For people who haven't seen this particular story, it was published in the *New Yorker* in a very innovative format. If you're familiar with the *New Yorker*, sometimes they'll have a single-column illustration that runs down one-third of a page. How this story works is that there's a single column here, and you turn the page and suddenly there's this two-page spread, and you're not expecting this, especially in the *New Yorker*.

AS: Well, one way *Maus* changed my life is that when I got the Pulitzer Prize, I had lunch with Jules Feiffer, who said, "This is either going to ruin your life, or it's a license to kill." And I said, "OK, I'll take license to kill." All of a sudden, things that one would never be allowed to do became possible. I believe that Tina Brown never read *Maus*, but she heard that I had gotten the Pulitzer Prize for it. And so she invited me into the magazine. This was a magazine that I had never aspired to—it was like from a different social class than my parents and me. I sort of had looked at cartoons from one place or another as a kid, and as about a fifteen year old, Jay Lynch and I (he's an underground cartoonist and my oldest cartooning friend) decided to try to sell cartoons to the *New Yorker*. I looked at them and thought that the whole operating principle of *New Yorker* cartoons was, you did a picture and then put a non-sequitur below it. [laughter] So I made up like a sheet of fifteen cartoons I didn't understand. And I sent them to the *New Yorker*, and I got a rejection slip, then after this Pulitzer Prize I get invited into the magazine.

This was pretty much one of the very, very first things I did for them. And since I was off on a book tour for *Maus* in Germany, and I was told that the book was going to be launched at the Frankfurt book fair, and I said, "You know, that's interesting, except the Frankfurt book fair isn't Germany; it's this international place. I'd like to have a book signing in Germany," and he said, "Fine, where?" Like "I live in Hamburg," said the publisher, "we can do it there." I said, "How about Rostock?" which was where there had been this anti-foreigner skinhead activity, where the gypsies who were living in a housing project were burned out of their homes, with swastikas all over. So I figured, if there's a bookstore in East Germany in Rostock, I want to have a book-signing there. And this was just after I had hooked up with the *New Yorker*, so I proposed to the magazine that I do a report on my trip to Rostock. And so the first column was just meeting a German at the Frankfurt Book Fair who— I don't even remember what his story was—oh, I'd had an interview where I had given the answer to the question, "How does it feel to have your book published in Germany?" I said, "Well, it's interesting to me, and ultimately Germany isn't that far away from America; it's only a seven-hour flight," or something like that. And then he complimented me, this guy comes up to me and says, "A very interesting answer you gave, but it's really seven hours and forty minutes." So I had a really great punch line for the first part of the strip; that was the lead-in to the trip to Rostock. And then when I got to Rostock there were these housing projects. And everything looked identical—East Germany was like a three-dimensional version of a Xerox machine running amok. They're all the same building, mile after mile of the same building. And then one vertical row of this same building that was like all the other same buildings had all been burned out and had all the windows broken. And so I figured, I've said it before but here was a real overt place to put it into effect, which was that comics are stories in the sense of going back to the root word for stories, "historia," stories of a building, coming from the picture windows in churches, which were pre-press comics. So I figured the building was the story here, so that it's basically a double-page spread of a building, with insets of the little anecdotes and incidents that happened while I was there. And it was a way of doing a kind of comics journalism.

GK: That's something that I know you've been working on, that you've actually started a section of comics journalism in *Details* magazine.
AS: A totally absurd venue. What happened is that somebody I had met years before at the *Village Voice* became the editor and asked if I could work for him. I said, "I'm under contract to the *New Yorker*, but they've just fired me as an editor for badmouthing Tina Brown, so I'm allowed to edit since I don't do it for them anymore." And he said, "Fine, edit for me." I said, "It's not easy to do comics for a fashion magazine." He said, "What would you like to do?," and I said, "What really should be happening in magazines is that the articles should be done in panels with balloons." Because newspapers are already slow, they can't deliver news. They can give you detailed information, and magazines even more so. Therefore, a magazine is the perfect place to have the kind of distillation and reflection that comics can offer, and so he let me do it.

We did these insane things; we sent cartoonist Ben Katchor on assignment, because they wanted me to cover some subjects which would be interesting to *Details* readers, which included a surfing competition.

I figured the only thing that would make a surfing competition interesting would be to send someone who knows less about surfing than I do, and so we sent Ben Katchor. His first response was, "Why couldn't it be Coney Island?" I said, "You get a free trip to Hawaii." And then he comes back, and I said, "Do you have a way to handle this?" He says, "Yeah, now I can do it. Y'know, surfing is basically an extension of the garment industry."

This is one of the fact-comics pieces, which is his report, a very good one on surfing, and then for a men's fashion magazine, we got to send Joe Sacco to The Hague to cover the World Court, that's an amazing one. We sent Kim Deitch to cover an execution. It was amazing.

The one with Kim Deitch was really interesting. He took it very seriously. And he went in sort of approving of the death penalty, and then came back having made friends with the family of the guy, who he talks with quite a lot before he dies. The strip actually I found really touching, and it was totally out of place in this magazine. I don't know who saw it, but it was a great moment, I was very pleased with it.

It just seems like [comics journalism] now seems to be more possible. The *New Yorker* occasionally allows cartoonists to do that sort of thing. I did a piece for the *New Yorker* a few years back about the picture collection of the New York Public Library that's reprinted in that book [*Comix, Essays, Graphics, and Scraps*]. That was interesting to me, because it was the kind of thing that in the old *New Yorker* would have been a very typical kind of piece for the *New Yorker* to do; it was about this obscure librarian and a strange collection.

GK: So in a way you thought you were kind of getting back to what the *New Yorker* had been?

AS: Yes, doing the old kind of *New Yorker* article. There was very little room for it in the very souped-up version of the magazine at the beginning of Tina's tenure, and it was a way of doing it in a form that people could kind of find novel-looking enough to belong in this new incarnation of the magazine.

GK: I just realized what time it is. We haven't got through a third of the slides. It's already nine o'clock, and we want to have time for questions. We were going to talk about a *lot* of things.

AS: Why don't we just look at the slides and I'll do two-word sentences.

GK: Let's do that. This slide of "A Day at the Circuits" is related to the comics formalism panel that's going to be tomorrow morning at ICAF on thinking about doing comics about comics.

AS: Well, at a certain point I was getting more and more interested in the formal aspects of comics. This wasn't an especially well-drawn one, but it was like getting inspired by all the arrows that have to be used once somebody does a comic page badly. It's a comic that you can read in fifteen different directions, and it ends in the center panel. The center panel is a picture of the world that says, "Dead end—start again." But it loops back on itself with the magenta, the blue.

GK: I like it that the color is itself a narrative element.

AS: So, that's an easy-to-understand one, but I do a lot of things where I was interested in breaking apart what was being told and what was being seen, so that the words would refer to a picture which was in a panel before or a panel after, as in this particular page, "Don't Get Around Much Anymore." This was all about how in two panels this kid is bouncing a ball, how it's the only what Scott McCloud has called moment-to-moment [transition], so that was the only place where there's some kind of moment-to-moment movement, and everything else was different kinds of movement. It was built around getting the eye to go back and forth and seeing the ball bounce. Doing these comics in the middle of the sex-and-drugs comix moment of the '60s and '70s, I was finding that I was backing myself into a corner of more and more good comics that didn't even have to be published (since I considered it an art for publication), since about three people seemed to care about what it was I was doing. I could just pass out the original and let them look at it. [laughter] At that period, a lot of the stuff that got gathered in *Breakdowns* was work that was involved with and very interested in the formal aspects of comics. And then I realized that if I wanted to have an audience—part of the definition of comics was that it was a narrative medium—I had to have a story worth telling, and that became *Maus*.

Moving right along, moving right along, ["Malpractice Suite"] is more formalist comics, taking *Rex Morgan* and grafittiing it by expand-ing the panels. Then, the *New Yorker* [September 24, 2001, cover]; I think of that as a two-panel comic strip, one where the second panel gets delivered a week after the first. We get to see the shadow of the World Trade Center towers vaguely, after thinking it's a black cover. This is being done after being with my wife, Françoise, who will talk to you

"Don't Get Around Much Anymore" (1973).

tomorrow about the *New Yorker* and will talk about some of this stuff as well. After finding ourselves in the rubble of the World Trade Center, because our daughter had just started going to school there, we had seen the plane crash and we went out that morning; the building is near our house. We went running down there and got there just in time to have the second tower collapse behind us. Really traumatic. Then we got home and there were some calls on our machine from friends who had survived and were letting us know they were OK—and then one call on the machine was this traumatic voice saying, "Françoise, get your ass up here! We're putting out a magazine in two days." So, all of a sudden there's going to be a special issue of the New Yorker while we're still shaking from the actual event. We just thought the uptown people were so insensitive. [laughter] And it was only when I left the scene that I realized that everybody uptown was traumatized too. Anyway, so, the result was I didn't know what to do with myself that day, and I began thinking about seeing if I could come up with a cover.

This image is now the cover of a book called 110 Stories, which just came out from NYU Press. That's what I was working on the 11th. And it was one of these simple-minded thoughts of, it's just such a nice day, the sky is so blue, there's so much death in the air, so this shroud is in the middle of the city. So I started out channeling Magritte and Christo, and ended up with Ad Reinhardt, finally. But this seemed wrong-headed. A year later it's possible, but at that time it wasn't going to fly.

I also was traumatized enough that day to want to make comics again, so what I've started doing now is going to begin running in a German newspaper, called "In the Shadow of No Towers." And they're very large comics pages. I can do big buildings because they're big pages there. Each page is the size of the New York Times, and they're broadsheets, in color, and I get to do about a dozen of them over as long a period of time as I need, reflecting on September 11th, and wherever I'm at now. So this will be the first one. The only place it will run in America right now is the weekly Forward, and maybe sideways in the L.A. Weekly, because it has to be broadsheet-size. But it's made me, basically, work on comics full-time again. But the New Yorker covers, which are also about children under threat, included this one which was done on September 11, 1995, and has a kid in a newspaper hat which says, "Terrorist Bombers" on it. Actually, it only had that because Tina didn't like some of the other headlines I had on the paper, and we had to argue about it. I can put "Terrorist Bombers" in, rather than something like the word "Murder," if I took out the word "AIDS" on the big headline, because she found that the idea of AIDS and children was just too depressing. So I put in "DRUGS," which wasn't depressing. [laughter]

[Slide of rejected *New Yorker* cover] This started out as a cover that I rejected, rather than the magazine. I was going to do a cover last Thanksgiving that was a parody of the Norman Rockwell Thanksgiving picture, just because there was a Rockwell show in New York as well. So this was an accepted picture, and there was a dinner with Arab-Americans having a Thanksgiving dinner, but a rock being thrown through a window behind them. So it seemed like it was an interesting example of something, kinda condensed too much. It was an interesting example of something I've now started calling "neo-sincerity," which is using the arsenal of ironic techniques perfected by *Mad*, which have now become the same techniques that are used to sell cigarettes and soap, to say something worth saying, rather than just say "everything sucks," which is what it's degenerated into. I was going to do that as an example of doing something that was a parody, but also allowed one to make a statement that needed making, but right when I was beginning to work on it, there were all these—I had CNN on a lot in those days—there were all these Arab-Americans saying, "The Jews did it," and I fig-ured, "Fuck 'em, let them get their own cartoonists." [laughter]

[Slide of November 26, 2002, *New Yorker* cover] This is juxtaposed with another cover image, because this insane project in Afghanistan had just started, where they were dropping yellow canisters that had bombs in them, and then yellow boxes that had food in them. And then they dropped flyers in English saying, "Don't pick up the yellow canis-ters—they'll kill you." And that became the turkey bomber cover.

[Slide of rejected "Bound Justice" cover] This was the one cover I'm really the most unhappy about having had rejected, and Françoise, who is the editor of the covers, I think agrees, because she still has the sketchboard up in her office as a recriminating thing. What it was, was, in the wake of the Republican impeachment hearings, this was justice bound and gagged, with an S/M ball-gag in her mouth. This didn't go over, and yet, I thought it was a good image for the moment, but even better, the week it came out, the week it would have been in print, was the week that Larry Flynt became America's hero, and started outing all these Republican senators for their extramarital affairs.

GK: So the cover would have been incredibly prescient at that point.

AS: Exactly, it would have been a news cover. So anyway, I regret that was never printed. That was a sketch done on a computer.

This one I finished and it was accepted and then rejected, and then ran in the *Nation* magazine, in the wake of the O.J. Simpson verdict. It was "The Race Card," which everybody had talked about, but nobody had shown. And it was the KKK of clubs and the O.J. of spades being held by a bloody glove, with a little bit of a credit card behind it. And there was a caption for it; at some point it was going to run inside the magazine rather than be killed entirely, it said, "Rules: Race Card Beats Gender Card Except When Player Holds Gold Card." So the *Nation* magazine ran it [in 1995], but they wouldn't run it with the caption; they ran it under the title "National Rorschach."

[Slide of *Short Order* #1] Early days of comics, underground comix, *Short Order* was a book I did with Bill Griffith, who I then did *Arcade* with at a time when the underground comix boat seemed to be sinking and we wanted a life raft. The problem was we produced it on a quarterly schedule without having had distribution that would even begin to accommodate such a thing, because it was underground comix distribution—*Zap* 1 came out, *Zap* 5, *Zap* 6 several years later, they'd all be put on the stands next to each other. Here in the course of one and half years we got six issues out, despite the anarchic inability of the cartoonists we were working with to meet deadlines. Amazingly, every three months we had one, but the underground comix shops were begging for mercy. They didn't need seven copies of the book on sale at the same time. It was as if every issue of the *New Yorker* just stayed on sale.

GK: How did it do on the newsstands, or did it not make it there?
AS: Barely. Actually, after it folded, I ended up meeting a distributor when we were first talking about *RAW*, and he said, "You know, we had our eyes on this magazine you were doing, *Arcade*. If you had just lasted two more issues we would have picked you up." But he wanted to see if we had any longevity.

One of the lessons I learned from *Arcade*, though, was that there was no place for it on the newsstand, so when Françoise and I started doing *RAW*, we realized that we needed to have a common denominator; there wasn't any other comics magazine to be with, but there were a lot of large-sized "New Wave," as they were called, magazines coming out, like one called *Wet, For Gourmet Bathers*, another one called *Skyscraper*, about architecture, one called *Stuff*, about getting and spending, and so, by being large-sized, they thought, "Oh, it's another New Wave magazine. It's got comics," but they didn't care. So it was able to get distributed.

Cover of *RAW* (vol. 1, issue 7, 1985).

So we became "Raw Publishers, the 'torn-again' graphics magazine."
Our newsstand experience meant that they wanted to rip off the logos
to show us which copies they didn't sell, and we didn't want them to do
that, but the idea of ripping off logos to count unsold magazines led to
this cover where we actually ripped corners off the magazine and made

that part of the cover design, so that part of the contents page extended up beyond the right-hand corner.

Read Yourself RAW was an anthology; it was useful in terms of talking about what *RAW* was about. There are these three symbols on it—there's the Munch picture to represent the high arts, the fine arts cartoon, then there was a middle-aged Tintin, representing the Euro content, and a slutty version of a grown-up Little Lulu, representing American comics and underground comix, as they all defenestrate.

[Slide of Garbage Candy] This was another part of my "children's" work career. My original Medicis were Topps Bubblegum, where I worked for them from the time I was eighteen until I was about thirty-eight. So for years I had a relationship with this bubblegum company, and came up with things like Garbage Candy, candy in the shape of garbage.

GK: I still have my plastic garbage pails somewhere in my parents' basement.
AS: As do a lot of people who smoke hash.

GK: "Children's" comics!
AS: So, then we had, back to this Camels pack here, Wacky Packages, Garbage Pail Kids, which were very different approaches to children's literature, because this was an I/Thou relationship, just bilk a kid out of twenty-five cents, basically. But in more recent projects, we're doing children's books; you have to actually convince the parent it's a good idea to have this, because it's the parent who has the twenty bucks, which is what our kids' book is, or fifteen dollars. But after I had kids I became interested in this thing in a very different way, and ultimately, this was the book idea I'd had years and years before, but figured it's now or never. Now when you have kids if you ever want to do a kids' book you should do it now.

GK: You've got a receptive audience to test it on, too.
AS: Yeah. And ultimately, what Françoise and I were finding—our kids learned to read because I was willing to sacrifice my comics collection. They've destroyed fantastic Barks comics, Walt Kelly comics, early *Mads*.

GK: And it all comes out of their allowance, right?
AS: They'll pay back, they'll pay back. They may grow up and have to buy them all back at whatever price they cost. In any case, it made us realize that comics really were a useful teaching tool. Without wanting to be didactic, it somehow led us to doing this *RAW* for kids, *RAW* as an

applied art rather than a pure art. In a way, like, you know, one of the reasons I was hesitating to even come to this SPX thing was I thought that I'd be met with hostility. The reviews in Comics Journal—I'm not sure if they're a barometer of anything—but they've been so hostile to Little Lit. And I felt it was sort of like I was being excoriated, like . . . I was trying to pass for white [laughter] by getting mixed up in the so-called "real world." And the fact that at this point there's now the beginnings of this thing we were talking about earlier today that there's so much evidence of here, that it's possible to make comics as a means of expression. There's no reason to do RAW anymore; there's ways for all these cartoonists to get published now. There weren't when we started RAW. Now there's a need for us to ensure that there's another generation of readers—let alone comics readers—and certainly comics readers would be nice if there's going to be comics in the future. And the way to do this was to bring in that world of children's librarians, and chil-dren's book stores, and parents who would read to their kids and let kids feed an appetite which is very easily won—which is to read comics.

[Short gap in transcript as tape is changed.]

 . . . Maurice Sendak would have become a comics artist if there was a world that could have accommodated him when he was coming of age. And so we invited children's book artists who were moving in that direc-tion to make comics, so David Macaulay and William Joyce and many others joined people like Kim Deitch and Chris Ware.

GK: Posy Simmonds . . .
AS: Yeah, exactly. And so we're doing a third book now. We're finding that we're doing something that is finding a degree of success, but not the kind of success that, say, Olivia the Pig is having, the four hundred thousand copy print runs, but successful enough so they'll let us keep going, and have other work by the guy who does Olivia [Ian Falconer]. And I realize that one of the problems is that I'm moving way too fast. I mean, I thought, "the comics world is coming of age with comics as a means of self-expression," to then go around to talking about, "No, no, you should make an applied art out of what you're doing, and find a way to actually make something understandable for kids and adults, and not just to do anything you want to do, but make it work here." And make it a story that's worth re-reading and living with intensively, because kids are very close readers, and will read something many,

many, many times. So it's not like the disposable, sometimes really great and very disposable mediocre kid comics of the forties, but like something really worth holding on to.

GK: And, so again, as with the *RAW* impulse, you're taking some history and putting it in there as well, and not just publishing new material.

AS: It's finding stuff that had legs like *Barnaby*, and finding a section that we thought would be kid-friendly. In the third one that we're working on now, we're trying to find a common denominator so that librarians and book reviewers have an easier handle on it, because it's such a dense world of material in any issue of *Little Lit*. Like the fact that you have to move from, ultimately, Chris Ware to William Joyce—it's a big jump. And in order to make it possible to even talk about and understand, we figured we'd give it a tighter theme next issue, so the next book that we're doing is called, "It Was a Dark and Silly Night." And every comics artist will have that as the title and first line of his strip, and then can take it anywhere he wants. So there will be this feeling of what it is to make a story, but each person spinning a different yarn off of that first sentence.

GK: Do you have a date on that yet?

AS: It's going to be next fall. And I think we've got Kaz doing one again, he's found it a very congenial area to work in, we have Lemony Snicket working with Richard Sala, we have Neil Gaiman and Gahan Wilson doing a story together. This one guy who I discovered who I really love is Carlos Nine; I don't know how many people in America know him, but if we had *RAW* he'd be in *RAW*, so one way to make it happen is in *Little Lit*. And he's an artist with very, very different styles; you have the classical way of drawing that maybe is in the same vein as the things that influenced David Levine, that nineteenth-century kind of illustration and cartooning from *Puck* is one way he draws. Then he has a way he started drawing recently that's just delirious, and it's hard to believe it's the same person; he looks like a very, very talented, very young cartoonist. He works in Argentina, and it looks nothing like *Krazy Kat*, but the only thing it can remind me of is *Krazy Kat*.

GK: Purity of expression, sort of?

AS: Well, it's a doodle drawing—it looks like somebody who can draw meticulously doing this image that just rolls off his hand, and it's very privately, whimsically amusing work. So we got him to do a story where he's using both styles.

Audience question: Is your artwork for Topps your own property?

AS: No. I was following Harvey Kurtzman's footsteps, repeating those lessons of the early *Mad*, working for pitchmen. In fact it was the reason I left Topps.

Question: Did you try to get the artwork back at some point?

AS: No, it was hopeless, hopeless. I left over the humiliation of an auction in which I saw work of mine auctioned off that I couldn't afford to buy. After they promised that the only reason they were keeping it was that they needed it to reprint from, which was a specious excuse. It was actually the catalyst for leaving that whole thing.

Audience question about drawing and writing at the same time:

AS: I do it both ways. I've done comics where I've had the visual conception; in fact sometimes these pages I'm doing for this [German] paper come as visual ideas first, then I figure out the language as I'm working on it. It moves back and forth. Ultimately, it's usually not either drawing or writing; it's this framework of what happens on a page. Even *Maus*— ultimately they're built around visual ideas for a page, very often, as a way of parsing how much information, or how much content can be in that page. So it's really moving back and forth between prose and pictures, and the part that's hardest for me is drawing. I writhe; it's painful.

I mean, September 11, on the one hand we're about to live through this horrible second attack on America in the form of CBS and ABC [laughter], and on the other hand, something genuinely happened. It did feel like it was a transforming moment in a sense. I mean, now I'm as back asleep as everybody else, but for at least three or four months I'd take a day off the calendar and it would still be September 11. On the very morning, when we first were outrunning this toxic cloud and got back onto our street, there were a few things that were realizations. And one of them was, "Geez, I really do love my family, and there I was in a building which I thought was going to collapse on us, looking for my daughter," so OK, family values, Bush helped me there; I'm impressed. The other things really were twofold—I saw Canal Street again. It was the first time we were out of line of sight of the Ground Zero itself, and I realized how much I really loved Canal Street. And then the first coherent sentence I said to Françoise while we were walking down was, "Shit, I now understand why the Jews didn't leave Berlin after Krystallnacht." It was my first rational thought—semi-rational thought. So I ended up realizing that, no, I'm not a rootless cosmopolitan, I'm a rooted cosmopolitan, and although I'll never buy the mug nor wear the T-shirt, I do love at least my part of the city. Then I also realized that I really wanted to make comics again, that it would be a pity to just stop doing so much of it. I really was only doing like maybe three or four pages a year. Now I'm also doing only three or four pages a year, but it's full-time.

GK: But they're really big pages!

AS: Really big pages! It looks like it's a weekly page, except each one takes five weeks, so to do something on September 11, I should have started in 1995.

Charles Hatfield: Do you get any inquiries or any demand for repackaging some of the *Breakdowns*-era strips?

AS: Well, yeah, I started doing it and then put it aside only because it started to feel posthumous to me or something, like I was looking back on my older work. I did it with this catalogue, which was for a show of my work, instead of doing *Breakdowns* again, because I began to get uptight about how much the Zipatone had peeled on the separations, and what am I going to print from on these pages, and the work of actually curating it enough to republish it was slowing me down. On the other hand, there's now a French publisher who wants to do it. Now that I'm making comics again—in the wake of *Maus* I really didn't want to put out that older work—now I'd like to see it out again, and if this French publisher comes through, then I'll go through the hassle of getting an American edition published at the same time.

Hatfield: Any more Comix 101 essays, in the wake of the Cole project?

AS: Eventually. Right now, I really want to do comics, so everything else is a distraction. But I also have one essay I really want to write, and I've wanted to write it for a long time, about Rodolphe Töpffer. I have an oral contract, I have permission from Pantheon to do a book. It came back to life again when I was talking to Chris Ware, who also wants to even if necessary self-publish a book of Töpffer, so we're going to do it together, where I'll write the essay and what Chris is going to do is letter in Rodolphe Töpffer's handwriting style in English, so it will really look like a facsimile of the original drawings by Töpffer. And he's really important, he's well-known in Europe, and here it doesn't exist. And he's really the first comics artist. I know many of you are involved in that Platinum Age comics-scholars list that Bob Beerbohm set up, and it's an amazing thing to watch people actually unearthing this prehistory of comics and how vital it is. So I want to write that essay.

Audience question: Do you have any regrets about the success of *Maus* kind of curtailing your career as a cartoonist?

AS: It's hard to regret it, because I was working on it for thirteen years. You know, it's late at night, you're working and kind of groggy and still doing it, you end up having these idle fantasies, like I imagined being on national television explaining what I was doing. Having all that stuff come to pass was a mixed blessing, but to complain about it really is like complaining about having a Rolls-Royce, but it's dirty. So it came with problems, and on the other hand, I made the thing to have a small but actual audience, and I'm glad to find that it stays in print. That was one of the reasons to make it all those nights. And it's my own neuroses and nothing else that's stopping me from doing whatever I want in life.

Audience question: I just wanted to say that I bought *Little Lit* for my nine-year-old niece, and she loved it, and ate it up, and we played the Chris Ware board game together.

AS: It's amazing—it actually is playable!

Audience: Yeah, she was totally into it, she actually wouldn't leave me alone. She just wanted to play it the whole time. But, with that in mind, and maybe this is more of a question for Chris than for you, there were some things in there that might have been a little racy for a nine-year-old. I was praying to God that she wouldn't land on Jack the Beanstalk's Gentlemen's Club.

AS: You know what it was, I found that working with the younger people who were working on *Little Lit*, in the age spectrum of people who were working, they had a much harder time with it, except for Kaz. I don't think Chris ever was a kid. He couldn't steer his ship in any other direction than his own—more power to him, he makes some great cartoons. And every time we tried to simplify what he was doing, he would come back with something more complex. So we said, "Just have the board. They're end pages. You have the board twice, once with instructions, and that's it." And no, no, he had to do a comic strip about it, and the comic strip was about this frog getting his legs cut off. It was so hard to work with him in that sense, because we're trying to do something very, very focused, like really an applied art. If I had been a really good editor I would have rejected it. The thing was, it was a brilliant, brilliant piece of work, and actually, with one editorial change it became a functional aspect of the book, which was, originally, the instructions were all written in that kind of quaint nineteenth-century style that he has, and they were very complex instructions. We said, "OK, you're going to have to write a short set of instructions." And we just labeled them to say, "Instructions for adults," and that was the short, simple ones; "Instructions for kids," and that was these long, long things in six-point type. We couldn't reject it, it was too good, and yet in a way I even now regret it, because it set a tone for *Little Lit*, it's the very first thing that opens it, and it made the other parts of *Little Lit* harder to beam in on and locate, even though I believe it's just propaganda [about] what kids can really take in. I at a very young age was reading stuff that was totally age-inappropriate. I genuinely read Kafka at the age of twelve. It was not in the young-adult fiction section. And so there's a certain latitude that if you can convince the librarians, children's-book critics, and comics critics that there actually is something that a kid can assimilate, it's amazing what kids can assimilate. And so we allowed it to run the gamut, including this crazy game.

Art Spiegelman, Cartoonist for the New Yorker, Resigns in Protest at Censorship

CORRIERE DELLA SERA / 2003

Original interview, *Corriere della Sera*
(Milan), 13 February 2003; re-translated
to English. Compiled and edited by
electronicIraq.net.

Art Spiegelman decided to leave the *New Yorker* in protest at what he calls "the widespread conformism of the mass media in the Bush era."

"The decision to leave was mine alone," the author of *Maus*, (the saga of Jewish mice exterminated by Nazi cats that won him the Pulitzer Prize—the first ever awarded for a comic book), explained in an interview with *Corriere della Sera*. "The editor of the *New Yorker*, David Remnick, was shocked when I announced my resignation. He attempted to dissuade me. But I told him that the kind of work that I'm now interested in doing is not suited to the present tone of the *New Yorker*. And seeing that we are living in extremely dangerous times, I don't feel like stooping to compromise."

Q: Do you consider yourself a victim of September 11?

A: Exactly so. From the time that the Twin Towers fell, it seems as if I've been living in internal exile, or like a political dissident confined to an island. I no longer feel in harmony with American culture, especially now that the entire media has become conservative and tremendously timid. Unfortunately, even the *New Yorker* has not escaped this trend: Remnick is unable to accept the challenge, while, on the contrary, I am more and more inclined to provocation.

Q: What kind of provocation?

A: I am working on the sixth installment of my new strip, "In the Shadow of No Towers," inspired both by memories of September 11— on that day, I had just left my apartment, a few steps from the tragedy— and a present in which one feels equally threatened by both Bush and bin Laden. The series was commissioned by the German newspaper *Die Zeit*, but here in the U.S.A., only the Jewish magazine the *Forward* has agreed to publish it.

Q: Did you feel snubbed by the refusal of the *New Yorker* to publish it?

A: Not at all. I knew from the beginning that the tone and content of the strip—which, at this point in time, is of most importance to me—were not in harmony with the *New Yorker*. A wonderful magazine, mind you, with delightful and refined covers, but also incredibly deferential to the present administration. If I were content to draw harmless strips about skateboarding and shopping in Manhattan, there would have been no problem; but, now, my inner life is inflamed with much different issues.

Q: For what do you reproach the *New Yorker*?

A: For marching to the same beat as the *New York Times* and all the other great American media that don't criticize the government for fear that the administration will take revenge by blocking their access to sources and information. Mass media today is in the hands of a limited group of extremely wealthy owners whose interests don't coincide at all with those of the average soul living in a country where the gap between rich and poor is now unbridgeable. In this context, all criticism of the administration is automatically branded unpatriotic and un-American. Our media choose to ignore news that in the rest of the world receives wide prominence; if it were not for the Internet, even my view of the world would be extremely limited.

Q: Then the Bush revolution has triumphed?

A: Yes. In Reagan's time, "liberal" was a dirty word and to be accused of such an offense was an insult. In the Bush Jr. era, the radical right so overwhelmingly dominates the debate that the Democrats have all had to move to the right just to be able to continue the conversation.

Q: Will the *New Yorker* be the same without Spiegelman?
A: The *New Yorker* existed long before I came on board. The great majority of the readers who adore the warm and relaxing bath of their accustomed *New Yorker* were very upset by the "shock treatment" of my covers. Those readers will feel more at ease with the calm and submissive *New Yorker* of the tradition which, since the 1920s, mixed intelligence, sophistication, snobbery, and complaisance with the status quo. Every time that I put pencil to paper, I was flooded with letters of protest.

Q: Which of your works caused the most controversy?
A: The cover with the atomic bomb issued on the 4th of July. The one from last Thanksgiving where turkeys fell from military aircraft. The only one universally well received was the September 24 cover with the Twin Towers in two-toned black. The censorship of my work began as soon as I first set foot in the magazine, long before the 11th of September.

Q: What kind of censorship?
A: Large and small. For the Thanksgiving cover with turkeys dropped in the place of bombs, I chose the title "Operation Enduring Turkey" to mimic "Operation Enduring Freedom" then begun by America in Afghanistan. But David Remnick forced me to change the title.

Q: Is it possible that the media is more reactionary than their readers?
A: I don't think so at all, not after reading in the polls that George W. Bush is the most admired man in America. The world I see is very different from what they see. Those who think like me are condemned to the margins because the critical alternative press of the Vietnam War era no longer exists. The *NYT* chose to remain silent about the enormous protest marches that took place during the summer; and the readers of the *Nation*, the only major publication with any guts, are at most fifty thousand: that's nothing in a country as large as ours.

Q: What does your wife Françoise Mouly, the artistic director of the *New Yorker*, think of all this?
A: She thinks that I've left her at the *New Yorker* as a hostage, but I don't think she wants to follow my example. Sometimes, I think I would

like to emigrate to Europe; and seeing that in America they won't even let me smoke, the temptation is very great.

Q: Your plans after the *New Yorker*?

A: In May, at the Nuage Gallery in Milano, there will be an exhibition that covers my ten years at the *New Yorker*. Ten is a better number than eleven and, who knows, perhaps I left the magazine simply because it better suited the book and catalog that accompany the exhibition.

Interview with Art Spiegelman

Joseph Witek / 2004

Previously unpublished interview, conducted 9 July 2004, at Art Spiegelman's
New York City apartment.

JW: I'd like to ask you some general, wide-ranging questions so as to
follow up on some things that you've talked about over the years. The
first one comes from an interview in *Cascade Comix Monthly* from
1979, where you were talking about comics and what you saw as the
need for comics that have a kind of "seriousness of intent." You used
that phrase, and then said that "Serious audiences are probably at least
as important as serious artists" in the comics world.

AS: Sounds like a smart guy, whoever I was back twenty years ago.

JW: It's amazing how that works sometimes, isn't it? I was wondering
about an issue that also works in with your consistent rejection of the
"high art/low art" distinction in terms of comics over the years. Where

it's possible to see people like Will Eisner or Harvey Kurtzman as artists with seriousness of intent, that is a kind of conscious intent, how does one make the case for people like Chester Gould or Carl Barks as artists with seriousness of intent?

AS: Well, I'm not going to defend everything that this schmuck twenty years ago said, I have no memory of the interview or where I was thinking from at the moment, but my quarrel with that phrase would only be that "seriousness of intent" would include those collage-y painted comics, and that's very serious in intent, but it's not for me. It seems very kitschy to me, and it seems like a different version of the wrong turn that Hal Foster and Alex Raymond dragged comics down, of moving it toward a mock-respectability, an ersatz respectability, because illustration was higher on the totem pole, and the same way illustrators were moving toward classical art, here these artists are moving toward modernist art. There's a whole brand of comics that I've seen now that seem to use collage and different visual styles, but in a way that makes them imitative of other arts and not keeping one's eye on the diagrammatic ball that has to be there even if somebody draws well.

All of which is to say that intentionality ain't enough—if the work cuts it, or don't cut it—and maybe we can just cross out the words "of intent" and just leave it with "seriousness," because I would posit that, in some deep way, Gould is *serious*. He's got a world that he believes in and he's putting it out there, and maybe that's part of it as well, the degree of conviction with which one enters the world of the comics one's making. With Gould, and certainly with Harold Gray, who remains a baffling monolith of a certain kind, it's that conviction that he has that carries this thing off. The stories are sappy, they're sentimental, they're politically Jurassic, they're not especially well drawn in Hal Foster/Alex Raymond terms, and yet there's a really convincing world that can actually have an emotional tug when you're reading it, for me, and that involves a real seriousness. "Seriousness of intent" begs a question, which is "intent toward what?"

JW: Let me put the question in a slightly different way. You're often called upon to be someone who talks to audiences that don't know very much about comics; you've been doing that "Comix 101" talk quite a bit, making the argument that this form is something that is intellectually serious, for lack of a better word, and I think that people often will look at someone like Chester Gould or Carl Barks—I'd like to hear you talk about Barks as well. To say, "Here are the comics that you as an intelligent person can take seriously, can look at with your full mind at work," and that person might look at Carl Barks's work and say, "He did this for kids, it's a kids' comic, what am I looking at?" What *are* they looking at?

AS: It's funny, because Barks was always the most difficult lecture. When I was teaching at the School for Visual Arts, each of these artists would get pretty much a full session, which might be me acting for two and half to three hours on end with slides, and Barks was always a hard sell. Because Barks comes with the baggage of having dealt with the Disney characters, so you've got to get past *that* even; it's the least likely place to look for something worth more than corporate-logo attention. The Disney corporate logo overshadows the characters, and one can't look at the strip directly. It really is children's adventure comics, and unless you're making the case for children's literature as well, it would be difficult to find a place for Barks as art. In other words, more than most, it is boys' adventure tales, and the fact that it's done so convincingly, and with a consistent ethic and aesthetic inside it, and done so masterfully in terms of its craftsmanship, that's where the powers of it reside, but it's slippery in terms of analysis—it's hard to analyze his work. It's possible; one can do it, but it was always a hard sell. The people who grew up with it without thinking about it much were perfectly willing to revisit it and think about it differently, and in Europe, especially in northern Europe, that's a no-brainer, everybody just assumes he's one of the great cartoonists. Still and all, it doesn't, for me, reverberate—it's somewhere between Roy Crane and Elzie Segar that the Donald Duck stuff got forged; it's an alloy of those two tendencies, and in a way, each of those artists are easier to explicate, even though the least interesting thing for me about Roy Crane is the characters and story, finally, but the kind of ruddy-cheeked adventurousness that underlies the content is certainly the same world that moves Donald and his nephews through their stories. The characters, the mythic-sized characters, are somehow to me easier to locate, and in a much more stern universe in the Segar world, so this seems like less graphically breathtaking than Roy Crane and less rigorous in some ways than Segar, but finding his own way through. And yet, I've taken great pleasure in them, it's just that slide lectures ain't the easiest way to put narrative across; it's good for the pictures. So, it's more difficult, and I wouldn't, at the moment—but this changes every few years—keep him at the very top of my pantheon, even though he's definitely made the temple.

JW: This comes up quite a bit in discussions of comics about the potential of comics, when there's a tendency to say, "Here are these people who are making great comics, but you have to put aside the content, you have to ignore or get past some of the context, and *then* you can see it, in some ways, as great art." But if you really want to do away with the "high/low" distinction, at some point you're going to be making the argument that Gary Panter is great, and Carl Barks is great, and in looking at this art form, you're looking at greatness.

AS: For me, at least, the form is what always seemed great. The form is great, and then there are things that manage to take place in that form on occasion that just are mind-blowing. After that, one is left with interesting pokings, explorations toward one area or another that indicates more of its potential. For example, there are moments in Carl Barks where Donald feels guilty, and it takes place over half a page, and it's so expressive, it's the essence of what it feels like to come to the realization that you've done something horrible to somebody else. (I think he'd sent Gladstone Gander to the North Pole in the example I'm thinking of.) All of a sudden there's a glimmer inside that of just how emotionally powerful this stuff can be, and how deep inside one's personality one can travel with this simple sign system. And yet when you get right down to it, there are these sequences where Gladstone is getting chased by a bear, and it's either amusing or not amusing depending on your tolerance for that sort of manic slapstick—manic isn't the right word with Barks, but slapstick.

You were talking about me demoing this stuff for other people, and it's much easier to make a case for comics by showing the best of Eisner or the best of Kurtzman, the best of McCay and Feininger, and then, once one develops the taste and language, then one's degree of forgiveness for the aspects of it that just aren't cutting it become easier. It's a little bit like cinema—you might want to start somebody off by showing them Orson Welles's *Touch of Evil* or *Citizen Kane*, and then after they're sort of halfway with you and saying, "Oh, yeah, maybe there's something to this cinema stuff," then you can start showing them Frank Tashlin. But you don't want to start there, because it's a much harder road to travel. Similarly, now I think we're living through this amazing moment where there's an attempt to make stories that are as worth the long time-consuming hours of rendering that are on the same level as what one might pick up from a novel of prose aimed at adults or a relatively serious independent film. But that's relatively recent—it was all done in the context of quick deadlines, children's entertainment.

JW: That brings up something that maybe I'll just ask you to react to. It's something that you said to the effect that when you're talking about the history of comics that you're really talking about the aberrations of the history of comics, the things that are *not* typical of comics are the things that you value.

AS: Fair enough, although I would say that's probably true of the history of painting as well. If you were really left with the warehouse of everything that's been painted, man, it would take a while before you got to Vermeer.

JW: You just mentioned the idea of comics as a simple sign system, and yet at other times you talk about as if it's *not* such a simple sign system. You've taken to saying that comics work like the human brain; are you suggesting that there's something actually more immediate about the apprehension of comics than there is in other art forms?

AS: I'm saying that the powers that reside specifically in comics are not mimetic the way cinematic things might be, and not as abstract as prose might be, and have a tendency to be able to deliver more narrative than many paintings, because paintings have to essentialize into one image, and the ways it goes about doing it are actually echoes of the way one remembers and takes in information. It's a very synthetic thing to remake that in comics form, but it's very immediate to take it in, because it's doing something that your brain does with the information it's trying to process anyway. It's a specific attribute of comics; there's no other medium that does that, and once comics have passed their moment of being mass culture, and in a way they have, even with all the success of manga and the graphic-novel sections of the bookstore, we ain't talking about movies or rock 'n' roll anymore. When it passes that moment it either reinvents itself or dies, and the reinvention now has to do with finding what it can do that can't be done elsewhere.

JW: That actually brings me to the next quotation I wanted to bring up. This was in the *Jewish Quarterly* in 1995, where you said, very patiently, "Comics are a medium. Any medium has its own parameters, what it can do easily, and what it can do only with great difficulty." I'd like you to be more specific—what is it that comics can do easily, and what is it that they can do only with great difficulty?

AS: Fortunately, you're picking quotes where I still sort of believe what I said, but I'm beginning to feel like one of those politicians where people say, "In 1998, you voted for NAFTA, and now . . ."

JW: I could have made it a lot worse, believe me!

AS: What I was thinking of then, probably, if it was a Jewish audience, was very specific things in *Maus* that I found very difficult to translate into comics form. At the time I was talking about that stuff, I was talking about a kind of horizontal rather than vertical information. Although comics invented some of this before movies, let's talk about some of the things that comics can do that's like storyboarding. At that point, it's pretty easy: "Hulk moves toward car; Hulk picks up car; Hulk throws car into building." Even as I say it, you can envision it any of several different ways, all of which your eyeball can track and see quite readily. Other things, like the specific example I used to use from *Maus* was trying to understand what Vladek got to eat in Auschwitz, not at a given meal, but more generally. Prose does that just like this: "Every day they would get either this or that or whatever." But finding a way to do that in comics is very difficult, because comics, like film, tend to deal in individual moments that are mimetic of a reality. And when you're trying to talk about something more general, you're really dealing with prose, and finding ways to do that without bringing the comic to a dead halt is difficult. So I was thinking of those moments as, rather than the horizontal "pick up car, throw car," a menu. A menu is a vertical structure, and how does one find ways to enter that information into what I was thinking of as this grand deposition of some kind and not bring the whole damned thing crashing to a halt. And there were many temptations to move in the direction that ultimately I've seen now Paul Karasik go into with his sister [Paul Karasik and Judy Karasik's *The Ride Together*], or Phoebe Gloeckner [in *The Diary of a Teenage Girl*] go into about her wild youth, in which you go, "Well, comics ain't working for this; we're going to go into prose for a while, folks, and then I'll see you in about ten pages." It was very tempting, but I felt that that would be a total failure. Not that I have any animus against those two books, they're interesting, but the idea was to really live out the notion that comics are a language. I must have said in that interview, it's a little bit like the mythic fifty words for snow in Inuit, that anything can be said, but it's harder to say some things. If I need to talk about snow in English, it's going to take a lot more adjectives to get there than it will for somebody who has a noun that means "slushy snow," and one that means "snow that melted and then re-packed itself again," and I had to find solutions for that throughout my working life when I wanted to move in those areas. There are other things that are difficult but can certainly be done in comics that just have to do with investing these things with emotional content.

JW: What do you mean by that?

AS: Maybe it's just because of the history of comics, but a lot of time what one's getting is either action or humor or commentary, but very rarely something that gives you the choke in your throat and the lightning bolt of recognition of how human behavior actually works and how you emotionally respond to things. And it can be done, but it's certainly not what most comics go to, so they tend to fall either on the side of bathos/pathos rather than something genuinely moving, or something rather distancing. But to actually evoke that emotional gasp is done on occasion—I, actually, as I said, have gotten this from Harold Gray—but I would say that it's clear that Chris Ware's going for that when he does his work, and that *Maus* moves into those territories. That's not the only territory, but it's one that can be accomplished only with really either great calibration to make it work so that it's not just sappy—and I actually met somebody recently who found Chris's work sappy rather than emotional, and I was shocked, but there it was—and it's a difficult trick to pull off because you're working with such simple means. It's much easier to do this, somehow, in film, because you automatically come in believing in that character as a person, because even if it ain't the person you're told it is, it's *some* person doing that, so you just have fewer of those barriers to climb over.

JW: So do you think that those barriers are a function of the form itself, or of the social reception of the form and its history?

AS: Well, the social reception of the form shaped the actual work that's been made, until now the possibilities are more open-ended. But that wasn't always the case. One didn't turn to comics for the same things one would go to Thomas Mann for. The form is capable of a lot, but it's really a limited set of tools that one's working with, and it's a difficult form to make a lot of things happen in. I don't think I even have ever read a sestina, but maybe I have, and it seems to me that there are certain forms that artists get attracted to that have their ways of making something told, but they have very rigorous rules. Comics rules may not seem rigorous, but to accomplish certain things in comics requires a real either brilliant unconscious or a lot of rigor. Or both.

Page 49 of *Maus II*.

JW: Is that different from any other art form, though?

AS: Every art form is rigorous, obviously, and requires mastering a discipline, but I think that prose, by its nature, allows a lot. There are so many things that get to be called a novel, and it's not as difficult to stretch and move once you're operating through the verbal neurons to see how one can shape things in very many ways. It's true that painting, in theory, couldn't deliver a full-fledged narrative rather than an essentialized moment, at which point it probably begins moving toward being comics with multiple images and using these things as signs. But there's a province for painting, and a province for prose, and it's what comics suffered from. The guy who wrote the essay called *Laocoön*, Gotthold Lessing, had pretty much queered it for comics by telling us that there's this proper province for painting and a proper province for prose, and don't try to mess with mixing it together, you'll come up with some mongrelization. As a result, in Western art, comics suffered from this. So I'm not trying to say that there's one thing comics *must* do and should do; all I'm saying is that one can stretch prose to becoming very visual, one can stretch painting to becoming very narrative, one can do comics that do this that or the other, and probably ditto for sculpture and music, but it's harder to make music deliver a complex narrative, until you start putting the verbal component in, than it is to make that happen with prose. And similarly with comics, there are things that it can do, but you have to want to do it. And you have to want to stay with the grammar of that medium to do it in order to find out *how* to do it, that's all.

JW: You've mentioned a number of times, and it's clear from your work, that you have a real love for and affinity for the popular culture of the 1920s and '30s, which is also true to a startling extent of a lot of other cartoonists, including people of your generation like Robert Crumb and Kim Deitch, but also now younger cartoonists like Seth and Chris Ware. What is it about this time period that is so attractive?
AS: I wouldn't start with the '20s necessarily.

JW: You seem to be going further back lately; the quote that I pulled was when you said, "Somehow my nostalgia ends with my birth."
AS: Yeah, that's about right. I think that's a critical part of the answer for me. Everything I lived through is way too fraught to get that pure glow of a self-contained world. In other words, anything I lived through moves through all of these other problematic things that are my personal history, the specifics of a political situation, the specifics of a love affair, the specifics of whatever, that don't let me just see this as a nicely self-contained universe. I'm sure if I was living in the 1930s, all I would remember is either economic deprivation or the nastiness of the bad plumbing in the small village I lived in or whatever.

But I think that there is a set of values that changed over the years, and the moments that attract me are the ones where an allegiance to and value in craft was combined with the newly industrialized world. That moment, where one is working for mass production of one kind or another, but not totally alienated labor. Labor that's invested with the pride of craftsmanship led to amazing buildings, amazing furniture, amazing comics, amazing graphics, even amazing paintings and litera- ture, because it didn't have that kind of hurried and uncontrollable vehi- cle-out-of-control feel that a lot of what's happened in the last fifty years has.

JW: I think of Gilbert Seldes, who when he first did his book *The Seven Lively Arts* was very sanguine about popular culture and about its effect on American culture, but by the time he reissued that book in the 1950s he had become almost despairing that it had been so corporatized.

AS: You have to confront television in the second round.

JW: I'm wondering, would it have been likely that people in the '20s and '30s would have been looking at this same stuff and saying, "Oh my God, it's the end of craftsmanship, it's the sign of the apocalypse!"?

AS: Probably. You were talking about the "history of the aberrations in comics"; it takes a fairly alert sensibility to see what's of value as the flood goes by, because that old Sturgeon's Law applies, what is it, 90 percent of everything is crap, and that's always been true and remains true. And it remains true when I go back over the old comics. There's a lot of stuff that has a kind of charm that comes with the patina of death and age, but it's not like, gee, every cartoonist was a master.

JW: As a matter of fact, when one looks at especially the comic *books* of the '40s, they're often quite bad.

AS: They can be unreadable.

JW: I'd like to talk about something that has been of intense interest to me for a number of years, the role of the page and page layouts in comics narrative and how that works. It's clear that, especially in the early days of comics, some artists treat each panel as if it's like a slide, with the assumption that the reader is looking at one panel at a time and none of them exist in relation to one another, while other artists arrange the panels in a somewhat pleasing shape on the page, and others are concerned with general compositional aspects like the spotting of blacks on the page. But then it's possible to get into some extremely complex effects, where the page itself works as a kind of narrative entity. When you're building a page of narrative, how do you build that?

AS: You're using the right word. To slide in one soundbite from my comics lecture, is this notion of the roots of the word "story," that the narrative component of comics comes from the same word that gave us the first comics made out of broken bits of glass, the story of that great superhero, JC, and the moments of his life presented as a story in churches that ultimately gives us the same word "story," as in stories of a building. That architectural notion of the page is, for me, what I'm scanning for. I get lots and lots of comics from lots of young cartoonists, and I scan by riffling through them in comics shops and bookshops, just to see what people are up to, and the ones who aren't interested or aware, either or both, in that particular aspect of comics, it takes me a much longer time to find out what might be interesting in their work, if I ever find out at all. It's that architectonics of a page that attracts me to comics, because otherwise, you really might as well go back into Lynd Ward-land and make individual compositions. It's the balancing act of trying to get the storytelling elements that have to be communicated balanced with the compositions of individual panels, and even more important the composition of all those panels together that make up the page. And so, when I'm doing something, I'm often trying to figure out how to make a paragraph out of a flow of information. It's like a visual paragraph.

JW: The page is?

AS: The page is a visual paragraph. I mean, it's a faulty metaphor, but the page is a unit of thought or action. I think it was only when I was talking to Joost Swarte years ago that I realized that there's one way of composing a page which is the Harvey Kurtzman method where every last panel is a period, and there's another way of doing it where every last panel is either three dots or a dash, which is the way that Hergé does it, so that the goal is to get you to flip over to the next page and keep reading. It's too sophisticated for me; I can't think that way. I have to think in terms of a unit of thought that has a shape of its own. Occasionally, the thought is too big and it has to be a long paragraph or two pages to make up that one chunk. But the idea that there's a chunk of thought that you're trying to give an overall shape to is just intrinsic, to me. The people who do it well, there's something that I start trembling and vibrating while I'm looking at the page, going "Wow! That's so cool!"

Like the page that's right behind you by Harvey Kurtzman, that never was published. It was his *avant le lettre* attempt at doing a graphic novel by adapting some Charles Dickens Christmas story into paperback format. It's a beautifully structured way of telling that particular chunk of story. The kind of things that Harvey Kurtzman was thinking about included the fact that each of these boxes on this page have to be the same size, and that meant that, if he has three lines of prose on the top of the first row of panels, and he doesn't have three lines on the second, but just short bursts of phrases above each of the panels that's only one line deep, he still had to leave the room for the other two lines so that the panels would stay the same size. It creates a certain kind of measure and beat; the fact that he has three panels in the first row, four equal-sized panels in the second row, and two in the third are part of the rhythm and structure of that page. It's more straightforward, since he's using just box shapes, than, say, the kinds of things that start happening in Fiction House comics, where all of a sudden the characters are standing on each others' heads, literally, because they been pulled out of the panels and turned into vignetted figures. Kim Deitch has done that on occasion in his work as well.

JW: What do you think the effect of that Fiction House mode is?
AS: Oh, it's chaotic, but it's exciting. It's visually exciting, and if you can balance those things so that you still keep the eyeball able to go back and forth between the whole composition and the narrative, that's cool, and there are probably ways to use that particular strategy that nobody's done yet, but it would involve really making the linkups more solidly between the figure that's burst out of the panel and what it's burst onto.

JW: Looking at the Kurtzman page, what do you think the effect is of having the captions not be in boxes? They seem to be free-floating; there don't seem to be lines around the captions.
AS: I think that if he did that on every page, it would probably start feeling either archaic, or if it's done well. . . .

JW: Why "archaic"?
AS: Well, back to Gotthold Lessing. At that point keeping the prose separate from the pictures makes you one step closer to following the "proper" course of aesthetic principle that keeps prose in its province

and pictures in its province. That's where you saw *Prince Valiant* go as an attempt for respectability, for example. The balloon is a much more problematic component in the page. On the other hand, we've certainly seen that that's not Harvey Kurtzman's problem; he can do both. There is something that comes from the power of narrative that exists as a separated prose component. Whole stories have probably been done this way that are just great.

JW: There is a whole series of devices in comics that serve to separate out the words from the pictures: balloons, the caption boxes, whether or not one uses sound effects. You seem to be suggesting that there's an ideological thrust to that.
AS: Gee, am I?

JW: Well, when you say that when you bracket them off from each other, you get to Lessing and the idea that these things are of different orders. But something like a sound effect, for example, functions both ways, and I think that in comics criticism, people who are thinking about these things in somewhat theoretical ways are pushing toward the idea of words and pictures becoming like each other in comics. You've talked about comics styles that become really almost like a kind of handwriting, where there's a mode of cartooning that is almost like calligraphy, and then there are these others where there's much more separation between the order of the word and the order of the picture. Is that something you look at when you look at comics?
AS: Yeah, but like I said, if somebody's got that feeling of structure, then the various kinds of handwriting and the different balances and modulations become the thrill. But if it's lacking that architectonic, I don't know how to find it, very often. But within that, you know, I forgive and admire Winsor McCay's draftsmanship; it doesn't get in the way of him being a great comics artist. So it's not like I say, "Oh, gee, unless it looks like handwriting, it's not gonna cook at all," but it just has to do with a feeling that somebody's made use of the ur-language, which has to do with being aware that the boxes are up in juxtaposition against each other, while doing all of the other things that it has to do. So the simplest way of doing it is keeping even-sized boxes going, so at that point at least many of the other things are allowed to foreground, the other things that happen in comics go forward unimpeded, because you're not dealing with these arbitrary-sized blocks that happen to be organized

into a page. It has to do with that feeling that there's something holding it all together that I'm looking for before I can actually focus on the individual elements.

JW: I'd like to ask you about some more specific things about the page. If you look at, say, a Carl Barks page, except for the splash panels or occasional splash pages, there are relatively few obvious manipulations of panel size or shape, but within the regular grid, the panels are slightly offset, so that the gutters don't line up all the way down the page.

AS: Which is why he's a harder person to demo, and a very interesting artist to read, because he doesn't have Harvey Kurtzman's grammatical rigor, and yet he has a very solid intuition of how to be a great storyteller. The pages look great; it's not like it's genuinely arbitrary. Things will either offset to the left, and then offset to the right, then offset to the left in the next row, so that you have some kind of rhythm set up. It seems to me that he works obviously in half-page units; if there's a period, the period happens after the second tier. That gives a feeling of structure as well. Sometimes when he does what you call these splash panels, he'll have a small panel on the left, then the rest of the half-page will open up into a picture, and your eye is really moved. If you start diagramming out what he's really doing, it diagrams. And maybe, when I'm talking about this comics stuff, when I'm talking about forgiving illustrators—or people who can draw better than me—it really has to do with, "Do I feel a diagram underneath it?" That's the thing that allows everything else to work. If the diagram is there, they can render it like Rembrandt, and it'll be great. If it doesn't have that, it just seems like a lot of lumps that have been put together, but not to make any kind of sculpted entity. If you're asking me something more specific, I'm game.

JW: No, this idea of the underlying diagram is exactly the sort of thing I'm interested in, especially the interaction between the shapes and sizes of the panels and the compositions within the panels, the trajectories, the lines of sight, the way people are pointing, and then the interaction of the textual elements as well, where your eye goes in terms of things like balloons or caption boxes.

AS: That's what's so swell about Jack Cole's work, which was interesting to me because I discovered Cole later. What now becomes this windy, theoretical thing once it's turned into language was very visceral for me when I was trying to understand what the hell these cartoonists I liked were doing, at a formative age for me. At that point, finding these structural elements was important, and as a result, certain artists just foregrounded; they were the people I was really thinking about a lot. Cole I just didn't have access to, for the most part, while I was taking shape, so it was something I got to do some of the same work with, but as a more encrusted artist. I already had my notions about how things should work, for me, at least. Cole was an interesting example of somebody who was, on the one hand, almost completely intuitive, as Barks is in that sense, and yet had such a clear sense of how your eyeball is bouncing around that page, so that every page is kind of breathtaking. Not every page, but many of his pages are really breathtaking in that way, and as I think I pointed out in a reductive diagram in one of the pages of the book form of that Jack Cole thing, there's almost like an arrow that you can make, and Plastic Man is a crucial element in showing you how your eyeball should move, does move, around that page.

JW: Will Eisner uses what I have always thought of as a wonderfully fraught term, "reader discipline," making the reader do what they're supposed to do on the page. That brings to mind Chris Ware and his approach to the page. If, say, Jack Cole is dancing you or pulling you along through the page, what do you see Chris Ware doing with his pages?

AS: Well, the reason I got KO'ed by Chris when I just saw a little part of a page on the back of a little interview with me in some college newspaper in Texas was, there it was, there's somebody who's thinking about these things as boxes and how they fit together and what they do. It's not to say that the artist's job is always to make his work invisible; boy, modernism smashed that as a notion. Chris kept coming to mind when you were talking about sound effects versus prose in boxes versus balloons. One of the strips that we ran in *RAW* was one in which the sound effects are just continuing the narrative along as if they were just more text. So if somebody's very cognizant of the use of the page and is moving very far along, that puts him at the top of the heap, as far as I'm concerned, in terms of what he's doing now.

JW: One of the things I'm thinking about with the Ware pages is, especially for someone whose eyes are not what they once were, that it's a lot of work to read a Chris Ware page. It's almost as if, where if Jack Cole is a sort of funhouse ride for the reader's eye, it's almost like a workhouse or prison, an enjoyable one, but you're *laboring* when you're really reading all of what Chris Ware has on a lot of these pages.

AS: I think that's why there's a certain degree of resistance to the work. Part of it is built in with this crazy six-point type; it's like nobody over forty should bother looking. I suspect that it's because Chris is so self-effacing that a) he just would tend to whisper rather than talk at a normal decibel level, and b) this way when he's in his fifties he won't have to look at his early work.

JW: He won't be able to!

AS: Exactly. I have to get special glasses to enter into *Jimmy Corrigan*, and I'm looking forward to the large-type edition that'll eventually get published by whoever does that kind of book publishing. But the more essential thing that makes it difficult, even at a large scale, even if these pages were blown up, is that it's a kind of comics that I think I've been engaged with, and that certainly Dan Clowes is involved with as well, that almost tells you up front, "This is going to take more than one reading." That way, that reader's discipline that Eisner's talking about is something that one learns. One learns how to read a specific artist. That's always true, like in terms of even just going, "This is a funhouse," (rather than, "This is just nuts," which is, I guess, a way to look at Cole's work), requires something that is afforded by comics, which is that you can kind of get the lay of the land, you can look at it as a map, before you read the story, by flipping through pages, by looking at the overall page before you slow down to get into it panel by panel, and that any one reading is the beginning of understanding. I think in that sense, maybe, comics, when they're done this way, have more to do with poetry than prose. I don't think anybody would enter into a poem saying, "Oh, I'll read it once and see what's up."

JW: Reading the poem for the plot.

AS: You might do that with a *Time* magazine essay, but not with a poem, and similarly, the comics thing you enter into, you begin to get a sense of it, and then you go back and read it again, and it begins to open up for you. With Chris, it's almost inevitable that the first reading isn't going to let you get through it all. It's just a very complexly built thing.

When I started lecturing about *Maus* years ago, because I was asked to, I found it very difficult to talk about the content, because the content is all there. There's not much I can really add to it except give you my sources. So I found myself more and more talking about the grammar, the ways in which I made *Maus* happen, because those are the things that remain invisible for most people who are prose-oriented. You see, I think with *Maus* specifically, since *Maus* was made in service to a text of sorts, like I used the word "deposition" sometimes, the prose always has to remain foregrounded. It's not okay to have lots of silent sequences. It's fine in the sections of *Maus* where I'm in the so-called present, because I'm there, and I can decide how to tell it. But in the part that I'm receiving from him, in Vladek's story, I have to not impose myself so overtly, so that *that* story can get told. That means that, at first glance, it's easy for somebody who's used to reading prose to work their way through this thing and feel that rosy euphoria of accomplishment—"I actually made it through a comic strip!"—for people who are used to not looking. On the other hand, when I force people in some of these lectures to look, they're going, "Wha? Huh? Cool, I didn't know that!" Because there's a lot of that kind of structuring that takes place for each one of these pages, and yet in *Maus* specifically I was trying to make that as seamless as possible so I wouldn't throw people into a disorientation on that level so that they could get disoriented by the actual content instead.

JW: This material that we're talking about here, essentially the theory and practice of page layout and leading a reader through the narrative, how much of this, in terms of articulating it, are things that you've had to learn on your own, or is there a secret cartoonists' knowledge that is passed on? Because it's clear that some cartoonists just absolutely will not talk about this kind of thing.

AS: A lot of it's so intuitive. I get self-conscious about it. On the other hand, I've tended to over-intellectualize too many aspects of my work life—it slows me down, even. But it's certainly the conscious motor for me to make my work; I wouldn't know how to go about it without that aspect of it because, unlike many other cartoonists, I don't take great pleasure in inking folds. It's not my thing—I'll do it because you've got to show that there's a fold somewhere, but it's not what gets me up in the morning and want to figure something out. And it's not, for me, the arduous perspective problems that you have to solve, or simply just figuring out what the story is you want to tell and how to tell it, even in a more rudimentary way, that moves other cartoonists. For me it really has to do with these issues of what happens when you've got a bunch of pictures together and you've got to work your way through them. So it's clear that this is an issue for the people I just mentioned before, Dan and

Chris, and it's what for me puts them at the top of the heap. It's something much more intuitive for artists even like Mark Beyer, whose work is very visually graphic on the page, but in some of the work I'm thinking about, he saw Feininger, a lightbulb went off in his head, and that way of having a page include small icons between panels, brackets that are holding the page together of one kind or another, struck him as, "This is good—I get it," and then just led him to making something that ain't like Feininger, but certainly comes from there. There are people who have the same experience with Winsor McCay. I don't think they even necessarily turn it into sentences in their head, but they'll find themselves making pages that way, and so on. I think that there's a certain amount of received vocabulary.

JW: Is there? For example, I've found it hard, when I first wanted to talk about 1940s pages, to label things like, for examples, round panels. Is there something beyond "round panels"? People don't use those much anymore, unless they're specifically trying to evoke the pages of the past. Do you simply call that a "round panel"? A "cameo" panel?
AS: "Cameo panel" sounds good, or "iris." I didn't even know that they're not being used that much anymore, because they are in a lot of the stuff I look at.

JW: Like what? Who uses them?
AS: Besides Chris and Dan? Me? I don't look at this Marvel stuff anymore.

JW: But even the Marvels of the '60s or '70s that you might have looked at don't use them. Jack Kirby used them in the '40s, but Kirby stopped using them by the '60s.
AS: This is what scholars are for. Again, it's just part of a vocabulary, so any minute now a Marvel cartoonists may be doing this on his page because it isn't as common and will attract attention.

JW: Is there a term for page layouts that are shaped like the things that are within then?
AS: You mean like a building?

JW: No, I mean things like a Fiction House comic I have, one of the air war comics, where one of the panels is shaped like the fuselage of a fighter plane, or I saw one where there was a scene of a king on his throne and the panel was shaped like a crown.

AS: Well, one is certainly welcome to find a word for it now that there's an academia, but I don't think that any artist had that in their head as verbal: "Wow, we can make this thing look like a gun, or an arrow!" I've seen lots of that over the years, and it's just one part of that thing that takes place on the page. I guess what it keeps coming back to is, let's stick with the word "diagramming." When you take a picture, and are involved in using it for its diagrammatic functions rather than for its illustrative functions, a lot of possibilities open up, which include the balloon as rain cloud or dripping ice, and include using a panel shape mimetically so that it moves toward an object, or when one has a page that's shattered by having a lot of panels exist as shard shapes. I don't know that we actually have to create a verbal taxonomy—but one might, because there are academic careers to be made, by God—but although I tend to talk about this a lot and intellectualize about it to a degree, I'm not sure that I'm even comfortable having it all isolated into its rigorous Linnaean categories. I'm not sure how useful the words might be. Maybe they would be. Maybe if it was just common parlance, people would say, "What I really need is a mimetiphone over here." The same way it's probably useful to know that something is an adjective rather than an adverb, it's something you tend to internalize. Even kids can use adjectives before they know that there is such a thing. I think that it's just part and parcel of thinking of drawing as having a diagrammatic aspect rather than a picture being used to do the job of a camera.

JW: Can you be a little more explicit about the difference between the "illustrative" and the "diagrammatic"? What's the difference between the diagram and the illustration?
AS: It's more important to know that the man is walking into the house than to see the five thousand fold concepts that make up that figure walking into the house, unless you're just obsessed with folds, in which case something else happens, as it does with George Wunder, where everything begins to look like it was made of aluminum foil in those *Terry and the Pirates* pages. But for the most part it's more important to make sure that it's clear that a man is walking into a house. At that point it's also important to understand what kind of house is he walking into, is he a tall man or a short man? These are the content parts of a picture that have to be diagrammed. Whereas it's possible in any given photograph to get a photograph of a guy walking, let's say, (photography having replaced the painter's task a while back now, so let's talk about it in terms

of photographs), it would be very possible to have a photograph of somebody walking into a house and have the shadows and stuff falling all over the place and only have it be the seventh thing that you notice, that somebody's walking into that house. It's possible to have this thing happen so you can't even tell whether the guy's tall or short, depending on where you put your camera. And it's the cartoonist's function, very often, to either intentionally disorient you so that you don't know, or intentionally orient you so you do know. Then we start moving into the diagrammatic functions, because that has to do with language, and the language of visual communication—I never really read Edward Tufte, although I have the books on my shelves and I've flicked through some of it—that has been codified for certain other purposes, like mapmaking and diagramming. That's an important part of a cartoonist's job; it's not okay to just make a "beautiful picture." Again, I'm sorry to be picking on Hal Foster or Alex Raymond, but they were the beginnings of, one way or another, moving people toward illustrative values, and on occasion, although they tended to be rather decent illustrators, they had to lose the more purely informational content that would allow you sometimes to move through a page well. It's actually something that Raymond got back later in his life in his *Rip Kirby* strips. But say with Foster, when he moves further away from his Winsor McCay roots, which is pretty quickly, you're just left with nice book illustrations stacked up on each other, and your eye isn't moved from one picture to the next, where a character points, he's facing the right way, the eye levels are staying consistent, or at least the eye lines, where the eyes of the characters are stay consistent, so that you can fluidly move through these things from box to box. And those are diagrammatic aspects.

JW: Over the years you've talked at some points as if you're reading a lot of contemporary cartoonists, and then at other times not so much, and yet again you've said in the *Comics Journal* that you haven't been reading very much at all except the work of friends who you know pretty well. Where are you right now, in terms of keeping up with what's out there?

AS: I go in phases. I'm looking around; I'm not as insular as I kept myself in the immediate post-*RAW* magazine period. There was a point where I just didn't want to have to function as an editor, and part of the editorial function included a fairly conscious and intensive scanning of what was around me to see what I should be trying to pull into this thing we were making. Now I just find it interesting to be looking around. I tend to not remember artists' names anymore, because I just don't have enough room; I'd have to throw out too many old addresses from my brain just to make room for it. So I tend to look and say, "Oh, this is cool," and only after a certain amount of repeated exposure does somebody actually get a name. I'm interested in seeing what's happening now in comics. I really can't say that I've looked at a Marvel or DC comic in a very long time, although even that's not true, but I haven't reached for one thinking, "Ah, I've got twenty minutes—I think I'll read a comic book." So it's really just looking around at stuff, for instance, like the stuff that's piled around at MOCCA, to see if somebody has moved into some terrain where he's going, "Hey look! Look what I've found!" Very often it takes me like an eighth of a second to see where somebody's setting up their tent and going, "Alright, cool, let's see if they find any gold if they dig there," but it's very easy to see where they're coming from, whether it's, "You know, I just think that S. Clay Wilson stuff is really cool," or "You know that really kind of exaggerated thing that Mark Beyer started doing—let's see, I could kind of do that," or "That Robert Crumb—he's pretty amazing. I'm going to try to draw like that," or, "That damned Clowes, he really discovered something; I think I could . . ." So there's a lot of stuff that just feels like it's in territory that's already there, and unless somebody comes up with a rather astounding narrative or develops something else there, like I said, I don't retain their names; I'm just interested that it's there, and I'm interested in what a relatively high degree of craft is beginning to happen. When I look back at the underground comix, which at the time I thought, "What a wonderful giddy breakthrough all this is!"—I look back on and go, "Man, a lot of this is really pretty crappy," just in terms of craft.

JW: So might you identify the underground breakthrough as more in terms of the social relations of comics? That is, people are now creating comics that they want to do, as opposed to comics they've been commissioned to do, say by Marvel or DC?

AS: Well, I would say that's basic. The fact that a comic should express one's personality shouldn't just be a parenthetical afterthought, but the core of what one's working with.

JW: In what we were talking about comics history, that's sort of to the point, since one wants to put forward as great comic artists all these people who weren't necessarily in that position. They were much more bound by expectations about what comics were, and certainly about what the content of the comic could be.

AS: Now we're in the same territory about what happens for painting, which is that something changes with the invention of the camera, something changes with the invention of the tube of paint that lets you get out of the chemical laboratory of your studio. If you look back at certain paintings, they've got a function. They've either got to tell the story of Jesus Christ or show how much money this guy who hired you has, or show you how beautiful this man's property is, or what this bourgeois family looked like, or any of the various functions that were taken over by the camera later. You know, there's a lot of Dutch genre painters, and then there's Vermeer. If you reduce it to its verbal content, there's kind of a lot of them that have interior scenes with a few figures in them. Vermeer got to do that part of the gig, but it obviously wasn't what was getting him to the table. And that's probably why the paintings were not looked at for hundreds of years as anything special, because you have to go back and say, "Wow, there's something going here just in terms of the composition that's underneath all this, the light that it's suffused with, and the textures that are making up this big rectangle that ain't like what the other folks are doing." I'm sure Mrs. Vermeer was like, "Can't you be more like DeHooch? Look, he's got twenty paintings done in the past month alone, and we're still trying to figure out how to afford enough money to get some butter." There's something really going on there; it's not just the magic of a name brand. There's a lot of people you get moved toward because you've been told that they're great, but there is something in the Vermeer paintings that I'm able to see that's clearly not what I see when I look at some other quite estimable Dutch painters from the same moment. It's not just the magic that's associated with Vermeer's name; the reason that his name is carrying magic is that there's something in those pictures that ain't elsewhere.

Similarly with the comics stuff, if somebody's job is really to tell you a racial slur to get you through your Sunday morning in 1907, well, cool, but it's only a few artists who manage to have this other set of concerns, either consciously or unconsciously or both, that's making something worth looking at other than sociologically years later. And those are the people who make up the real history of comics as art, as opposed to the many other ways that comics can be and have been looked at.

JW: Are we still in a post-underground moment of comics history, that is, "the underground comix and their successors," or have we moved into something else?

AS: We're moving toward something else. The underground comix couldn't have happened if there weren't comics before that to build from, so it's really one river, and it depends on what you're looking for. You can place the watershed moments at different spots along the river. Certainly there's a breakthrough that happens in the sixties, where cartoonists aren't any longer obligated to tell a joke or to tell an adventure story. So the social commentary that had been part of comics earlier in their history begins to make a stronger entry into the narrative parts of comics stories. The idea of talking in a more direct fashion to somebody who is your peer, rather than trying to deliver something to somebody in a way that's somehow condescending, and the possibility of entering human torment into the content in ways even more overt than Harry Tuttle did in *The Bungle Family* is new. The idea of moving toward strictly visual phenomena, so that one doesn't have to deliver much of a narrative at all, as in the Victor Moscoso/Rick Griffin moment in underground comix, opens up possibilities that are new.

What's been happening in the more recent past is a move toward, on the one hand, the pleasures of the picture and the iconography of comics that might come from something like Gary Panter's spelunking— and you can see a lot of it in places like *Kramers Ergot*—that's one place where things happen. And then there's another very strong thrust toward well-structured, tempered narrative. That thing that the word "graphic novel" was probably born for (that I'm not sure I can even buy into), but this thing of trying to tell a more nuanced story than before. It's certainly where a lot of the European comics have gone to over the past twenty years or so, and where I see a lot of energy being expended in the world of alternative comics now. To some degree those two places haven't been synthesized as interestingly as they might yet, in that, when one starts dealing with that kind of storytelling, the visual elements have to be very controlled and subsumed, and there's also a kind of suppression of the libido in those comics because of the pressures of getting that story told. As a result, some of this stuff feels, in some very deep way, conservative.

JW: I'm tempted to ask for an example, although I understand why you wouldn't want to give a name.

AS: I don't want to give people's names, because it's not like there's anything wrong with it. At its best, when it's done really well, we've got Dan Clowes. I have nothing but admiration for his work at this point, although I didn't like the first Krigstein-inflected stuff of his, and therefore regret that I missed out on noticing an important cartoonist early on. He was developing in ways that didn't allow me to enfold him into *RAW*. He's very smart and it's beautiful visually in its own way, but it involves a lot of suppression to get it told.

JW: What do you mean by "suppression"?
AS: Let me do it more broadly just by talking about Gary Panter at the other extreme, just to indicate what I mean, where if you have a visual need to just wail, you wail, and then you go back into some other mode to keep chugging along on whatever you're trying to tell. Or Chris Ware also, there's a lot of visual suppression. Like with most repressions, things leak out in other ways; the graphic design elements make up for the rigor required to make everything so thoroughly diagrammatic in Chris's work, where it wouldn't *have* to. If you look through his sketchbooks, there's a million different ways that Chris draws, all quite well. There's a certain thing that happens when you're trying to do a certain kind of story, where you've got to keep other things in check. It was true in *Maus*. It drove me nuts; I had to keep forging my drawing style for ten years. In order to make *Maus* happen, at a certain point I had to just forge the work of the guy who had gotten up the day before to do something. In order to do it, you've got to keep very focused in order to not let it veer off into becoming something else. That's one of the requirements of making that kind of extended narrative. One of the artists I admire the most is Crumb, and Crumb, by working so diligently from childhood on at his drawing, has—he insists that it's incredibly hard work, and I'm sure it is, because it always is—and yet he's got so many chops under his finger that there's a kind of organic fluidity of movement that allows him actually to move even into what would seem at first to be disparate vocabularies, and something that doesn't feel like that when you're reading through it. If I said those phrases to him, he'd probably just look at me like I'm some kind of, you know, "One more hebe intellectual—get away!," and yet, it's there just because his hand is so educated.

JW: So was something like *The Wild Party* something that you wanted to move toward that you had kept suppressed while doing *Maus*?

Panel from Joseph Mancure March's 1928 *The Wild Party*, illustrated by
Spiegelman and published in a new edition in 1994.

AS: Well, I wanted to do an *exercise de style* after *Maus*, and I certainly wanted to do something that allowed me to draw naked women.

JW: Who weren't mice.

AS: Something that just had room to draw, because the other drawings had to be so focused. I got really restless with it; by the time I finished *The Wild Party*, I felt I'd gotten out of a jail.

JW: In talking about the underground comix, and where comics have gone since then, do you see technology as changing comics in important ways? How has technology changed your work and your work habits?

AS: I had to give up having originals; it was a heartbreaker. Early on, I kept saying, "You want to show my original page, cool, but that's like showing a woodblock that turned into a print. It's interesting as sculpture, maybe, but it ain't the work." I didn't realize it at the time, but I had the luxury of having it both ways, because I would let people have this piece of bristol board and put it up somewhere. In the last five to ten years, I don't have originals, I have rubble. I have things that end up finding their way into the printed page, but there's no one piece of paper that's got it. These two tables used to both be drawing tables, and I'd be able to keep some longer term project on one, and not have to put my books away that I was using for reference, and have another project that was a shorter term project, like a *New Yorker* cover or something, and not have to clean up. It was great. But more and more I'd have to keep moving over to that computer, which at that point was in this other corner of the workspace. It became much more efficient eventually just to decide I'd have just this one longish work area made up of two tables, one of which has the computer, one of which has my nineteenth-century drawing tools, and I have a scanner in between. And what I don't know anymore, even when I'm looking at the "No Towers" pages, except for a couple of panels, I can't remember what was done how. Often I'll sketch directly onto the computer with a Wacom tablet, then print out something, bring it to the drawing table that has a light table on it, start building that picture differently and in more detail, then scan that in and begin working on it on the computer, and I can't tell where things started or ended anymore. There's some panels that look totally drawn, but they were just drawn, because I was in the mood, totally on the computer; there's no drawing on paper. There's other things where, it was a painting but I've scanned it in and changed the colors so completely that the painting is of no use to me anymore. It's really fluid. Certainly, even in the thinking process, I look back at what I was doing in *Maus*, and I've got these pages of reconfiguring balloons over and over again to try to get them shorter and more compressed so they're taking up less of that two or three square inches. It means rewriting the same phrase as if I was in some kind of mental hospital. Over and over and over again, finding, "Well, you know, if I say 'go' instead of 'walk' it's going to take up an eighth of an inch less in width and maybe that cadence works." Distilling the language that way involved a lot of pages of very small repetitious-seeming balloons, but that are different from each other. I've found that after I've made my first notations, this is a lot easier to do on Quark Express than it is by re-lettering everything to get it to happen. So now I, at a certain point, still am starting with thumbnails that I've made somewhere, but rather soon moving into blank squares or shapes on Quark Express, with prose that I can kind of yank horizontally or vertically and create different configurations so the balloon is still efficient in its space.

JW: At one point before you were using computers, you talked about not wanting to get into the Internet, that you didn't want to waste time doing it. Is that still true?

AS: I waste a lot of time now.

JW: Do you? Doing what?

AS: Oh, everything from eBay to doing news trawls. During the last few years especially, I've found that the *New York Times* was not as reliable a source as I used to think, so there's a ritual that must take me forty minutes—I'm not sure how much time I'm wasting because it used to all be spent on the *New York Times* newspaper page, and now the *New York Times* web page is part of the news trawl of the day that takes me over to the *Washington Post*, *Common Dreams*, the *Guardian*, Drudge and beyond, various blogs, and it's a way of trying to get a picture of what is happening that used to be much more finite.

JW: How important is it to you to know what's happening every day at that level?

AS: It's become more important ever since September 11th, because something's afoot. We went through a major sea change, and there's a lot being done to us. There are a lot of people who are getting information for the first time from Michael Moore's movie, *Fahrenheit 9/11*. I don't think there's anything in that movie that's a surprise to me, but from what I understand, this is the first time many people in America are realizing that there's a connection between the Saudis and the Bush family, for example. On the other hand, there are things that passed me by at the time that I was glad to see in that film, like I knew all about the black caucus trying to get this election called on account of rain, but I didn't realize that it was a senator's signature that would have changed the course of history, and the fact that there wasn't one man brave enough to sign that petition. That was a revelation to me, but for the most part that movie was stuff that was part of my daily information gathering that on some level was strictly survival-oriented at the beginning, like "What's the scope of this? How soon are they going to hit me in New York again?" And who's doing what to whom, and what is this coup d'etat? All of that was part of some trawl for information, but not in some abstract sense, and as I found myself drawn into drawing something related to political cartoons as part of the "No Towers" project as it developed, I found I had to do it. Now, it's just part of my day. It doesn't have the same degree of urgency as the September 12th, 13th, and 14th moment, when I was discovering things like, "Wait a minute, one of the people listed as dead inside the Pentagon was actually on one of the airplanes. What does that mean?" So that's part of it; part of it is that somebody will send me an Internet connection that gets me to a beautiful set of T. S. Sullivant drawings, and it's a great place to go, so that I'll use my computer window to do that rather than what used to happen, which is taking an eyeball refresher by picking one of the books off the shelves. So I'm not sure how much more time it's added into my time-wasting activities—they've always been a big part of my day—but it's certainly channeled them more.

JW: I've actually adopted a daily news round myself. In my case, it was less 9/11, although it began around that time, as much as when the buildup to the war in Iraq first started. I kept thinking, "There must be more to this than I know; it just seems so crazy that this is happening." I began to feel a little like it must have felt in the days of the Soviet Union, where you begin complaining about what's going on, and they say, "You're insane, obviously we have to invade Iraq." Just knowing that there were other people out there making arguments about this was crucial to sanity, to know that you're not the only person in the world saying, "This seems crazy."

AS: Because of the "No Towers" stuff, I was really aware of how out of step I was, in a way that I wouldn't even be able to remember now. In other words, the zeitgeist has changed yet again, and at this point the mainstream press isn't quite as sleepy and timid as it was, and it would be hard right now to remember that when I did certain frames and passages in the "No Towers" strips, they were really anathema, not just sort of invisible, but like you've just farted and puked and started talking in Tourette's gibberish. Now this is all part of a discourse again. The press is a pretty unreliable beast, and it's capable of falling down on the job all too easily, but it's not the same moment that it was. Through all that, it's been possible to get information, because there are English-language sources from India and Pakistan that are giving you a very different take on the same stories you're either reading or not reading in the *New York Times*.

JW: You talked earlier about working towards a new long work.
AS: I won't say a word about it. Yes, I would like to make a long work, I have some notions, but until I actually sit down and dig in I don't even want to present it to Pantheon, because I just want to make sure I can stay there. It's just too long a time commitment for me to try to get from beginning to end until I'm much further along in the process than I am now.

JW: What's the appeal of doing a long work?
AS: It keeps me from being as fragmented as I get when I'm doing short gigs. I'm not built to not work. I need to be making something; otherwise I wouldn't understand what I was doing with my days, even if I didn't need money to pay bills. It's not about that when I'm working anymore. I have to have something I'm thinking about and giving shape to, but if it's a series of short hits, like I got into doing for the *New Yorker* for a decade, it's over, and you've got to start again, and you didn't get to build on that thought directly, and I'd like to be able to follow something through in greater depth. Otherwise one can get lost in a series of essays, a series of single images, one-page strips. It's taken—it's still taking me—me about a year to clear out various things I said "yes" to in weak moments, so that I can actually do this. I'm now just about at the point where there's very little facing me, except a book tour that makes me tremble, and I don't really want to be on that book tour without an anchor, and that anchor would consist of knowing that I've got some roads I'm following on my own.

JW: Without being specific about the longer work, do you think that your future work will be more politically inflected than perhaps it was in the past?

AS: Not necessarily. I remember being in a public interview with Jules Feiffer, being onstage at the 92nd St. Y, and he was talking about something about his *Voice* strips, and then somebody from the audience asked me if I think of myself as a political cartoonist as well, and my response was, "Yeah, but I work really slow, so I just finished World War II." I think that there's a political element in *Maus* somewhere; it's not mere, sheer autobiography. The mix probably will be determined by world events. Right now, the distinction between what happens inside my little bubble of personal interest and personal reality and what's happening outside that bubble that threatens to shatter it is up close and against each other in ways that make it seem not volitional to ignore this stuff; it's not okay. So at the moment, that seems like it would have to enter into the work. But I'm not thinking of it in terms of political or not political. I can say this much, which is, what I'm trying to figure out is more to the point of what we were talking about before: the place between Gary Panter and Jason Lutes, between the visual license that comics can afford and the narrative rigors required to keep those drawings harnessed. I think the one thing that was a clue for me in this year of working on the "No Towers" stuff was it's allowing me to synthesize concerns that I had to suppress before *Maus* and the areas that *Maus* took me into. So that if one looks at the work in the *Breakdowns* anthology, there's a set of formal concerns that are easily visible that are coming back into the "No Towers" pages.

JW: To go back to that issue of the "serious audience," you've talked about the *Breakdowns* work as sort of reaching a dead-end, because it was easier to pass around the examples to the few people who cared about it than to actually go to the trouble of publishing it. Now do you feel that the audience has grown along with the comics?
AS: Yeah, I think when you talk about me going out there and yakking about comics under the rubric of these "Comix 101" lectures, at this point I think there's a more educated audience willing to accept the fact that you can have to read something more than once, that's willing to accept the fact that there's information that's not coming at you invisibly the way a *Nancy* comic strip comes at you, and it seems more plausible to be moving in this territory and still find a constituency. What you were quoting back to me, I said that in relation to why I turned to doing *Maus*, which had to do with the fact that people were so intent on getting a narrative, as the main thing they were turning to comics for, that

the rest of this stuff was like a dog whistle. Now it seems more reasonable that one can do this and find, if not the same size audience that will be available to *Dilbert, an* audience. I'm not interested in working in the total vacuum of non-communicative art; it's part of what drew me to comics to begin with. I respect certain things that I see that are totally insular, that you have to find your way into to understand and get something from, but I'm just somewhere on the spectrum short of that spot.

JW: There are elements in the "No Towers" strips that are insular as well. Figures like Happy Hooligan or the Katzenjammer Kids are in some ways as distant from a general audience as your more abstruse formal experiments.

AS: Yeah, but if you didn't know who Happy Hooligan was, you'd still know that there was this bum sitting among trash cans with a tin can on his head. If you didn't know much about *Little Nemo,* or *anything* about it—although at this point I think a kind of cultural literacy can demand that you do know—it's not invisible, it's not as obscure as making a reference to *The Incredible Upside-Downs,* let's say. So on the one hand I can assume that people know about it, and if not, then there's just this weird panel where somebody's waking up from a dream at the end, and it's functioning at a basic level. You're somehow missing something if you don't know that there's this older strip, but you know that it looks old-fashioned and somebody's waking up. There's enough information there. When I tried to figure out how to make this into a book, there's a comics supplement that actually deals with the issues that those old strips bring to the foreground and that are evoking an argument that's not about even the overt politics of the "No Towers" pages or the specifics of my experiences on September 11th, but that have to do with the nature of ephemera, and what happens when even buildings and civilizations become ephemera. Those are issues that concerned me and I got to obliquely get at them through this long comics supplement—no comic book should be without a comics supplement—that make that part of the reason for making a book out of this stuff.

JW: What was it like working in that larger format?

AS: Intoxicating. In fact, the reason I had to put the brakes on in trying to figure out this other long work is that in some ways I felt, "This is it—you've got a format and you can just keep making this stuff." But I am attracted to books, and until fairly late in the process I hadn't a clue as to how this thing could be turned into a book. This rather strange, novelty-like format of the Pantheon book that's about to come out was a fairly late development in thinking this thing through. I just figured, "It can't be a book." It wasn't thought of as a book, it wasn't meant to be a book. At best I could make some kind of portfolio or newspaper supplement reprinting it again in some other very ephemeral way, but the format is not conducive to bookmaking. Originally I just wanted to do a hardcover, very, very, very thin book the size of the *New York Times*. The publisher was not interested in talking to me about this. So it made me slow down and try to start from a different place.

But there's something intoxicating about moving into that main river of comics development, which is what started me channeling these old cartoon characters into the pages, and with the glories of being able to have different kinds of imagery butting up against itself without having to turn a page. I thought the use of the first couple of "No Towers" pages in the *McSweeney's* that just came out was not what I was after. It was part of the experiment in seeing if I could turn this into a "normal-sized" book, and something really gets lost in the translation. As soon as I have to separate out those components and make discrete pages out of it, it wasn't what I wanted. And the only other alternative would be to work in Chris-Ware-sized boxes to get that sense of juxtaposition. So it was intoxicating, and certainly it encouraged the kind of things we were talking about before: what is a page layout, and how does it articulate what you're making?

JW: Did it give you some insight into the early days of comics strips as to what it might it have been like to be an artist in those days?
AS: To a degree. It certainly let me know that there must have been something in the water back in 1900 that let these people produce prodigious amounts of work, because here I am trying to do the equivalent in some ways of a weekly strip, although more impacted, and it's taking me three weeks to get each one of these pages done. The idea that McCay was producing those on Sunday, producing stuff every other day of the week, and making an animated cartoon at the same time makes me feel like such a wimp.

JW: Yes, the film of McCay drawing is really quite astounding, isn't it? You think it *has* to have been done with special effects somehow.
AS: But in my own way I was working fast, believe it or not.

JW: I do believe it, and that's another thing I wanted to ask about. Does the time-intensive nature of comics-making militate against working in the longer form? Obviously economically it does, yet some people seem to be pushed into that direction, that the long form is something to aspire to. Is this perhaps one of the things that comics can't do as well, which is to be long?

AS: Well, clearly not, it's just that you have to want to make something long enough to be willing to work on it for a while. The joke of these "graphic novels" is that it takes years to do these things, and back in '86, all of a sudden there's a graphic-novel section in the wake of *Watchmen*, *Dark Knight*, and *Maus* where there's nothing to put on the shelves, so the section got overrun with Dungeons & Dragons how-to books or something. Because each of these works is quite an intense project, unless you're doing something with shortcuts, like, "I'll just xerox faces and make a book out of it" or something that involves a team of people working together. It takes a while, but there's something that can be done that way that can't be done any other way, and, yes, it attracts people to it, and they've got to be willing to understand that they're entering something that's going to take them anything from a couple of years to seven years. I mean, *Jimmy Corrigan*'s a long-term project; next year, presumably, Charles Burns's *Black Hole* will come out as a graphic novel, but it's, God, I don't know how many, but eight or ten years in the making. It means that you can't make a lot of them; you can't churn them out the way Simenon churned out his detective stories. You have to be obsessed, and that's probably good. It probably makes for better work to be obsessed.

JW: I'd like to ask one last question. This goes back to our discussion about the underground comix, specifically the role of drugs in their creation. You've talked about having had quite a psychedelicized period, Crumb has as well. Was there a legitimate creative element in the psychedelic experience?

AS: At this point my life is so overdetermined it's hard to figure out what strands fed something—I'm sorry to talk in fragments here, but it's a little hard to talk about this. For instance, there's the romance of the mad artist. But was Van Gogh great because he was nuts, or was he great because he managed to overcome his insanity long enough to get some painting done? These are anything but clear notions. Once you have taken drugs, it's impossible to not have taken them, so it becomes part of the process. If I look back on where my comics were before I took drugs, I was actually going someplace already implying where I would get to, and I don't look at the drug comics as my best work. That was where I actually took several steps backward into following the lead of other cartoonists, and did things that just wouldn't be my first choice for anthologizing. They were a necessary part of development, and it's affected how I think. From where I'm at now, no, I don't think it was either a good or a bad thing in terms of my work, it was just part of the trajectory.

JW: It's hard to imagine Crumb—I guess it's not hard to imagine Crumb without the drugs, because it would have been the greeting card stuff. **AS:** No, no—there'd be a Crumb, and it would be a very interesting Crumb. Certainly there was something he describes as an LSD experience that was the return of the repressed, the return of the blue-collar knobby-kneed Elzie Segar and Basil Wolverton drawing, which just came to him in a vision and affected the visual stylization of where he turned to. But the Fritz the Cat stuff and the stuff that was appearing in *Help!* magazine was already moving him toward something more ambitious than greeting cards. It would have gone into a different zone. It would be a *different* Crumb—it's so hypothetical, we're talking about Phillip-K.-Dickian alternate universes at this point—but the intelligence and the skill that he was bringing to his work, that completely snarled-up personality that needed to express itself through those particular vocabularies that he was mastering, would have found expression anyway, it seems clear. But he definitely became part of and a shaper of his moment, and that included the drug-taking.

JW: Thank you very much.

Comics as Serious Literature: Cartoonist Spiegelman Has Seen Change since Pioneering Maus

Laura T. Ryan / 2006

From the *Post-Standard* (Syracuse),
18 September 2006. The Herald Co.,
Syracuse, NY © 2006 The Post Standard.
All rights reserved. Reprinted with
permission.

Art Spiegelman turned the world of comics on its ear in 1992, when he won a special Pulitzer Prize for *Maus*, his graphic novel about the Holocaust, which portrayed Jews as mice and Nazis as cats.

In 2001, another tragedy sent Spiegelman to the drawing board: the attack on the World Trade Center. He lived just blocks from where the towers once stood, still does, in fact, and spent the morning of September 11 trying to reunite with his son and daughter, enrolled in nearby schools at the time.

First, he responded by creating the striking, black-on-black illustration of the twin towers for the cover of the *New Yorker*, where he was on staff. Then he published *In the Shadow of No Towers* in 2004, a graphic exploration of his own grief, anger, and healing, as well as an indictment of al Qaida and the Bush administration.

Spiegelman comes to town this week to deliver a talk, "COMIX 101.1," as part of the 2006 Syracuse Symposium at Syracuse University. He spoke by telephone last week.

Q: How has the world of comics changed since you entered?
A: Well, I would say while America has been going into an absolute nose dive and turning to (expletive), comics have been doing great, much to my happy astonishment . . . and I would say, during the last few years, more so than ever. Comics have just been kind of upgraded in their cultural status.

Q: They're more respected as a form of literature now.
A: Yeah, when I was first being a cartoonist, I would really hesitate to tell people what I did. It certainly didn't win me any points with the girls, I'll tell you.

Q: And now it's got cachet . . .
A: It's got cachet! It's like being a small-scale rock 'n' roll star.

Q: What do you attribute that to?
A: I could be as thumb-sucky as anybody else who wants to talk about a more visual culture or whatever, but I would say that there's several things. One is comics went into a tailspin in the '50s, thanks to the link-up that was made between comics and juvenile delinquency. . . . After the accusations that comics were the single biggest cause of juvenile delinquency and there were comic-book burnings across America, the generation that was denied grew up to become juvenile delinquents, and then adult delinquents. And made comics and read comics. . . . And then the ambitions of what cartoonists could be working on really changed in the '60s and after. And that helped slowly to get others to pay attention, so at this point we've got comics as a fairly important component in what's happening in cinema, what's happening in museums, even, and in the art world. What's happening in bookstores and libraries.

Q: Did *Maus* open the door for comics to become forums for serious subjects?
A: It was certainly a key moment, if one was trying to grasp the change, when *Maus* was given a special Pulitzer and got onto best-seller lists. First time that ever happened for a work of Holocaust literature, actually.

Q: Did that surprise you?

A: Absolutely. At first I thought it was joke, when I was called and told. And then I realized it was a special Pulitzer, so I associated it with Special Olympics.

Q: What made you want to open that door?

A: I wasn't trying to open the door for comics as serious subjects. I was just trying to deal with what was important to me in the medium that was best suited for me to tackle it through. I mean, I'm a terrible dancer. I could not have done a modern dance of my parents' lives in Auschwitz.

Q: Did you brace yourself for a negative reaction?

A: I was braced by my publisher, certainly. In fact, the book had been rejected by every publisher it was brought to, which was upwards of twenty. Sometimes really gruffly and perfunctorily, and sometimes with soul-searching, agony, because an editor really liked it but couldn't figure out how on earth to put such a book out. At that point, I was being consoled before it came out. You know, "We do lots of books that only sell two or three thousand copies. And if they're good books, by God, we're glad we did them. But, incidentally, when this comes out, you might just want to go to the country and take a holiday somewhere, so you don't get too depressed."

Q: What do you think of the new graphic adaptation of the 9/11 Commission Report?

A: It seemed like an interesting antithesis to my *No Towers* book, in that it was trying so desperately hard to be so-called objective.

Q: Do you think it could have happened without your *No Towers* book coming first?

A: Yeah, I'm sure it would have. There were other comics with crying firemen on the cover, too, that came out in comic-book format right after 9/11. Like a bunch of superheroes going, "Boo-hoo, I wish we were as brave as the fire- and policemen in New York City," or something like that. So the more sanctimonious side of our culture is always well represented. And now that graphic novels seem to be at the center of the culture, well, this was the perfect storm.

Q: What are you working on now?

A: The project I'm really trying to keep ahold of is one that sort of metastasized into a monster. It was supposed to be really easy. The very first collection of comics I did was in 1978, a book called *Breakdowns*, gathering the best of what I'd done up to that point. Very thin book. And, although it fetches very high prices on eBay and such, it hasn't been around for a long time. . . . Then I very blithely said, "Oh, I'll do an introduction" (to a new edition). And then I realized, I don't want to write an introduction. Because I vowed to return to comics after September 11, I'll draw the introduction. And now I've got about thirty pages of the introduction drawn for the forty-page book. . . . And I'm about halfway through.

Q: You vowed to return to comics after 9/11?
A: Yeah, on 9/11 actually. . . . My life at the *New Yorker* was a little bit too comfortable. I was encouraged to do essays or strips, if I wanted, or covers. And found it so much easier to write or draw separately, rather than have to make it all work as comics, that I was getting the perks of being better paid and more visible when I was doing either an essay or the covers. So like a farmer who's paid to not grow wheat, I just sort of got flabby. And when I thought I would die on September 11, which I did, one of the things that was among those realizations I had was, "Oh, schmuck. You really should have done more comics. That's what you do better than anything else."

Q: Lucky for us.
A: Depends who you talk to.

Index

Aberrations (atypical comics), 271, 276

Abie the Agent, 18

"Abstract Art is a Warm Puppy," xxii, 243

Abstraction, 43–45, 108–9, 130

Accessibility, 90

"Ace Hole, Midget Detective," 6, 37, 39, 120

Actors vs. stars, 6–7, 34

Adult comics, 30, 185

Adult readers, ix

Aesop, 72

African Americans, 90–91, 144, 149

AIDS, 252

Alex, 104

Allen, Woody, 246

Alternative comics, 289

Alternative Media, 6

American Repertory Theatre, 212

American Society of Magazine Editors, xxii

American Tail, An, 72, 153

Among the Thugs, 177

ANC (African National Congress), 93

Angelou, Maya, 221

Angoulême, xx, 204, 210, 217

Animals, anthropomorphic, 69, 72, 81, 91, 113, 197, 230–33

Anticommunism, 103, 105

Apex Treasury of Underground Comics, 85

Arab Americans, 253

Arafat, Yasir, 159

Arcade: The Comics Revue, x, xii, xix, 13, 16, 20–23, 28, 98–99, 134, 165, 182–84, 201, 224–25, 254

Arnolfini Wedding, 199

Arrow of Time, The, 177

Art history, 188

Art vs. entertainment, 52

ArtForum, xx

Artie X, 75

Artiness, 99–100, 108

Artists' political role, 142

Audience (readership), 7–8, 12, 26, 30, 49–50, 117, 134, 156, 217, 297

Auschwitz, 123–24, 143, 232, 272

Autobiography, xiii–xiv, 137, 156, 168, 178, 296
Avant-garde, 36, 101, 152, 184
Awards, 109, 204

Backstreet Boys, 101
Balzac, Honoré de, 69
Banalization, 132, 193
Bar Mitzvah, 145
Barks, Carl, 36, 61, 256, 268–70, 280–81
Barnaby, 209, 258
Barry, Lynda, 118, 132, 173
Batman, 100, 165, 242
Bazooka Group, 183
Bazooka Joe, 99, 186
Beano, 84, 95
Beatles, 58
Beckett, Samuel, 73, 131
Beerbohm, Bob, 241, 260
Being John Malkovich, 218
Benigni, Roberto, 193
Benson, John, 42
Bergdoll, Alfred, 3
Bernstein, Leonard, 214–15
Beyer, Mark, 4–5, 15–16, 21, 43–45, 119, 164, 183, 217–18, 284, 287
Big Fat Little Lit, xxiii
Big foot style, 31
Bijou Funnies, xviii
Binghamton University, xxi
Binky Brown Meets the Holy Virgin Mary, 156, 168
Bizarre Sex, 144
Blab!, 216
Black Hole, 299
Blackbeard, Bill, 18
Blasé, xvii, 75
Bliss, Harry, 211
Board games, 261–62
Book tours, 295
Bookmarks, 168, 215

Bookstores, 116–17, 302
Bosnia, 175, 181, 192, 222
"Bound Justice," 253
Bourdieu, Pierre, xi
Bowart, Walter, 97
Bracelets, 74
Brain function, 39, 90, 109, 127, 271
Brakhage, Stan, 167, 218
Brando, Marlon, 7
Breakdowns, xii, xix, 7, 20, 36, 48, 78–79, 163, 208, 250, 260, 296, 304
Breaker Morant, 52
Brief Interviews with Hideous Men, 218
Briggs, Raymond, 123
British comics, 84, 105
Broken English, 88
Brooklyn Museum, 206
Brown, Chester, 179, 185
Brown, Mary K., 16
Brown, Tina, 247–48, 252
Buford, Bill, 177
Bukowski, Charles, 134
Bungle Family, The, 289
Burns, Charles, 101, 105, 164, 183, 186, 210, 299
Busch, Wilhelm, 29
Bush, George, 127, 294
Bush, George W., 265
Buster Brown, 165

Cady, Harrison, 241
Cain, James M., 139
Caire, Patricia, 36
Caligari, 77
Calvino, Italo, 50
Campbell, Eddie, 216
Camus, Albert, 64
Caniff, Milton, 120
Caniff school, 31
Caran D'Ache, 15

Carracci, 188

Cartoons vs. comics, 188

Cascade Comix Monthly, 3, 15, 267

Catharsis, 110–11, 169–71

Cathy, 244

Cavalier, xviii

Cavalieri, Joey, 35

Censorship, xiii, 265

Cerebus the Aardvark, 120

Chandler, Raymond, 139

Chaplin, Charlie, 154

Chevalier del'Ordre des Arts et
  Lettres, xxiii

Chick, Jack T., 209

Children of Holocaust survivors,
  110–11, 143, 156–57, 160, 162,
  191, 195

China, 221

Christian bashing, 176

Chronicle Books, xxii

Cinematic layout, 61–62

Citizen Kane, 63, 270

City Limits, 95–96

City of Glass, xxi

Clear line style, 210

Clowes, Dan, 185, 210, 214, 216–17,
  228, 282–84, 287, 290

Cocteau, Jean, 29

Coe, Sue, 118, 181, 183

Cole, Jack, xxii, 18, 154, 218, 244,
  260, 280–82

Color separations, 32–33

Colwell, Guy, 45

Comanche Moon, 52

Comedian Harmonists, 151

Comic Book Confidential, xx, 114–15

Comics (the word), 25–27

Comics Code, 105, 107, 203, 211

Comics Feature, 20

Comics Journal, The, xii, 35, 55, 66,
  240, 257, 286

Comics journalism, 181, 248–49

Comics shops, 117, 119, 203, 217

Comics vs. cartoons, 188

*Comix, Essays and Graphics and
  Scraps*, xxi, 213, 249

Comix Book, xix, 22

"Comix 101," xiii, 187, 191, 196,
  205, 209, 242, 260, 268, 296, 302

"Commix: An Idiosyncratic Historical
  and Aesthetic Overview," xx

Communism, 141

Complete Maus, The, xxi, 160

Concentration camps, 141

Constructivists, 31

Content vs. form, 39–40, 65, 201

Corben, Richard, 31

"Corpse on the Imjin," 39

Corriere della Sera, 263

Cotler, Joanna, 228–29

Crackerjack, 32

Craft, 11, 13

Crane, Roy, 269

Creepy, 28

Crime comics, 107

Critical radar, 238

Crumb, R., 5, 13, 31, 70, 73, 84, 90,
  96, 119–20, 136, 138, 163, 165,
  173, 183, 218, 224, 275, 287, 290,
  299–300

Cruse, Howard, 185

Crystalline ambiguity, 74, 194

Dachau, 141

Dada, 31

Dandy, 95

Dangerous Drawings, 163, 213

Danish cartoon controversy, xxiii

Darger, Henry, 127–29

Dark Knight, The, 116, 120, 299

Dauntless Durham, 18

"Day at the Circuits, A," 250

DC Comics, 62, 116, 119–20, 195,
  287

Death penalty, 249

Deconstruction, 38, 167

Deitch, Kim, 17, 23, 103–4, 119, 218, 249, 257, 275

Demographics, 118

Detachment, 42

Details, 215, 248

Deutsch (publisher), 93–94

Diagramming, 280, 285–86, 290

Diaries, 92–93

Diary of a Teenage Girl, The, 272

Diaspora novels, 222

Dick, Philip K., 54, 177–79, 300

Dick Tracy, 127

Dickens, Charles, 106, 278

Die Zeit, xxii, 235, 264

Dilbert, 244, 297

Direct-sales shops, 117, 119, 203, 217

Disney, 72, 269

Distancing, 88–89, 108, 131, 157

Distribution, 28, 99–100, 254

Ditko, Steve, 119

Donald Duck, 82, 269–70

"Don't Get Around Much Anymore," 6, 250–51

Doodling, 146

Doonesbury, 127

Doré, Gustave, 27, 29, 165

Doubleday, 116

Doucet, Julie, 185

Doury, Pascal, 132

"Drawing Blood," xxiii

Drawing tables, 292

Drawing tools, 6, 292

Drawn & Quarterly, 216

"Drawn Over Two Weeks While on the Phone," 21

Drawn to Death: A Three Panel Opera, 212, 218

Dreams, 144–51

Dreams of a Rarebit Fiend, 154

Drechsler, Debbie, 216, 218

Dude, xviii

East Village Other, 97

Easter Bunny cover, xxi, 175–76

EC Comics, 27, 106–7

Eco, Umberto, 204

Ed Head, 18–19

Editing, 66, 182–84, 248, 286

Eightball, 216

Eisner, Will, 5, 18, 20, 102, 116, 136, 268, 270, 281–82

Elfquest, 120

Emotional content, 273

Emotional response, 49, 89, 129

Emotional vs. intellectual content, 41–43, 51, 57

Empires, 105, 141

Enlightenment, The, 222

Entertainment vs. art, 52–53

Epel, Naomi, 143

Epic Illustrated, 22, 30

Escapist entertainment, 126

"Essay on Physiognomy," 189

Eternal Jew, The, 91

Ethnic cleansing, 159

Europe, 269

European comics, 23, 66, 70, 103, 105, 164, 183, 204, 289

"Every Dog Has Its Day," 15

Existentialism, 139

Fabulous Furry Freak Brothers, 22, 84–85

Fahrenheit 9/11, 293–94

Fairy tales, 228

Falconer, Ian, 257

Fame, 214–15

Family Feud, 177–78

Fantagraphics Books, 216

Fantasy, 30

Fanzines, xvii, 5

Fatherhood, 150

Fathers, Michael, 122

Faulkner, William, 90, 131, 139

Faustian bargains, 239–41

Fearless Fosdick, 127

"Fears of July," xxiii

Feiffer, Jules, 69, 247, 296

Feininger, Lionel, 18, 242, 270, 284

Fetish, 99

Fiction House, 278, 284

Figurative drawing, 43–44, 166, 198

Filmmakers, 113, 115, 167

Fine art, 11, 13, 32

Firesign Theater, 58

Fish Rap Live!, 136

Fisher, Bud, 31

Flash Gordon, 200

Flynt, Larry, 253

Ford, Gerald, 166

Foreshadowing, 133

Form vs. content, 39–40, 65, 201

Formal experimentation, x, 166, 168, 250, 296

"Forms Stretched to Their Limits," xxii

"41 Shots 10¢," xxii

Forward, xxii, 234, 252, 264

Foster, Hal, 44, 200, 268, 286

France, xxiii, 23

Freaks, 139

Freudian interpretations, 138, 147–48

Friedman, Drew, 103, 183, 225

Fritz the Cat, 173, 300

Fumettis, 96

Funny Aminals, xviii, 7, 78, 81

Gaiman, Neil, 258

Gaines, William, 116

Garbage Pail Kids, xi, 164, 172, 211, 256

Garfield, 100–1, 202

Gazeta Wyborcza, 231

Gehr, Ernie, 167

Gen of Hiroshima, 52, 135

Generation gaps, 74

"Genocide Now," 175

Gent, xviii

German expressionism, 31, 168

Germany, 247–48

"Getting in Touch with My Inner Racist," xxi

Ghetto, 113

Ghost World, 216

Giacoia, Frank, 242

Gibberish, 60

Gilliam, Terry, 96

Gladstone Gander, 270

Gloeckner, Phoebe, 272

Godard, Jean-Luc, 26

Goethe, Johann von, 29, 189

Goethe awards, 29

Goffard, Chris, 136

Good Morning America, 169

Goodman Beaver, 96

Gopnik, Adam, 187–88

Gothic Blimp Works, xviii

Gould, Chester, 18, 44, 268

Grammar of comics, 280, 282

Grandville, J. J., 210

Grants, 203, 240

Graphic novels, 116, 132, 167, 185, 289, 299

Gray, Harold, 268, 273

Great Santini, The, 52

Green, Justin, 17, 23, 39, 156, 163, 168, 224

Greenberg, Clement, 198

Greeting cards, 300

Griffin, Rick, 120, 289

Griffith, Bill, x, xix, 15, 17, 20–21, 23, 97, 135, 165, 179, 181–84, 224, 254

Griffith, D. W., 63

Groening, Matt, 173

Groensteen, Thierry, 210, 240–41

Grof, Stanislav, 179–80

Gross, Milt, 57, 154

Grosz, George, 120

Groth, Gary, 35, 240

Guggenheim Fellowships, xi, xx, 203–4, 240

Guggenheim Museum, 197, 202, 205

"Guns of September, The," xx

Halgren, Gary, 25

Hallmark cards, 201

Hammett, Dashiell, 139

Happy Hooligan, 146, 297

Haring, Keith, 207

HarperCollins, 224, 228

Harper's, xxiii

Harpur College, xvii, xviii, 75

Hate mail, 176

Hawaii, 249

Hawks, Howard, 26, 187

Hearst, William Randolph, 29

Heavy Metal, 22, 30

Hefner, Hugh, 18, 96

Help!, 96, 300

Hemingway, Ernest, 138

Hernandez, Jaime, 116

Herriman, George, 18, 154, 187, 207

Hergé, 245, 277

Hershfield, Harry, 18

Hide and Seek, 205, 219

High and low art, 99, 197, 267, 270

"High Art Lowdown," xx, 241

High School of Art and Design, 6, 75

High Times, 19, 182, 225

"High/Low" exhibition, xx, 241–42

History of Holy Russia, The, 27

Hitchcock, Alfred, 48

Hitler, Adolf, 91

Hoberman, J., 197

Hogarth, William, 188–89, 207–8

Holocaust, xiii, 141, 145, 157, 167. See also Children of Holocaust survivors

Holocaust, The, miniseries, 113, 158

Holocaust literature, 68–69, 89, 109, 112–13, 129, 174, 192–93, 222, 302

Holocaust Museum, 158, 174–75

Honesty, 50

Honorary degrees, xxi

Houston, Whitney, 176

Hulk, The, 64, 117

Humor, 220–22

ICAF, 250

Identity politics, 175

Idiot-savants, 246

Illustration, 44, 199–200, 268, 285–86

Immediacy, 90

Immigrants, 164

In the Shadow of No Towers, xiii, xv, xxii–xxiii, 235–36, 252, 264, 292, 294–97, 302–3

Incredible Upside-Downs, The, 297

Independent films, 167

Independent on Sunday, 122

Index on Censorship, 220

Instantaneousness, 55

Intellectual art, 99

Intellectual vs. emotional content, 41–43, 51, 57

Internet, 226, 264, 293–94

Interview, 28, 99

Interview process, xiv–xv, 85–87, 169

Irony, 222, 227–28

Israel, 124, 158, 221

"It Was a Dark and Silly Night," 258

It's a Good Life, If You Don't Weaken, 185

Jack Cole and Plastic Man, xxii

Jacobowitz, Susan, 152

Jacobs, Ken, 81, 167, 218

Japanese comics, 70, 89, 103–4, 135, 164, 204–5

Jarry, Alfred, 15, 29
Jaxon, 52
Jazz, 51
Jesus Christ, 277
"Jew in Rostock, A," xx, 247–48
Jew of New York, The, 216
Jewish Quarterly, 271
Jewishness, 154, 173–74
Jews, as vermin, 81, 91, 232–33
Jimmy Corrigan, 282, 299
Joel H. Cavior Present Tense Award,
    109
Johnson, Crockett, 209
Johnston, Philip, 212
Jonze, Spike, 218
"Josephine the Singer, or the Mouse
    Folk," 82
Joyce, James, 53–54, 58, 90, 189
Joyce, William, 211, 228, 257–58
Julius Knipl: Real Estate
    Photographer, 185
Jungian interpretations, 138
Jungle Book (Kurtzman), 96
Juno, Andrea, 163, 213–14
Juvenile delinquency, 302

Kafka, Franz, 69, 75, 82, 131, 139,
    154, 262
Kannenberg, Gene, 238
Karasik, Paul and Judy, 272
Karl, Deborah, 229
"Karla in Commieland," 103
Katchor, Ben, 36, 183, 185, 204, 216,
    240, 248–49
Katzenjammer Kids, The, 29, 297
Kaz, 51, 183, 210, 225, 258, 261
Keane, Walter, 135
Kelley, Mike, 218–19
Kelly, Walt, 200, 210, 228, 256
Kidd, Chip, xxii
Kirby, Jack, 115, 120, 136, 284
Kitchen, Denis, 4, 16

Kitsch, 219, 268
Kominsky, Aline, 16
Kosher, 232
Kramer's Ergot, 289
Krantz, Judith, 50
Krazy Kat, 154, 187, 258
Krigstein, Bernard, 18, 290
Kristallnacht, 191, 259
Ku Klux Klan, 221, 254
Kunzle, David, 208
Kurtzman, Harvey, 5, 18, 20, 39,
    41–42, 57, 61, 96, 154, 181–82,
    259, 268, 270, 277–80

La Centrale dell'Arte, xxi, 213
LA Weekly, 191
Laing, R. D., 179
Lang, Fritz, 63
Language of comics, xviii, 5, 165–66,
    194
L'Assiette au Beurre, 15
Le Police, Pierre, 185
Lessing, Gotthold, 275, 278–79
Levine, David, 69, 258
Libraries, ix, 138, 208, 302
Library of Congress, 205
Life Is Beautiful, 193, 222
Li'l Abner, 127
Lingua Franca, 230
Lissitzky, El, 31
Literary Dog, The, 15
Little Annie Fanny, 96
Little King, 242
Little Lit, x, xiii, xxii–xxiii, 210–11,
    213, 215, 224, 226–29, 240, 246,
    257–58, 261–62
Little Lulu, 256
Little Nemo in Slumberland, 129–30,
    154, 165, 297
Long comics, 295, 299
Long Island Post, xvii, 75, 144
Lorenz, Lee, xx

Los Angeles Times, 173
Love & Rockets, 118
Love comics, 41, 107, 154
LSD, 76, 120, 162, 180, 300
Lutes, Jason, 296
Lynch, Jay, 15, 96, 180, 247

MacArthur Fellowships, 240
Macauley, David, 210, 228, 257
Macbeth, 148
Mad magazine, 75, 96, 100, 107,
    139, 154, 228, 253, 256, 259
Magazine format, 28, 99
Mail books, 14–15
Mainstream, 161–62
"Making of Maus, The," 123, 144
Male readers, 217
"Malpractice Suite, The," 38–39, 250
"Manhattan," 40
Manipulative writing, 41, 47–50, 53,
    129
Mann, Ron, 114, 116
Mann, Thomas, 273
March, Joseph Moncure, xiii, xxi,
    153, 291
Marey, Etienne-Jules, 190
Mariscal, Javier, 21, 41–42, 45, 183
Mark Trail, 19
Marsalis, Wynton, 215
Marvel Comics, xix, 5, 19, 22, 26–27,
    62, 89, 116, 118–19, 284, 287
Marxist interpretations, 138
Masereel, Frans, 129
Masks, 92, 108, 221
Mass culture, 271
Mass media, 171, 203
Masse, Francis, 35
"Master Race," 39
Mattotti, Lorenzo, 210, 228
"Maus" (1972 story), xviii, xix, 7–8,
    78, 82, 85, 90, 168
Max and Moritz, 29

Mayakovsky, Vladimir, 31
Mazzucchelli, David, xxi, 210, 218
McCarthy, Joe, 105
McCay, Winsor, 17–18, 130, 154,
    183, 207, 242, 270, 279, 284, 286,
    298
McClintock, Barbara, 210
McCloud, Scott, 201, 204, 209, 250
McDonald's, 73, 174
McGee, Barry, 219
McLuhan, Marshall, 239
McSweeney's, 298
Medium of comics, 271
"Mein Kampf," xxi, 192, 195
Meltdown, 217
Melville, Herman, 161
Memory, 131–32
Mencken, H. L., 140
Metaphors, 91, 232
Metropolitan Museum of Art, 206
Mickey Mouse, 78, 81, 91, 232
Milan, 266
Miller, Frank, 62, 120
Millet, Cathy, 16, 45–48
Minstrel shows, 221
Moby Dick, 64
MOCCA (Museum of Comic and
    Cartoon Art), 287
Modern art, 43–44
Mongrelized art, 275
Monroe, Marilyn, 34
Moore, Alan, 121
Moore, Michael, 293
Moore, Suzanne, 96
Moral centers, 134
Moscoso, Victor, 120, 289
Mother Jones, xxi
Mouly, Françoise, x, xii, xix–xx,
    3, 14, 20–21, 24, 70, 164, 182–83,
    210–11, 215–16, 223–25, 228–29,
    250–51, 253, 265
Movie offers, 138, 194

Movies, 52, 54–55, 61, 63, 112, 142, 190, 270

Mullaney, Dean, 20

Munch, Edvard, 77

Munich, 141

Muñoz, José, 35

Museum of Comic and Cartoon Art, 287

Museum of Modern Art, xi–xii, xx, 123, 144, 186–87, 205–6, 219, 241

Museums, ix–xii, 141, 154, 174, 184, 186–87, 204, 302

Musical theater, 212, 214

Mustaches, 148–49

Mutt 'n Jeff, 201

Muybridge, Eadweard, 190

Nabokov, Vladimir, 139

Nancy, 296

Narrative, 8, 36, 40, 45, 54–55, 58, 62, 130, 156, 198

Narrative Corpse, The, xxi

Nation, xxiii, 254, 265

National Book Critics Circle Award, xix–xx, 109

National Lampoon, 28, 100

National Public Radio, 126

"National Rorschach," 254

Nationalism, 222

Nazis, 148, 232

Neo-sincerity, 228, 253

"Nervous Rex: The Malpractice Suite," 38–39, 250

Netherlands, 23

New Comics, The, 160

New Republic, 187

New Wave comics, 119

New Wave magazines, 100, 254

New York, 4, 6, 164, 259–60

New York *Journal*, 165

New York Public Library, 181, 249

New York Times, 123, 147, 185, 225, 252, 264–65, 293–94, 298

New York Times Book Review, 11

New York Times Magazine, xxi, 195

New York *World*, 165

New Yorker, The, xiii, 185–86, 213, 229, 247, 251–52, 254, 263–66, 295, 304; covers, xx–xxiii, 164, 172, 175–76, 193, 211, 221, 228, 235, 250, 253, 292, 301; editorship, xii, xx, 153, 211, 226; features, xxi–xxii, 160, 181, 218, 243–44, 249

Newgarden, Mark, 103, 225

Newhouse, Alana, 234

Nietzsche, Friedrich, 170

Night Watch, The, 59

Nine, Carlos, 258

9/11 attacks, xiii, xxii, 235–37, 239, 251–52, 259, 264, 293–94, 297, 301, 304

9/11 Commission Report, 303

Nixon, Richard, 151

Noomin, Diane, 16

Nostalgia, 275

Novels, 133–34, 274

Nuage Gallery, 266

Oblomov, 52

Olivia the Pig, 257

110 Stories, 252

Open Me . . . I'm a Dog!, xxi, 197, 246

Operation Enduring Freedom, 265

Oral History Journal, 84

Original art, xi, 131, 292

Out Our Way, 241

Outsider art, 198

Packing, 245

Page layout, 61, 89, 276–84, 298

Page rates, 19

Paintings, 54–55

Palestine, 181

Panels, 42

Panter, Gary, 132, 164, 181, 183, 218, 270, 289–90, 296

Pantheon Books, xx, xxi, 73, 109, 116, 216–17, 295, 298

Parks, Van Dyke, 212

Parshas Trumah, 145

PBS, 214–15

Peanuts, 217, 243–44

Pedagogic tool, *Maus* as, 141, 158

Pencil sharpening, 11

Penguin Books, xix, xx, 93–95, 102, 109, 116, 226

Penny dreadfuls, 106

People Weekly, 169

Personal comics, 5

Phelps, Donald, 240

Philbin, Ann, 207

Photographs, 159, 190, 285–86

Picasso, Kiki, 183

Picasso, Lulu, 183

Picasso, Pablo, 58, 120

Pierre, 161

Pigs, 92, 230–33

Ping-pong, 76

"Plastic Arts, The," xxii

Plastic Man, xxii, 154, 218, 281

Playboy, 11, 18–19, 96, 121, 182, 225

Plots, 8, 46–47, 49, 58, 63–64

Poetry, 12, 56, 60, 101, 217, 282

Poland, xix, 91–92, 112, 123, 148, 230, 232

Polish people, 159, 193, 231–33

Politically Incorrect, 221

Politics in comics, 295–96

Pollock, Jackson, 59, 170

Polti, Georges, 8

Popeye, 127, 134

Popular culture, 192, 276

Populism, 202

Porky Pig, 232

"Portrait of the Artist as a Young %@?*!," xxiii

Postmodernism, 197

Post-Standard (Syracuse), 301

Priest, 176

Primitive art, 45

Prince Valiant, 200, 279

Princess Daisy, 50

Print magazine, xx, 98, 109

Print medium, 32

Print Mint, 98

Printing presses, 3, 9, 14, 182, 225

Printing process, 33

"Prisoner on the Hell Planet," xviii, 6, 77–78, 82, 133, 137, 156, 168–69

Progressive, The, 137

Protests, of Spiegelman work, xxi–xxiii, 265

Proto-comics, 106

Proust, Marcel, 73

Prozac, 180

Psychedelics, 76, 180, 299–300

Psychotherapy, 76–77, 111, 124, 134, 137, 145, 150

Psychotic breakdowns, 76

Publisher's Weekly, 223, 234

Puck, 258

Pulitzer Prize, ix, xi, xx, 138, 144, 152, 162, 165, 204, 225, 234, 247, 302–3

Pyle, Howard, 31

Quark Express, 293

Queneau, Raymond, 56

"Race Card, The," 221, 254

RAW, x, xii–xiii, xix–xx, 20–21, 23–26, 28–34, 39–43, 48, 51, 57, 66, 68, 70, 79, 85, 95, 98–105, 118, 128, 132, 134, 137, 144, 153, 164–65, 170, 182–85, 189, 201, 210, 215, 218, 223, 225–26, 254–57, 290

Raw Books and Graphics, xix, 3, 14–15, 225
Rawness, 130
Raymond, Alex, 200, 268, 286
Raymond school, 31
Read Yourself Raw, xix, 256
Reader discipline, 281–82
Readership (audience), 7–8, 12, 26, 30, 49–50, 117, 134, 156, 217, 297
Reading the Funnies, 240
Reagan, Ronald, 265
"Real Dreams," 148–50
Real Pulp Comics, 144
Reality, 45
"Red Flowers," 103
Redefining comics, 26
Reid, Calvin, 223
Rembrandt, 59, 280
Remnick, David, 263–65
Representational art, 43–45
"Representations of the Shoah in *Maus*," 191
Reproduced art, 11–12, 32, 167
Research, 7, 112
Resnais, Alain, 204
Respectability, 185–86, 202, 279
Rex Morgan, 39, 250
Richard, Bruno, 183
Ride Together, The, 272
Rigor of form, 273–74
Rip Kirby, 286
Rockwell, Norman, 197–202, 253
Rodriguez, Spain, 15, 17, 218
Romita, John, 119
Rootless cosmopolitans, 174, 183, 259
Ross, Alex, 200
Roth, Philip, 166, 175
Round panels, 284

Sabin, Roger, 95, 238
Sacco, Joe, xxiii, 181, 240, 249

Sala, Richard, 258
Sampayo, Carlos, 35
San Francisco, 4, 21, 23, 97, 178
Sausages, 148
Scanners, 292
Schindler's List, 194, 222
Schizophrenia, 178–79
Schmidt, Natasha, 220
Schneider, Bob, xviii
School of Visual Arts, xiii, xix, 5, 20, 26, 98, 102, 209, 225, 245, 269
Schulz, Charles M., xxii, 197, 201, 218, 243–44
Science fiction, 30, 178
Sears, 73
Second Generation, 191, 195
Segar, Elzie, 269, 300
Seldes, Gilbert, 276
Sendak, Maurice, xxi, 160, 257
Sentimentality, 199
Serious intent, 11, 267–68
Seth, 185, 217, 275
Seurat, Georges, 59–60
Seven Lively Arts, The, 276
Sex and drugs, 22, 97, 182
Sgt. Fury, 48
Shapinsky's Karma, Bogg's Bills, and Other True-Life Tales, 68
Shaw, Jim, 218
Shelton, Gilbert, 224
Shoah, 114
Short Order Comix, xviii, 77, 254
Siebold, Otto, 211
Sign systems, 90, 200, 271
Sikoryak, R., xxi
Silverblatt, Michael, 126, 197, 218
Simenon, Georges, 299
Simmonds, Posy, 257
Simplicissimus, 15
Simplification, 12
Simpson, O. J., 221, 254
Sister Wendy, 214

Skyline, 99
Skyscraper, 254
Slapstick, 270
Slash, 28
Sleazy Scandals of the Silver Screen, 144
Slow Death, 22
Smiley faces, 166
Smith, Graham, 84
Smithsonian Collection of Newspaper Comics, The, 18
Smoking, xiv–xv, 70, 72–73, 79–80, 82, 136, 140, 182, 223, 231, 233, 240, 266
Snicket, Lemony, 258
Sobol, Joshua, 113
Social commentary, 289
Socialism, 141
Soglow, Otto, 187, 242
Sophistication, 8, 201
Sosnowiec, 79, 232–33
Sound effects, 281
South Africa, 93–94
South Park, 244
Spain, 23
Spider-Man, 119
Spiegelman, Anya, xvii, xviii, 69, 74, 77, 79–80
Spiegelman, Dashiell, xx, 246
Spiegelman, Lolek, 87, 93
Spiegelman, Mala, 79, 87, 93, 113
Spiegelman, Nadja, xix, xxii, 150, 161, 246
Spiegelman, Richieu, 74
Spiegelman, Vladek, xvii, xix, 69, 73–74, 79–80, 82, 134–35, 209
Spielberg, Steven, 72–73, 83, 153, 155, 222
Spirit, The, 102
SPX (Small Press Expo), 257
Stained glass windows, 188, 208, 248, 277

Stalin, Josef, 31, 174
Stars vs. actors, 6–7, 34
Statue of Liberty, 72
Stein, Gertrude, 53, 60, 139
Steranko, Jim, 62
Stereotypes, 221
Sterne, Laurence, 189
Stranger, The, 64
Structure, 63–65
Stuck Rubber Baby, 185
Stuff, 254
Sturgeon's Law, 276
Success, 137–38, 162, 172
Suicide, 77, 93, 170
Sullivant, T. S., 294
Superheroes, 31, 106, 119, 154, 168, 303
Superman, 195, 211
Suppression, 290
Surfing competitions, 248–49
Swarte, Joost, 40, 210, 225, 277
Swift, Jonathan, 203
Syracuse University, 302
Szasz, Thomas, 179

Taboos, 111, 221
Talk radio, 151
Tampa Review, 126
Tan, Amy, 175
Tape recordings, 62, 86, 125
Tardi, Jacques, 35, 183, 225
Tashlin, Frank, 270
Taylor, Ella, 191
Tchelitchew, Pavel, 205, 219
Teaching, xiii, xix, 5, 17–18, 20, 26, 98, 102, 161, 209, 225, 245, 269
Teaching tool, *Maus* as, 141, 158
Technology of comics, 292
"Teen Plague," 101
Teen Titans, 101
Teenage angst, 169
Temporal media, 55–56, 58

"Ten Thousand Billion Poems," 56
Terry and the Pirates, 285
Testaments, 135
"Theology of the Tax Cut," xxi, 175–76
Thompson, Kim, 35
Three Stigmata of Palmer Eldritch, The, 178
Tijuana bibles, x, xxi, 127
Time magazine, xxiii, 185, 282
Tintin, 245, 256
Today show, 110
Top Shelf Productions, 216
Töpffer, Rodolphe, x, 15, 29, 189–90, 207–8, 218, 241, 260
Topps Chewing Gum, Inc., xi, xvii–xviii, 17, 164, 172, 256, 259
Torah, 145
Touch of Evil, 270
Transcriptions, 87
Transgressive comics, 166
Translations, 183
Trial and Error, 46
Tristram Shandy, 189
Trivializing, 90
Trump, 96, 107
Tsuge, Yoshiharu, 103–4
Tucker, Brian, 196
Tufte, Edward, 286
Turner, Ron, 22
Tuttle, Harry, 289
Twilight Zone, 154
2000 A.D., 105
"Two-Fisted Painters," xix
Two-Fisted Tales, 42
Typography, 200

UCLA Hammer Museum, 207, 242
Uncle Scrooge, 61
Underground comix, x–xi, xviii, 4–5, 19, 21–23, 25, 27, 77–78, 84–85, 90, 97, 99, 105, 120, 144, 183, 201, 224–25, 287, 289, 292

Understanding Comics, 201
University of California, Santa Cruz, 136
Urry, Michelle, 18

"Valentine's Day," xx, 175
Van Gogh, Vincent, 299
Vermeer, Johannes, 58–59, 242, 271, 288
Vermin, 81
Victimization, culture of, 198–99
Vidal, Gore, 221
Village Voice, xxi, 194, 248, 296
Virginia Quarterly Review, xxiii
Visual paragraphs, 277
Viz, 104
Vocabulary of comics, 284, 290
Volkswagens, 125
Voyager Company, xxi

Wacky Packages, xi, xviii, 164, 172, 211, 256
Wacom tablets, 292
Walker, Alice, 175
Wallace, David Foster, 218
War comics, 41–42, 57, 107
Ward, Lynd, 277
Ware, Chris, 164, 185, 208, 210, 216–17, 224, 228, 257–58, 260–62, 273, 275, 281–82, 284, 290, 298
Watchmen, 121, 299
Weirdo, 165
Weisel, Elie, 159
Welles, Orson, 270
Wells, H. G., 141
Weschler, Lawrence, 68, 194, 230
Wet, 28, 99, 127, 254
Wet dreams, 147
Whimsy, 129, 189
"Whiteman Meets Bigfoot," 5
Whitney Museum, 205–7, 242

Whole Grains: A Book of Quotations, xviii, 163

Wild, 75

Wild Party, The, xiii, xxi, 153, 290–92

Will Eisner Award, xxii

Williams, J. R., 241

Williamson, Judith, 96

Williamson, Skip, 18

Wilson, Gahan, 258

Wilson, S. Clay, 163, 224, 287

Windows, 248

Winfrey, Oprah, 171

Witek, Joseph, 95, 238, 267

Wolfe, Tom, 240

Wolverton, Basil, 18, 217, 219, 300

Women artists, 16, 118

Women readers, 117–18, 217

Women superheroes, 154

Women's comics, 16, 118

Woodford, Jack, 46–47

Word balloons, 87–88, 195, 279, 293

Work and Turn, 15

World Court, 249

World Trade Center, 234, 251–52, 301

Writers Dreaming, 143

Writing on the Edge, 152

Wunder, George, 285

Wyborny, Klaus, 63

X-Men, 36, 55, 66, 101, 202, 217

X-Tra, 196, 240

Yellow Kid, The, 164–65

Young Lust, xviii, 144

Zap Comix, 13, 100, 254

Zap Gun, 178

Zionism, 124, 158, 222

Zippy the Pinhead, 15, 97–98, 184, 224